THE HOSTAGE HANDBOOK

THE
HOSTAGE
HANDBOOK

To Bryan and Pauline
with real love and my
warmest good wishes

ANTHONY GREY

Tony
28/3/10
NORWICH

www.tagmanpress.co.uk

THE HOSTAGE HANDBOOK

First published in Great Britain in a hardcover
and trade paperback edition in November 2009
by Tagman Worldwide Ltd in The Tagman Press imprint .
Tagman Worldwide Ltd
The Lovemore Suite, Media House,
Burrel Road, St Ives, Huntingdon,
Cambridgeshire, PE27 3LE
Tel: 0845 644 4186
Fax: 0845 644 4187
www.tagmanpress.co.uk
email: editorial@tagmanpress.co.uk

© 2009 Anthony Grey

The right of Anthony Grey to be identified as the author of this work has been
asserted by him in accordance with the Copyright, Designs & Patents Act 1988.

ISBN
Hardcover 978-1-903571-61-3
Paperback 978-1-903571-62-0

A CIP catalogue record for this book is available from the British Library

Edited by Bridget Lely
Cover design: e-Digital
Text: Richard Legg, Ben Taylor and Cathy Gibbs

Printed by CLE Print Ltd, St Ives, PE27 3LE, UK

www.tagmanpress.co.uk

Dedicated
with much love and deep gratitude to
Agnes, Alfred, June, Geoffrey, Shirley, Bernard and Lucy Shibko,
Clarissa, Lucy, Angela, Nawal and Treeva.

Seek the stillness,
Quiet the moment,
Feel the joy
Of here and now,
Unending peace
Resides internal
Embracing unseen
All we do

To find the way
To love and beauty
Simply be
And rest within,
Our halls of wisdom
Our own cathedral,
Exist inside us,
Let's go in!

AUTHOR'S NOTE

The Chinese names and words in this book are mostly rendered in the now outdated Wade-Giles system of romanisation since that system was still in use in China and internationally during my time in Beijing. China had introduced its own phonetic system called Pinyin starting in 1958 and later after I left China it became standard international usage. I have occasionally added the Pinyin version of a word or name in brackets where it might be helpful.

CONTENTS

Part Three: 1969 – The Year of the Rooster

FOREWORD
John Clements

'The depth and strength of an individual human character', Leonardo da
Vinci once wrote, 'are defined by its moral reserves.' He went on to add:
'People reveal themselves completely only when they are thrown out of the
customary conditions of their life – for only then do they have to fall back
on their reserves.'

The quotation, to my mind, is tailor-made to stand at the start of this
remarkable book, whose text amply and unwittingly bears out the truth of
da Vinci's insightful statement. For perhaps the first thing to be emphasised
about the diary that forms the core of this work is that it was not written
with any expectation that it would be published like this in its entirety. Its
revelations are in a way unconscious and unselfconscious, because it was
compiled secretly in shorthand purely as a survival tool in a hostage's cell.
Its publication now in full, over 40 years after it was written, takes the
reader very vividly back into that cell in the heart of China's capital at the
height of the violent and protracted Cultural Revolution. Yet it also does
much more than that.

While reading Anthony Grey's diary entries, I was quickly reminded that
in the year 1192, King Richard I of England, popularly called 'Lionheart',
was captured in the guise of a Knight Templar, and held by King Leopold
V of Austria for a ransom of 150,000 marks. Not until February 1194 was
he allowed to return to England, where his brother Prince John, who
features in the Robin Hood folk tales, had been acting as Regent in his
absence.

In the year 1967 – and I believe for the first time in the modern era –
another Englishman was taken as an international hostage for a similar
two-year period by a foreign power. Anthony Grey was not a king in
disguise, but a foreign correspondent for Reuters international news
agency; and he just happened to be in the wrong place at the wrong time.
Further, he was held – not for ransom but for reasons of political muscle-

flexing – by the Chinese Communist regime of Mao Tse-tung, which sought leverage against the British Government over actions taken in the then British colony of Hong Kong.

Tony, an innocent man caught up in the maelstrom, spent over two years in solitary confinement, monitored by Mao's youthful Red Guards and Public Security Bureau men day and night, awaiting an unknown term and an unknown fate. A 200-strong mob of Red Guards chanted 'Hang Grey! Hang Grey!' as they stormed his house at midnight in midsummer 1967 and roughed him up, symbolically and bloodily stabbing to death a pet house cat and hanging it before his face before confining him to a room only eight feet square. Yet as this diary reveals, he fought doggedly against desperation and despair and used his time positively whenever he could: by amusedly organising ant races across the floor of his 'cell', by later teaching himself Chinese, keeping fit both physically and mentally by constant practice of yoga, and devising many other different ingenious methods to constantly encourage and motivate himself in the certain belief that freedom and survival would arrive sooner or later.

As you read the pages of Tony's hostage diary, written originally in careful and meticulous shorthand symbols during his captivity, I'm confident that you, like me, will come to regard him as another more modern 'Lionheart'.

During my 20 years' practice as a life strategist, I have been in a position to observe, identify and help cultivate the qualities necessary for a man or a woman to become the kind of character we call a 'leader'. So it can be imagined how rare a pleasure it has been for me to find not only a genuine leader, but also a true friend in such an environment. I do not mean Tony is a leader in the political or military sphere, of course; I apply the term more widely in the sense that real leaders serve as role models, they inspire others as someone once said 'to be bigger than our doubts and fears'. They also have vision and by their writing or example encourage others to share that vision.

Reading this remarkable diary, I was staggered at Tony's inventiveness in transforming endless, ostensibly hopeless days into manifestations of a single aspiration: that his captivity would eventually come to an end and he was determined to survive it with mind, body and spirit fully intact. Anthony Grey is the quintessential Englishman; and, as you will discover, also an articulate, intelligent and sensitive man who has practiced self-mastery, and cultivated a perennial spiritual dimension in his life and work.

Adversity is an all-too-common component of our earthly existence. What separates the small soul from the great soul is the response to these events. The seeds of potential greatness lie dormant within all of us. So, we can choose either to diminish ourselves by becoming embittered, bemoaning our losses, craving revenge and recompense for our misfortunes, or we can become ennobled and enlarged in our moral character, choosing to use the adverse circumstances as stepping stones on our pathway to personal excellence and spiritual enrichment.

Though Tony would not, by any stretch of the imagination, claim to have enjoyed his two years of captivity, he nevertheless recognises that period as a profound turning point in his life, one which has ultimately produced great beneficial effects. He might even echo the words of Henry Ford (1863–1947) in saying that, when everything seems to be going against you, it's good to remember that the airplane takes off against the wind, not with it.

Tony's spirit remains indomitable as he continues, more than 40 years later, to overcome – seemingly by sheer optimism – all kinds of personal challenges; and he does this not only on his own behalf, but also for others whom he endeavours to assist in fulfilling their aspirations in particular through the published and printed word.

For my own part, I'm grateful to Tony for allowing me a privileged glimpse of these pages in advance of publication. Not many men have the strength to allow the broad spectrum of humanity into their unedited private world. And I know for certain that Tony's sole motivation in doing this after more than four decades of reflection, is to enrich and challenge all our lives – as he has done for many others, in so many other ways, in his historical novels, his non-fiction books and his radio and television broadcasting and publishing. It is my firm conviction that modern-day readers will relish and benefit greatly from the opportunity to browse and reflect on the extraordinary contents of *The Hostage Handbook*.

Dr John L. Clements is the author of *How to Get What Money Can't Buy - Peace of Mind in a World of Unrest*, and *Fruitful Prospects - Ripe for the Picking*.

'Nothing but good can befall you! Peace, happiness and contentment lie ahead. Prepare yourself for happier climes with a calm untroubled mind, free from worry or fear. You have a good future; your fate is in God's hands. God will deliver you. Something good is coming.'
24 October 1967

'Each day crouches huge and menacing at the window
And only at midnight steals reluctantly away.'
9 January 1968

'Fight! Fuck you! Fuck you! Fight!'
24 February 1968

'This evening there has been a very powerful sense of almost supernatural quality ... the pink and white blossoms on the tree, blowing in a strong breeze in the evening sunlight, were very beautiful. ... There was an almost tangible feeling of goodness and beauty. ... Now at this minute the sun has set and the courtyard is in shadow. The magic moment has passed.'
11 April 1968

INTRODUCTION

Berlin ... Budapest ... Prague ... Sofia ... Bucharest ... Warsaw ... and eventually Peking – known today as Beijing – these were some of the exciting world datelines of the Cold War era to which I travelled avidly in search of truth during my first two years as a foreign correspondent. They were all capitals of Communist states when the world was divided rigidly against itself, not by a largely Muslim–Christian conflict as it is today, but by the East–West, communist–capitalist schism that grew out of the aftermath of the Second World War.

As a Western journalist in those Communist countries, I was effectively a representative of 'the enemy' and this fact engendered the cloak-and-dagger atmosphere in which I and other visiting Western reporters and businessmen worked. Perhaps there is a similarity today for Western journalists operating from predominantly Muslim and Arab countries, although the sense of danger now must be even more intense and acute.

We journalists were tolerated rather than welcomed in each of these Communist world capitals. More often than not I found my telephone calls were bugged by the respective intelligence services of those nations, I was sometimes shadowed openly by car or on foot, my reports were unfailingly monitored by those same intelligence services and I became accustomed to recognising that my every word and deed would be subjected to the meticulous scrutiny accorded to any suspected visiting spy.

Despite or because of this, I felt I was right up there where it mattered, visiting some of the most significant places in the contemporary world. Above all else I felt quietly privileged to be writing about the secrecy-shrouded events unfolding in such places. By seeking out and reporting daily snippets of history, in the form of breaking news, in each of these world capitals during the tense days of the European Cold War and later the frenetic Chinese Cultural Revolution, I felt sure I was operating, at the age of 27 or 28, at the very cutting edge of understanding of our world and its destiny.

There were no finer places, I thought then, to gather enlightenment about daily life globally, no finer way of seeking understanding of the deep complexities of the human condition and gaining insights into how we might best resolve our chronic national and international dilemmas.

I had no idea then how limited and shallow was such an impression. However, in July 1967 amid a flurry of dramatic events in Hong Kong and the People's Republic of China, I was destined to find out. Although I did not know it then, I now realise I was about to travel, for the first time, to the most important, challenging and enlightening 'dateline' of them all. I was about to fly, via an unfamiliar and little used route, into the capital of that highly complex sovereign 'state' that exists independently and interdependently inside each and every one of us. The only world capital, so to speak, that really and truly deserves that epithet – since the word 'capital' comes originally from the Latin word *capitalis*, which means 'concerning the head'.

I was about to be given the opportunity, over a two-year period of enforced isolation as a hostage held in solitary confinement in a slogan-daubed room, to appreciate where the future of our joint world and our individual worlds will most likely be decided – deep inside of us all.

In presenting here for the first time the full transcript of the secret diaries I kept in shorthand during my two years as a hostage in China more than 40 years ago, it is not simply my wish to share the minute details of that strange experience. Although I admit that is a part of the intent, it is not the only reason. I wrote my first fundamental book describing the experience very rapidly during six weeks in January and February 1970. That was entitled *Hostage in Peking* and writing it was for me first and foremost a catharsis, a very deliberate exercise to get the trauma of the experience out of me, to exorcise the after-effects. That it was published in seven countries, and was something of a bestseller on the back of the worldwide coverage of my news story, was at the time essentially secondary to that main purpose.

Everything about the experience was so fresh in my mind then, that I scarcely needed to refer to my diaries in writing the book. I did quote from the texts of the entries in a few places to add immediacy to the story, and to do this I simply transcribed those particular bits I needed. A year or so went by after that book's publication before I finally settled down for a couple of weeks or more and slowly 'translated' and transcribed the entire text of the shorthand diaries word by word and line by line into clear typewritten English.

Over the three or four intervening decades I had preserved those transcripts and a copy, very carefully, in a deed box deposited at my bank. I did this because I always harboured an instinct that perhaps some day I might consider publishing the full text with some kind of reflective commentary. Yet I mostly shied away from doing anything to make that thought a reality, because part of me felt it might seem unduly egotistical or too self-regarding to offer for public consumption a warts-and-all unexpurgated version of the day-in-and-day-out thoughts of a single man forcibly cut off alone from the world in such circumstances.

Nevertheless I continued to preserve them because I suspected that value of some kind resided in them. I came to see, as time passed, that my first eight-foot-square hostage cell in Peking had been a kind of microcosm of the larger world, where nations get into conflict with each other for good or ill and individuals, through no fault of their own, get caught up in the crossfire. It seemed likely that there might be longer term lessons to be learned from all this and so I preserved the diaries and their transcripts and in the recent years, as hostage-taking in Iraq and elsewhere in the Middle East has reached new levels of brutality and intensity, I again from time to time found myself wondering whether they might contain something of current and contemporary value.

The experience of the solitary state in a hostile land had obviously stimulated a whole new way of seeing the world for me and had changed the course of my life markedly. Also people, I have found, even all these years after the event, remain endlessly curious about the predicament a hostage has faced and how he or she has coped, and what results and impacts have been produced.

After more reflection I realised that, as it was possibly a decision I could not responsibly take unaided, it would be best to seek the opinion of a few close friends and colleagues. So I had the transcripts carefully retyped in up-to-the-minute electronic form, then circulated them. Without exception all those who read the transcripts said they found them compelling and that they gave a very different perspective from my first published book on the subject. All, for varying reasons, urged me to consider publishing them at long last.

One of the wisest heads said that perhaps it was impossible for the author of such writings to assess and understand in advance what might be of value in them, since this might vary greatly from reader to reader. Perhaps, the wise head added, people facing up to many different kinds of challenges in life far removed from being held hostage, might benefit from reading the story and in particular realising, among other things, how keeping a diary could help an individual marshal and integrate their resources.

I did not read the texts myself at that time of retyping or later because something indefinable always stopped me doing that. In fact I had not read the diaries at all since I finished transcribing them in the summer of 1971 – and I have to confess that even now as I write these words of introduction in draft form for the first time late in the year of 2006, I have still not yet re-

read any of the diary entries. I don't think this is because I am reluctant overall or apprehensive to go back into that unpleasant and prolonged written experience of 'solitary'. I think it is more that I have put it off because I have not wished to embark on it again until I am really sure I am ready – and that there is a specific and worthwhile and thorough-going purpose involved in reading every word again carefully from beginning to end.

So now, after finishing the first draft of this introduction, I will begin re-reading the entries from those distant dates once more, revisiting them certainly for the first time and almost certainly for the last time, and I will record any feelings or interpretations that seem worthwhile as I progress through them.

At this point I should add that the first draft of the above paragraph and all above it, was first written nearly three years ago – and therefore the writing and preparation of this book for publication has unexpectedly spanned almost three years, starting in mid-December 2006. I originally planned to publish it in the summer of 2007 but I was more surprised than perhaps I should have been, that raking back among the details of my hostaage experience proved to have a destabilising effect on my life. During the years following my release I had encountered and eventually overcome several periods of depression with the help and support of my family. Remaining true to my questionable decision on release not to seek psychiatric help, I had never resorted over the years to consulting the medical profession. But after getting this book to its final prooof stage in early 2007, a prolonged and intense depressive period ensued, which was harder to shake off than anything I had ever known before.

I struggled with it for several months, but eventually felt compelled to seek help through my GP. This led to my first-ever discusion with consultant psychiatrists about my personal history. Consequently I put the book on one side in order to deal with these unexpected consequences. Even though four decades or so, had passed since my time in China, PTSD, post traumatic stress disorder, was diagnosed as being at the heart of my problems. I will say more about this whole subject later in these pages but for now as I redraft the end of this finalised Introduction in the autumn of 2009, I am glad and relieved to have been helped with these problems in a new way – and I trust, to have put them firmly behind me once and for all.

At first I was very self-conscious about admitting to suffering from depression because of the stigma that still lingeringly attaches itself to such illnesses – and I went out of my way to keep quiet about it. But after enduring a second bout of low morale earlier this year and coming through it again with generous professional help, I found that I was more relaxed about admitting to the difficulties. All this also helped me to decide that it was now right to publish this book. I outline all this here essentially to explain why my present-day 'Reflections' on the diaries – which are interspersed at intervals following each chapter of the transcribed shorthand notes, are dated as they were originally first written in the winter of December 2006 and January 2007, rather than the more immediate date of this Introduction itself.

Perhaps, in closing, I might usefully say something about the structure and title of this book. I have divided it into three parts naming each after the appropriate Chinese zodiac animal for those three years 1967, 1968 and 1969 – the Ram, the Monkey and the Rooster – because this somehow conveys symbollically how totally I was absorbed and swallowed up by China and its ancient and modern culture for that period. I hasten to add I have found no profound astrological clues or insights as to why I had that experience at that time in those particular Ram, Monkey and Rooster years – unless the 'Ram' applied to the implement the Red Guards might have used to smash down my heavy red courtyard gates in Beijing in mid-August 1967, and a 'Monkey' is what they made of me in my small cage for the following year, and then a 'Rooster' might symbolise my flying home at the end of that time to 'roost' among flocks of my own kind once again. But no deeper significance than these dubious 'facts' has declared itself.

As for the book's title, I must confess I did not dream it up myself but was given it by fellow writer Liz Jensen, author of the outstanding humorous novels *Ark Baby, My Dirty Little Book of Stolen Time* and *Egg Dancing* who came up with the suggestion instantly when we shared a lunch table at the annual Kings Lynn Fiction Festival and I was tentatively outlining to her what I thought I might possibly do with the diaries. It would be very much like a handbook, Liz said, because it would be portraying something of the essential experiences that each and any hostage must face up to if subjected to such misfortune. And that was that, the idea stuck, although I suppose first and foremost this is my own handbook.

It was not long after that meeting that I discovered that the keeping of a diary, or 'journalling' to give it its more modern formal name, is now taught in some further education colleges, in particular in sociology and similar courses which are designed to help people shape and develop their lives more consciously and with greater awareness with the help of a regular personal journal. Keeping my hostage diaries led me to resume keeping a fairly regular journal myself – though not by any means daily – from the early 1970's onwards until now. So I was also delighted to discover a few years ago that research into the subject has shown very clearly that those who keep a diary or a journal tend to live longer. So it was all these discoveries and new understandings rolled together that seemed to support my hunch that there might be some residual value in these 'ancient' documents, and this helped cement my decision to publish them.

Perhaps finally before going any further, I should add a brief word or two of apology about language. Occasionally flurries of vehement four-letter words will appear here and there in the text. I ask that they be excused in advance. They have been left unedited in their raw state like most of the entries, in the interests of what might perhaps lightly be termed 'historical accuracy' or 'authenticity'. In any event they acted as some kind of release valve, I suppose and although deciding not to use bad language, even in my mind, was sometimes part of the monthly self-discipline regimes I imposed on myself, just occassionally the flesh was weak and these vows were broken. Yes, that's my excuse, and I am sticking to it!

Anthony Grey
Norwich, England
3 November 2009

PART ONE

1967

THE YEAR
OF
THE RAM

PRELUDE

Over four decades ago, on Tuesday, 7 March 1967, I flew to Hong Kong from London *en route* to taking up my new post as Reuters' correspondent in China. I had just spent 20 months as the agency's correspondent in East Berlin.

After four months' reporting on Mao Tse-tung's 'Great Proletarian Cultural Revolution' from Peking, the political campaign entered its wildest phase. China was being seized, it seemed then, by a kind of political epilepsy. The nation, as far as the outside world could see, appeared to go into spasm. Demonstrations and factional in-fighting of many kinds were seen daily in the streets of the capital and other major cities, involving youthful Red Guards and 'Revolutionary Rebels' workers' groups formed at Mao's instigation.

The aging leader was using his enormous prestige to deliberately set the country on its ear and embroil the whole population in the confusing struggle as he strove to terrorise and remove from power the many pragmatists in the party and government who he imagined were opposed to his brand of revolutionary purity and his political legacy. Confusion reigned supreme and almost by the way Mao also appeared to be trying to change human nature in China, by permanently transforming people into selfless revolutionary automatons. Foreign diplomats, journalists and businessmen from more than a dozen countries of all political persuasions – communist, capitalist and Third World – became increasingly embroiled in the impenetrable chaos, and some of their embassies were defaced with slogans and targeted day and night by orchestrated demonstrations of up to a million screaming marchers. The British Embassy, at the climax to that summer's violence in mid-August, was set ablaze with all the diplomats and their families inside, and they had to flee for their lives through the flames and molesting mobs as the buildings were burned to the ground around them.

The Reuters house, where I lived alone close beside the walled moat of the Forbidden City, was being repeatedly covered with insulting wall-poster slogans and effigies during those sweltering summer months. Late one night a straw effigy of Britain's then prime minister, Harold Wilson, was burned in the street in front of me by a group of chanting Red Guards.

This aside, the assignment was a foreign correspondent's dream. I was filing news cables several times each day from Peking's central telegraph office, which were feeding hungry newspaper and broadcasting news bulletins worldwide. The outside world then scarcely understood what was going on in the planet's most populous country and I was the only British journalist reporting from there! I recorded almost daily voice reports for BBC's 'Radio Newsreel' via a telephone link to Tokyo and filmed whatever I could with a rudimentary Bell and Howell 'Pipsqueak' news camera for the Visnews television news film agency, then affiliated to Reuters. I got the film cassettes hand-carried out of the country by friendly journalists and businessmen who were flying out of Peking. No other outside broadcast or print journalists who were not already accredited in Peking, could get into China during that wild summer.

While all this was going on, in Britain's anachronistic colony of Hong Kong, over a thousand miles away on China's southern seaboard, local communist workers began demonstrations of their own, inspired by the chaotic events on the mainland.

Emergency laws were brought in to deal with very unpleasant riots and some street bombs. On about 19 July 1967 a local Communist Chinese journalist, named Hsueh Ping (Xue Ping), who was then working for Peking's New China News Agency in the colony, was sentenced by a court to two years' imprisonment for 'inciting a riot'. At that period of the Cold War, Western journalists who got into trouble in communist countries expected nothing worse than to be expelled back to their home country. The modern phenomenon of international hostage-taking by guerrilla groups, pirates and sometimes governments, which has become commonplace since the early 1970s, was then unknown. At that time it was still something that had happened largely in ancient history. So China led the way in modernising and updating this historic form of political and criminal action.

On the afternoon of 21 July I was called to Peking's Foreign Ministry and put under house arrest as a reprisal for Hsueh Ping's sentence. There was talk at the brief meeting of 'fascist suppression' and 'illegal persecution' of Chinese correspondents by the British authorities in Hong Kong. This diary begins on the day my house arrest started.

1
HOUSE ARREST

Friday 21 July 1967

Finished reading *Thought Reform* in the morning, rang Jean Vincent and he told me Tao Chu had been criticised openly for the first time in the Shanghai *Wen Wei Pao*. I went to his flat and wrote and filed a story. After lunching with Donald Hopson I read and slept, then as I arrived at the swimming pool outside the British Office at 5 pm, John Weston came out to say the Chinese Foreign Ministry was trying to reach me. They wanted to speak to me 'about my work'.

Eventually after telling the Minister, who was playing bridge, John took me to the Foreign Ministry in his car. A not-unpleasant woman official with a loose blouse hanging outside her trousers came in with Mr Chi. She offered her hand and I shook it and noticed, out of the corner of my eye, tea being brought in and so thought everything would be all right. But the tea wasn't touched. The woman read the statement and Chi translated. I wrote it down in shorthand.

"We have asked you here to discuss one question. It is regarding the repeated serious warnings to the British Government and the British authorities in Hong Kong that are becoming more savage and frenzied in their fascist suppression of our patriotic countrymen in Hong Kong. They have gone to the lengths of unreasonably kidnapping, brutally beating and illegally trying Hsueh Ping, and brazenly and unreasonably sentencing him on 19 July to two years on totally groundless charges. The British Hong Kong authorities further brutally persecuted correspondents Chen Fen-ying and Chen Teh-mu and five other patriotic Chinese correspondents by unreasonably kidnapping them and subjecting them to illegal interrogation. This is a gross political provocation by the British Government and Hong Kong authorities that the 700 million Chinese people will absolutely not tolerate."

The woman continued, 'I am now instructed to declare as follows: in view of the illegal persecution and the fascist atrocities in Hong Kong against Chinese correspondents, the Chinese Government deems it necessary to adopt measures to restrict the freedom of movement of Grey of Reuters in Peking. From this moment onwards you must remain in your residence and not depart from it. The visa for exit and re-entry issued to you is declared withdrawn from today. You must immediately abide by this decision or you yourself will be held responsible. That is all we have to say to you.'

I pointed out that since neither I nor Reuters were connected with the British Government, the affairs referred to in Hong Kong were nothing to do with me and this action was therefore unjustified.

The woman official replied, 'Do you think the atrocities are justified?' Without waiting for me to reply, she added, 'You know what the relations are between you and the British Government.' Then after a pause she said, 'We are expressing the greatest indignation and adopting measures against you.'

I then asked how long the restriction on me would last. Her reply was, 'There is no need for me to answer you now. The British authorities in Hong Kong should release the correspondents immediately without conditions.'

I asked whether visitors to the house would be allowed and the woman said, 'We have dealt with the main points. You can think it over for yourself.'

As the key part of the statement was reached, I managed to keep writing in shorthand, but some relief was mixed in my reaction to this blow. I sat unmoving when the interview ended until they motioned me out. They gave me only non-committal replies to my questions. When I asked how long I was to be restricted, she consulted her notes before replying offensively and ungraciously. I was taken by the arm as I made to leave the Ministry building. It was a little member of the Public Security Bureau. 'Come this way, Mr Grey,' he said.

He led me to a dun-coloured Warsawza outside and got into the back seat with me as another member of the Bureau got in to flank me on the back seat. Squashed in between them I was driven through pouring rain to my house. Had to wait ten minutes to cross Chang An Boulevard because of the main bodies of demonstrations going by. Finally on arriving home the chief told me to sit in the car and went to ring my bell. After a while I was asked to get out and open the door. Other policemen had gathered and six came inside with me. I stopped at the door when he asked me to show them which room I was going to sit in. I argued and told him eventually that the Foreign Ministry had only said to restrict my movement.

He went off and came back some minutes later. He called me down and told me the police would stay in the yard. I asked for a guarantee they would not come into the house and he said, 'That would depend.'

Then they motioned me in and went away. The little man said two men would stay in the yard. This they did, sheltering under the gate porch.

Every time I looked out of the window they gazed balefully at me. Some youths climbed up on to the adjoining roofs and shouted 'British Imperialist Bastard' through the window of my office ('*Ying-ti Hung Tan*'). This was sporadic and didn't last long. I drank several whiskies and soda, had a bowl of cornflakes and milk and eventually went to bed and read Henry Miller's *Sexus*. I listened to the crackly BBC World Service news at midnight on my shortwave radio and just caught a mention of Reuters Peking correspondent being ordered not to leave his house in the headlines.

The last friendly face I saw was John Weston as he left the Foreign Ministry. Several people telephoned during the evening. First Harald Munthe-Kaas, then Tony Blishen, the Minister, Mirec, Khan of India, Ray Witney, John Weston, Jean Vincent. The Minister remained in his office and telegrammed details to London. State of mind, first relief – that I had not been imprisoned or put on trial – gave way to curiosity as to how the situation would develop. The novelty of it prevented me feeling depressed; I feel a small sense of how unjust the measure. I was quickly asleep after listening to the news and saying a prayer.

Notes: Thought Reform was a book about what we in the West then called 'brainwashing' by American writer Robert Jay Lifton and I was reading it in a none too successful effort to get my head round contemporary Chinese political thought processes.

Jean Vincent was the Agence France Presse correspondent in Peking, a very good and admired friend, and I believe a wounded veteran himself of France's historic colonial defeat in Vietnam at Dien Bien Phu.

Tao Chu was a member of the elite Standing Committee of the Politburo of the Chinese Communist Party and along with President Liu Shao-chi and the durable Communist Party General Secretary Teng Hsiao-ping, was one of the three highest-level targets of Mao and his supporters during that phase of the Cultural Revolution. Tao Chu's naming for the first time in an official party newspaper was a significant confirmation of his political demise.

Donald Hopson, was Britain's Chargé d'Affaires in Peking (also known as the Minister, since diplomatic relations had not yet been raised to ambassador level). Donald Hopson later received head wounds at the hands of Red Guards during the burning and sacking of the British Mission. Courageous and soldierly, he became Sir Donald Hopson on return home.

John Weston - then third secretary and now Sir John Weston, having served as British Ambassador to the United Nations in New York and NATO in Brussels - is a lifelong friend, along with Sally his wife.

Mr Chi – Chi Min-tsung in full – was the official press spokesman for China's Foreign Ministry, famed among foreign journalists and diplomats alike for his clipped and assiduous Oxford English.

Harald Munthe-Kaas was correspondent for the Norwegian news agency; Tony Blishen was British Consul in Peking who was thrashed unconscious by Red Guards on the night of the Mission fire; Mirec was Peking correspondent of Ceteka, the Czechoslovak news agency, a good friend and Chinese speaker; Khan was a diplomat at India's Embassy; Ray Witney was First Secretary at the British Mission and later a Conservative MP and a Health Minister.

Saturday 22 July 1967

Woke to listen to the eight o'clock news. Heard it only faintly, but I was still in the headlines. The Minister called early to say a message from Reuters indicated they were getting in touch with my mother. He also offered to transmit a message to her so I said, 'In no personal danger, don't worry, love Tony.' Or words to that effect. They asked how things were domestically, but having only just got out of bed, I didn't know. He told me that in London last night a British Foreign Office official had summoned the Chinese Chargé d'Affaires and made a strong protest at the 'outrageous treatment' and demanded my immediate release; failing this, consular access was demanded.

I learned that several people came to visit me without success. Crowds gathered sometimes out of interest, apparently. Munthe-Kaas, Jean Vincent, John Weston, Samojima, the Japanese correspondent, and Tony Blishen all tried. I called Donald Hopson later to say I had cook and driver. He also told me Kevin Garry had called from Reuters in Tokyo to say he was unable to get through.

Many calls came in during the morning, from Ranga the Indian, the Norwegian Chargé d'Affaires, Magnus the Swede, Arne Belling of Denmark, Munthe-Kaas – he called the Foreign Ministry and was reprimanded for trying to visit me, but he was told to call in a few days time – Jean Vincent, Milo the Yugoslav, Vladimir Mikunov the Russian, Lulinski the Pole, Noleen the British nurse, Suzanne Vincent and Emerita.

I asked Lao Wang to get the car from the British Mission where I had left it, but he made a lot of excuses, said there were no buses, no pedicabs, the streets were full of demonstrations. He would go on Monday. I called the Foreign Ministry to ask that belongings I had left at the Mission be allowed in to me. But I was not allowed to speak to anyone in English.

While being driven home last night, I had tried to speak to the Public Security Bureau guards. I asked why was it necessary to escort me. No reply. After a while I said, 'Are you from the Public Security Bureau?' and a little guy said, 'Yes.'

I contented myself with staring at the one on my right who stared ahead and looked uncomfortable. The little guy had shaken his head three times and muttered an inaudible word at my first question.

Emerita rang and offered to send a letter to my mum, which I dictated and she took in shorthand. This afternoon I felt the first sense of being caged. It was fleeting and soon gone.

(10.30 pm)

I 'beat my bounds' round the courtyard just now, before locking up. When I went near the gate, the 'Wizened Guy' guard flapped his hands and said, *'Bu-shi,'* repeatedly.

I replied a little ridiculously, 'This is my territory up to here,' and went in. Emerita rang to read a telegram from home addressed to the Minister, which said, 'Thinking of you, good luck, Sue.'

BBC World Service radio just reported me to be 'still under house arrest but with ample food supplies'. It also said Hsieh Fu-chih and Wang Li had reportedly been arrested in Wuhan. John Weston said he had tried to deliver a bottle of whisky. (I saw him from the bathroom window during this attempt.) I sunbathed much of the afternoon and got a slightly red face. I spoke to Jean Vincent and Milo the Yugoslav correspondent and told them how telephone calls from abroad were being intercepted, my own foreign cables were being refused and sent back from the central Telegraph Office and the usual newspapers and mail were not being not delivered. I am only allowed telephone contact in Peking.

Had good dinner of salad, tomatoes, eggs, fried prawns dipped in sauce, watercress clear soup, fruit and beer. As I write this, someone is standing outside the window of my office on the adjoining flat roof shining a torch at me. I turn off the lights and leave the room and after a pause he continues shining the torch on the opposite wall. Cricket commentary comes in over the radio, but not clear enough to identify much. At one point I heard, 'They're looking for a single there,' and 'He got a nasty one just then!' Somehow the very Englishness of this was comforting, coming from my radio lying on the bed. Had a late call from Ray Witney, Pat and Anne.

Sue Turner was a television producer whom I had met when she came to East Berlin during my time there to make a TV documentary about the city, then still under international four-power control.

Emerita, Pat and Anne were all very kind secretaries at the British Mission. Emerita in particular often went out of her way to be helpful as far as she could, writing letters and conveying messages from my family and friends at home during the rest of her difficult spell of duty in Peking.

Lao Wang was the normally amiable Reuters driver who would later suffer grossly at the hands of Red Guards for his long-term employment with Reuters.

Hsieh Fu-chih was Minster for Public Security and he and Wang Li, a top party official, were believed to have been temporarily captured by opponents of Mao in the central industrial city of Wuhan when sent there as trouble-shooters. Chinese Navy units deployed on the River Yangtse and rival Peoples Liberation Army troops were then believed to have clashed in a rumoured bout of civil war.

Sunday 23 July 1967: Third day, 6.00 pm

The guard has just changed. I look out of the window of the lounge and see a water bottle hanging on the wall of the porch. Then I see one of the Public Security Bureau members carrying a khaki cape. I realise it is a shift change. All four present wear black canvas shoes with rubber soles, blue cotton trousers, khaki jackets with red collar tabs, soft round khaki caps with a red badge depicting the Gate of Heavenly Peace. There is no sign of arms. They take up position in the centre of the courtyard with their *Red Books*, then standing in a square they read; first a little introduction, then the chanting. Tried to record it, but wasn't quick enough. Two went away and two stayed and sat down on two chairs they had brought earlier to read their Red Books by themselves. I noticed yesterday that, as the day wore on, they moved their chairs round the courtyard in the shade of the walls.

Munthe-Kaas told me by telephone that when he took a 400-word story to the cable office he was told, 'We wish to look through this to see if everything is all right, since it is about Grey.'

Munthe-Kaas protested that he was allowed to file what he liked, but they said if there was anything 'not right', they would call him by phone. They didn't call. A number of people telephoned during the day (too numerous to mention). Noleen told me I was born in the 'Year of the Tiger'; Sally said a toast was drunk to me last night at the Pakistan reception; Jean Vincent said the *Peoples Daily* carried a front-page report of Hsieh Fu-chih and Wang Li 'returning triumphantly' to Peking.

Donald Hopson told me he had raised my case regarding the question of access, when called to the Consular Department last night to receive a protest that British seamen were insulting Chairman Mao somewhere. But he said he was surprised to hear himself told by the Consular official that it was none of his business. He said it was to do with the department that had issued the statement. Application had to be made to them.

The passage of time had not occurred to me until I was writing this. But even after it occurred to me that it was the third day, it still doesn't worry me much. Goodness only knows how long it will go on. At the moment I am not worried about that. Yesterday in the *Peoples Daily*, I had a three-column heading on my story and was mentioned in the Commentary. Last night I locked all the doors and windows, so I had to get up and let Sao

Kao in this morning. I got up, read the New China News Agency printer in the basement, put my clothing in order (found a cheroot with a cry of delight), vacuum-cleaned my bedroom and tidied the bathroom. I lunched off kebab in good sauce, salad, wheat cakes, soup, yellow melon and beer. Lazed and continued reading Charles Taylor's *Reporter in Red China* and after lunch went on the roof and listened to the Japan news and the news from London, neither of which mentioned me.

At midnight last night I was said by the BBC to be 'still under house arrest' and my food was ample and I was able to telephone in Peking. In addition to Munthe-Kaas's experience about his cable today, I learned Jean Vincent and David Oancia had cables refused on Wang Li's arrest.

Tonight I surreptitiously tried to watch guards' change shift – but when they thought they saw me at the window they stopped, turned off the light in the courtyard and shone their torches up at the window. While talking on the phone tonight with Emerita, a torch was shone on me from the roof. Uncomfortable-making! Had cold supper of meat sandwiches and beer, because Sao Kao had a ticket for a film, *Chairman Mao is the Red Sun in Our Hearts*. Went to bed, read *Reporter in Red China* and slept soundly.

Sao Kao was the likeable Reuters cook. Like Lao Wang he was polite and friendly in normal times. Under the eyes of the guards and Red Guards, both were uncomfortably obliged to behave towards me after my arrest in a 'revolutionary' manner.

David Oancia was the Toronto Globe and Mail correspondent and a good friend. He took both stills and newsreel photographs of me outside of the house before my arrest.

Monday 24 July 1967

Wakened at 7.15 by door buzzer, rose and let in Sao Kao, then returned and slept in a dream-laced doze until ten o'clock. After breakfast of tomato juice, cornflakes and milk, scrambled eggs, toast and coffee, I read the New China News Agency and sorted out the previous three days' copy. A talk with David Oancia revealed that his car was smashed up by the masses last night. He and Munthe-Kaas and a Swedish diplomat were caught in the crowds near Tien An Men Square, when trying to watch big demonstrations, apparently connected with the return of Hsieh Fu-chih and Wang Li. The windscreen and windows were smashed and the roof was jumped on. David was interrogated until 2.30 in the morning – and the incident began around 7 in the evening, he said.

He asked for normal protection, but was told the police didn't interfere in the actions of the masses. I spoke with Donald Hopson, who had nothing to tell me. It was the weekend and hardly Monday in London yet, he said. While lying on my bed after a heavy lunch of fried liver in breadcrumbs, sauce, salad, wheat cakes and beer, I felt for the first time a sense of 'imprisonment'. Twinges of depression came and went. When I went downstairs to talk to Lao Wang, the face of one of the guards stared in at me and I thought at that moment it was one of the most hateful faces I had ever seen.

I wrote a cable, but before sending it rang the Foreign Ministry. For the first time ever I got to talk to someone straight away. I asked for clarification of whether I was forbidden to file news. The immediate reply was, 'We have made all points clear. You should know the answer.'

I made it clear I didn't, but he repeated this and said, 'This is our answer.'

I then asked that belongings of mine in another residence be allowed to be brought in. I was asked to hold on. Then he said, 'We have made all points clear. That point should be clear to you. Think it over. You should know.'

These answers may have been in a slightly different order to that I have given them, but there was nothing beyond that. I am trying to adopt unshakeable confidence and calm – but a clear feeling that my freedom has been taken away arrived this afternoon. I was looking out through the wooden slats of the sun-blind at the waters of the moat and the roofs of the Forbidden City, when my 'Two Worlds' situation dawned fully on me. That outside my window – to me at least – is freedom. And 15 Nan Chihtze is now a jail. And I have done nothing to deserve it!

I sent my second personal cable to Angel, but it was returned. I sent the first one on Saturday. Lao Wang collected the car from Donald Hopson's residence and said he had been told not to use it and it was locked away in the garage.

As I was having dinner tonight, the guard walked round the side of the house craning his neck to look at me. Spent an hour on the roof today, because the sun didn't shine most of the day. Dictated message to the British Office for transferring to Tokyo if they ring. 'Fourth day no change – guard changes every three hours, posters saying "Down with British imperialism" are on outside walls. I can't send any cables, have received none and cannot make or receive overseas calls.'

John Weston told me tonight that slogans on the walls outside the house here say, 'Strongly support the stringent actions of our government.' I didn't send the cable I wrote. I am just going to lock the doors and the ironic thought occurred to me as I clanked my rather large key-ring – I am my own jailer!

Angel was Shirley McGuinn. I had met Shirley when she was senior lecturer in German, teaching in a language laboratory at Westminster College, behind the

Army and Navy Department Store in Victoria. I was brushing up my German just before departing for my first Reuters assignment in East Berlin. Shirley later visited me in Berlin as our romance flourished. When I left for China, we planned that she would visit me in China too - but that never became possible.

Tuesday 25 July 1967

Woke at 7.15, let in Sao Kao, then slept until 10, when Sally rang. (She had tried several times before.) I dictated a letter to her for Shirley saying, 'This is somewhere between extremely boring and exceedingly boring, but I am eating and drinking and sleeping well. Not as pleasant as house-arrest at your place would be.'

Donald Hopson rang with query about Munthe-Kaas's piece in *The Times*, saying my release depended on the release of Hsueh-Ping. I said this wasn't strictly so and then dictated the question and answer exchange from the Foreign Ministry. 'I wish we had known that before,' he said. (I am sure this was because *The Times* had it, not because of any intrinsic meaning it held.)

Sally sent off the letter to Shirley and wrote one to my mum, saying she could reply 'through the correct channels'. When Ray Witney rang in the afternoon, I asked with some annoyance whether there was any news of what was being done and he said the 'termites were at work', but it might be another week. I explained that house-arrest effectively nullified the Reuters operation here, which wasn't so in Hong Kong or London. He said he got the message.

Jean Vincent told me today that David Oancia had been recalled 'for consultations' after the car incident with the masses. David himself told me he had been called to the Foreign Ministry and given a serious warning. They said he had 'contravened revolutionary law and order' and the masses had been justified. The precise act of contravening law and order wasn't specified. Jean Vincent also told me he had a second cable refused – this time about Japanese businessmen whose rooms were searched at the Hsin Chiao Hotel. Slogans outside said, 'Crush the Japanese spies.' They had reportedly photographed wall posters. Jean is concerned that Japanese are able to go on filing the contents of wall posters and this story, but the Revolutionary Rebels in the cable office say they will not send those of Jean, because they don't agree with them.

John Weston rang tonight and we began a chess game by phone. During the morning, Chinese marched by my house and during the afternoon a huge rally got underway in the Square of Heavenly Peace. About nine giant red balloons flew above the square, indicating a top-level attendance of leaders, we thought. The sounds that came to me as I sat on the roof were fiendish and crazy sounding. I clearly heard the shouts, *'Ta tao* (down with) *Liu Tung-tĭ* and possibly the names of two local leaders at Wuhan. Today's *People's Daily* again praised the return of Hsieh Fu-chih from Wuhan, which suggests they were held or captured for a time. ... For most of the day I read the back numbers of the papers and clipped them and read the New China News Agency printer. I realise I am becoming terribly lazy and must discipline myself.

This afternoon, with a great thrill, I received a cable via Jean Vincent which said, 'Thanks Tony's cable, mine apparently obstructed Saturday. Love you, miss you, wish you here. Love Shirley.' What an angel! In the afternoon I continued browsing through the backlog of papers; I began to feel heavy and unexercised, and made a weak resolve to make a more disciplined effort tomorrow.

Wednesday 26 July 1967

Today was very orderly, with some measurable 'achievement'. I filed all the material that had piled up in my filing tray in the morning and finished the accounts in the afternoon. Quite a day! Also continued a chess game by telephone with John Weston in the evening. While having dinner the most interesting event of my arrest so far occurred. Lao Chiao, who returned from holiday today, came to me with a cable receipt form and it turned out that it was a cable sent from Reuters in Tokyo by Lee Casey last Friday, acknowledging receipt of my Tao Chu story.

At this moment I have just thought for the first time of being free and what I would do if I was. I decided I would drive to the British pool and swim before doing anything else. I conjectured what the arrival of the cable means, although five days late, having resulted from some firm decision somewhere and construed this as a promising sign and perhaps the first crack in the dam.

Harald Munthe-Kaas telephoned to say David Oancia had been given 'a serious warning' for refusing to admit his guilt in provoking the masses. Today's papers revealed that Mao's deputy Lin Piao, Premier Chou En-lai and other top leaders were present at yesterday's rally, which the reports indicated was connected with Wuhan. BBC news from London said tonight that trains between Canton and Hong Kong had been resumed after a break, which was not explained. Today was comparatively uneventful. Even had a crazy fear that this all would end soon, before I had caught up on all the things I should have done – among them making detailed notes on the Cultural Revolution's history.

Lao Chiao was the Reuters house 'boy' although white haired and aging. He looked after the boiler and jobs around the house and assisted Sao Kao with the cooking and shopping. He was the most genial of all the Reuters staff who came to the house every day. With Mrs Hou, a 'wash Amah' who did my laundry, and a translator, a Mr Wu, who suddenly ceased to arrive for work without any explanation long before my arrest, I and Reuters had a Chinese staff of five working for us. So many people were not really needed, but any foreign operation in China at that time was compelled to employ a minimum number of Chinese people. Sao Kao, Lao Chiao and Amah continued to staff the house each day under the strict supervision of the guards throughout my entire imprisonment.

Thursday 27 July 1967

Despite earlier resolve to resume taking notes from past files on the Cultural Revolution, I spent most of the morning on the roof soaking up the first sunny day since I was restricted. I took to shorts and singlet because of the heat. It turned out that I got as red as a beetroot. Had to oil myself and was even a little sore in the evening. Today I heard that the story about me got front-page play in the London *Times* (by Jean Vincent) and also in the *Telegraph* and that there was an editorial in the *Telegraph* about the incident of Oancia and Munthe-Kaas and my case.

Ray Witney spoke to Kevin Garry from Tokyo and he sent his regards and those from other people, especially David Chipp. Today I tried to reply to the cable I received last night, but it was returned. Munthe-Kaas had a story returned today, quoting the *Wen Wei Pao* newspaper on Wuhan. He said Hsieh Fu-chih and others were kidnapped, interrogated, humiliated and illegally arrested. *The Peoples Liberation Army Daily* said unless the 'Wuhan handful' surrendered, they would be destroyed.

My game of chess with John really got going today and we spent some half an hour at it. In the evening after dinner I went up to the roof, since it was quite a balmy evening. I sat and watched the swallows wheeling and dipping over the golden roofs of the Forbidden City in the fading sunset. It was a beautiful, tranquil setting, far removed from the peculiarity of my position. Peace and timelessness were in the air. The clouds on which the setting sun shone seemed to form themselves into two figures – an old be-robed magician, with outstretched arms and a flying cloak, who appeared to be chasing after a pink-tinged form of a beautiful girl, who remained just out of his reach. It seemed to depict the magician's wild chase, forgetful of his other powers in the beauty of the young form.

As time slipped by, the pink cloud faded from his grasp and as the sun went down, the dark blue cloud that was the magician turned into purple and seemed to be falling in a disintegrating mass over the horizon. Bats, with their clumsy flapping action only serving to emphasise the grace of the swallows, became more numerous as darkness fell. It must have been a bad time for small flying insects!

Lao Wang used the car to go to the cable office – for the first time. Hopson told me a note had been sent to the Foreign Ministry and he expected some reply to this. My mood today – the sixth day – was rather tranquil. I am a little horrified at how lazy I am and have decided my true vocation is 'Time waster'!

Thinking of endless days stretching ahead somehow doesn't enter my head. I suppose vaguely I am thinking of 1 August as having some significance. I wrote a loving letter to Shirley today, but goodness knows when it will get posted. Mrs Sathi was among those who called tonight; she prompted, through her gentle concerned femininity, my first real train of thought about the female of the species since my arrest began. The hours really seem to flash by. Time doesn't hang heavy. Lao Chiao is cooking well, Amah is back in action on my laundry and all is right in this peculiar world!

David Chipp was Reuters manager for Asia in London when I left for Peking. He had been the first Peking correspondent, opening the bureau for Reuters there in the late 1950s. He later left Reuters to become editor of the domestic Press Association in London. He showed great kindness to my mother during my imprisonment, several times driving from London to visit her at her home in Norwich to give her any scraps of information about me and my case.

Mrs Sathi, was if I remember rightly, the charming wife of the Indian ambassador.

Friday 28 July 1967

Began studying and noting Cultural Revolution history from Reuters files today. In the afternoon, as I went downstairs for a cold drink, I discovered the London and Hong Kong papers had arrived and some mail also from London (Ed Middleton, Sue Turner). I was so delighted that I celebrated with three or four whiskies and sodas, and went down to dinner in something of a euphoria. My story was fronted in *The Times* and on Monday on an inside page over two columns.

I later listened over the telephone to my Beatles' records, which I had loaned out to Noleen. While I was doing so from her flat, the telephone was cut off. I was unable to make contact with her again and also she was unable to contact me. Interesting little incident: David Chipp sent message through Donald Hopson this morning saying he had been in touch with Mum and June, all was well at home and they sent their love. As soon as he got his car repaired, he would visit Norwich and tell Mother about the house.

No real development in the Cultural Revolution, except Japanese correspondents' reporting that aeroplanes and gunboats had been sent to Wuhan. Radio Australia saw it as an armed insurrection! I became very depressed for the first time towards the end of the evening. Feel the British Government is weak in not doing something strong about this. Fed up with continual confinement with no apparent immediate hope of release. Fucked off in fact! Said aloud in the bedroom I would commit suicide tomorrow if nothing happens! (For the benefit of the microphones, if only to see if it had any result.) Sally Weston told me my photograph was on the front page of the *Guardian*. BBC news from London said tonight Hong Kong had introduced new emergency measures today to detain people for up to a year without trial. It was aimed at those who 'instigated trouble from the background'.

'Ed' Middleton - real name Brian - is one of my greatest friends from school days at the City of Norwich School.

June was my dear sister, three years older than me. She later died an untimely death in 1984.

Saturday 29 July 1967

High point of today was my winning of a chess game with John. He resigned to my very aggressive play. Today a normal delivery of papers came, four Chinese papers, *Herald Tribune* from Paris and *Peking Review*, as well as circulars. I continued noting the Cultural Revolution and finished up to the middle of September last year. When I let the cat, Ming Ming, out into the courtyard tonight, the guards shone torches inside and continued to do so although they couldn't see me.

I served myself tomato and potato sandwiches at my desk with beer late at night, wrote up this diary and bedded down. Jean Vincent told me had a third cable on Wuhan refused yesterday. David Oancia called before he left for Canada and redeemed his reputation with me a little. No feeling of depression, elation or anything today. Just not even thinking about it. Emerita rang to say *The Observer*, in a short front-page piece headed 'Reuters Man Well', referred to me as 'Sir Anthony Grey', thus giving me an early erroneous knighthood!

It is eight days today. Hell!

Wuhan stories are taking second place in the world news today. The New China News Agency in their foreign service reported that military leaders there had 'confessed their crimes'. BBC London news quoted Japanese sources as saying paratroops and gunboats went in. But there was still some continuing opposition, it said.

Ming Ming was the Peking Reuters cat I inherited on my arrival in March. An endearing, affectionate long-haired white and gold young male with a slightly nervous disposition, he had been taken on as a pre-Cultural Revolution pet by Joyanne, the American wife of my predecessor in the Reuters Peking post, Virgil Berger. In the early stages of the Cultural Revolution in late 1966, the keeping of all pets, including goldfish and songbirds, by ordinary Chinese was decreed 'bourgeois' and therefore unrevolutionary by the Mao-inspired Red Guard zealots. Consequently by the time of my arrival, Peking appeared to have been almost denuded of pets of all kinds, because Red Guard gangs had triumphantly rampaged through the city's narrow lanes, known as hutungs, smashing goldfish bowls and tiny birdcages to slaughter their occupants, as well as hunting cats and dogs to their death in the name of their brave new Maoist world.

Ming Ming, because he had lived a fortunate sheltered life inside the foreign-occupied walled courtyard of the Reuters house up to then, was one of the few remaining survivors of this fish, bird and animal holocaust. During the enforced idleness of those early days of my house arrest, when the house was quiet and empty in the evenings I devised a great game with a table-tennis ball, which I would roll for Ming Ming in a certain way at the top of the stairs outside my office. He would dab at it with his paws and chase it happily and erratically down the stairs all the way into the cook's basement kitchen. Then I would fetch it back up and we would do it all over again. I took what became a famous photograph of Ming Ming, dabbing an advisory paw at the queen or bishop on the chessboard set up on my office desk for my games with John Weston.

Sunday 30 July 1967

I spent an hour or so in the sun on the roof before lunch after rising late and breakfasting on fruit and coffee – at a small table on the roof. Then after lunch I read some more copies of *The Times*, which arrived on Thursday – sonic booms and the Abortion Bill were current topics in England. Then I got down to work on more of the Cultural Revolution files.

Two more *Times* copies arrived today with the Chinese papers. I played chess with John and lost after a very tight and demanding game – I lost my Queen early on but put up a good fight without it. Munthe-Kaas called and wanted to do a story. I told him to base it on there having been no further action so far, with a bit of description of my circumstances. On the London news at five o'clock it was reported that another five Chinese journalists had been arrested in Hong Kong, including one new New China News Agency man. Fuck! That doesn't help at all!

I am again feeling cross with the apparent reluctance of the British Government to take any strong measures to get me out of here. What a bloody wet-kneed apparatus the British Government is! The Americans would never have allowed this! My thoughts are again a little low tonight. I now find it difficult to foresee my staying here after this. I can also hazard absolutely no guess at how long it will go on. Could even be six months – or more. Considered later writing to the National Union of Journalists in UK to try to get something done. This I shall do if it goes on long. I have a feeling everyone has forgotten about the case.

Monday 31 July 1967

(Written after a bath and hair wash and with clean pair of green pyjamas on – I feel good.)

Have eaten nothing for some 29 hours. I am now sipping pineapple juice. Decided to fast for my own good, to give the cook a day off and to appreciate more the food the next day. Haven't felt at all hungry really. And it increases alertness I think. This rest can perhaps do me a lot of good. Developments: more Hong Kong newspapers arrived today. My arrest was front-page lead in two papers and back-page lead in the third. Some mail (circulars) from London and Hong Kong, and China papers now arriving regularly.

I tried to phone Tokyo today. After hearing the Tokyo number and my own number the operator said, 'Are you Mr Grey of Reuters?'

'Yes.'

'I can't accept your call.'

'Why?'

'Because of the statement of our Foreign Ministry restricting your freedom of movement.'

'But I don't want to move, I only want to call.'

'The operator refuses your call.'

Click!

I rose late and wrote a story from a *Red Flag* editorial commenting on Army Day. It said, 'Overthrow the "handful" in the Army'. After a glass of water for lunch, I waded into the November and December back files on the Cultural Revolution and kept at it until midnight, with interruptions for chess (third game) with John. I dictated a letter to Mother via Emerita and had some other chats. I continued breathing exercises on the roof in the morning. I suppose I am getting used to it now. The five Hong Kong journalists arrested yesterday were remanded in custody for three weeks. Hell! The 'official' news quoted by BBC London news said Chinese Air Force planes had dropped leaflets on Wuhan.

REFLECTIONS - 1
Thursday 7 December 2006

Looking back at my twenty-nine year-old self from this vantage point in a very changed world, I find myself smiling broadly at these forgotten facts I have just read. 'Four whiskies and sodas and an hour or two spent reading Henry Miller's book *Sexus!*' seems a relatively 'cool' reaction to potential disaster in the eye of the storm that was Beijing on that sweltering, rain-drenched summer evening. Even two whiskies and sodas today would probably set me singing or swaying, or both.

Anyway, several 'medicinal' doses of whisky mixed liberally with shots of Henry Miller – that was my private response to being apprehended at the Foreign Ministry and driven home across Peking through torrential rain and massive, street blocking political demonstrations. Sounds very bizarre now – yet events even more bizarre, it turns out, were unfolding around me without my then knowing how extreme things had become.

On that very day, I've just discovered, the Cultural Revolution was in fact flaring to one of its white-hot climaxes in Wuhan in central China. I had always been aware that it was events there which had triggered those massive demonstrations in the capital on the afternoon of my arrest, without knowing fully why. Now I have just discovered some fascinating new detail in an outstanding recent book by Jung Chang, author of the worldwide bestseller *Wild Swans*. In *Mao: The Unknown Story*, co-written with her husband Jon Halliday, Jung explains that Mao had gone secretly to Wuhan in person in mid-July, convinced he could personally bring into line a 'conservative' or 'moderate' general who until then had fiercely opposed the confused lawlessness of the Cultural Revolution in his region. Mao planned to use this example of a major convert backing his wild plans to help him swing rebellious leaders in other provinces behind him.

In the event, the Wuhan general, Chen Zai-dao, who commanded a powerful force loyal to him called the 'Peerless Million Troops', amazed Mao by defying him outright, face to face. Briefly a brutal civil war ensued in the area, as was to happen in many other regions during the Cultural Revolution, contributing to the believed death toll of over three million people. As an upshot of General Chen's defiance, a mob of hundreds of his supporters, armed with guns and iron bars, invaded the grounds of Mao's heavily guarded temporary villa situated beside the Yangtse, baying for his blood.

Swarming towards the buildings, they are said to have 'got within a stone's throw of Mao'. In the process they captured and ferociously beat a top member of Mao's entourage, Wang Li. Mao's special train, personal aircraft and warships were all standing by and the badly-frightened chairman of China's Communist Party was reportedly whisked out of the back door of his villa by Premier Chou En-lai (Zhou Enlai) at 2 am on 21 July. Mao switched quickly from his official train to the plane and fled for his life to Shanghai.

Chou En-lai eventually engineered the release of Wang Li and it was Wang Li's 'triumphant arrival' back in Peking and the sound of the extraordinary celebration rally of over a million people held in nearby Tien An Men Square that I now know I heard and wrote about in the opening pages of this diary on 25 July. General Chen's name was almost certainly one of those that I heard being screamed by a million throats to herald his downfall.

Later General Chen and his deputy generals of the Peerless Million Troops were, according to Jung Chang, brought to Peking and 'jet-planed' at an official formal meeting of the Party's Politburo, held either in the Great Hall of the People or the walled Chung Nan Hai leadership compound, both locations relatively close to my house. At the meeting, General Chen and his supporters were bent double with their arms held twisted up behind them, just as I had been on the steps of my house, while they were beaten and kicked unmercifully by a group of other leaders, led by the commander in chief of the Chinese Air Force, Wu Fa-hsien (Wu Fa-xian). General Chen was knocked to the floor and trampled on – all reportedly watched by Premier Chou En-lai, who was formally chairing the meeting.

'Even in Mao's gangster world', say the book's authors, 'for the Politburo to become the scene of physical violence was unprecedented.'

In addition to the surprise memory of those four first-night whiskies and Henry Miller's book, as I read on through the July diary entries, I was surprised too by the references indicating that glasses of wine and beer were also not infrequently quaffed in the next ten days. Such things had slipped entirely from my memory with much of the other detail. Already, too, in those first ten days of relatively comfortable restriction, it is very clear that, without my being particularly conscious of it, the diary was fast becoming a vital tool helping me to focus my wayward self-discipline and determination. I don't think I was particularly aware of it then – yet perhaps writing the diary itself was a kind of unconscious limbering up for what, if I had really allowed myself to be realistic, might soon be to come.

When I took a first glance at the transcript of this first ten-day period of these diaries some weeks ago, I found after the first page or two I became quickly overwhelmed and could not read on. Although the entries showed I was still relatively free inside the house, telephoning friends, reading newspapers from England and listening to BBC World Service radio, I was struck very forcibly by the fact that the unfortunate individual who was writing those diary entries in relative comfort in those very early days had no idea then that things were going to get very much worse for him. In fact without knowing it, he had two long harrowing years of isolation and inner trauma to endure still ahead of him.

I say quite deliberately 'the unfortunate individual who was writing it', because that is truly how it seemed – that I was reading about this happening to somebody else, not me. My heart sank for 'him'. How on earth is he going to get through all that, I felt. At that first encounter it was too painful to contemplate 'his' unknowingness. When I eventually was able to pick up the diary again in the last few days, I steeled myself to concentrate on re-discovering progressively exactly how I was reacting to the situation day by day. Then I found one or two spots in the transcripts that had small gaps and were not entirely precise in their meaning. I decided if I was really going to do this job properly, I must go to my bank in the centre of Norwich and get the original carefully-preserved shorthand diaries out of their locked deed-box, so that I could have them available to double-check any unclear passages.

So as we move on from July into August 1967, my two close supportive companions from those strange days cut off from the world in China are with me again after a very long absence. Two square scuffed Chinese exercises books, one with a hard blue cover, the other with a hard maroon cover, both of them very worn at the spines, are lying beside my computer keyboard as I write. One was originally the notebook where my translator listed the office postal expenses, the other was the cook's record of money regularly spent on vegetables and other groceries. The tiny hieroglyphics of my shorthand that took over from their handwritten Chinese characters about domestic expenses, are still amazingly clear, yet not easily comprehensible to me, as it is a very long time indeed since I read or wrote shorthand. Yet how extraordinary a written record can be! And in re-reading these diary entries, my chief realisation is about how much our memories lose routinely if we don't write things down. That is the thought filling my mind as I return to re-discovering how I was managing as the increasingly hot and humid days of August began in China's capital in 1967.

2
SKIPPING ON THE ROOF

Tuesday 1 August 1967

I rose late again and read the New China News Agency, and wrote a piece about Chu Teh appearing at the Army Day banquet. I received a letter from Angel and a card in an envelope from New York. Shirley's letter told me how worried she was. She was in Bad Godesberg, in Germany. I was pictured (like a convict) in *The Times* and *Guardian* and *Mail*. I also received a Beatles' record, a book and card and a picture from Bob in Norwich. I read the book with great delight – Michael Bentine's *Square Games*. Another message from David Chipp said he had visited Mum and June and they were very well and sent their love. Shirley said in her letter, 'Please God keep my Tony safe.'

After my daylong fast I resumed eating at breakfast with scrambled eggs, juice and fruit and coffee. It was so hot today I could hardly eat any lunch. Dinner, when I was hungry, was an omelette. On the BBC news there was mention of new Hong Kong measures to impose longer sentences, and a report of premier Chou En-lai reviewing a Red Guard parade.

Marshall Chu Teh was a greatly revered Communist Long March general who had not until then been seen in public during the chaos of the Cultural Revolution. This appearance seemed to suggest he had not been disgraced.

Bob is Robert Corless, another much appreciated lifelong friend from Norwich with a highly developed sense of humour.

Wednesday 2 August 1967

In the morning, after messing around doing very little until 10.30 am, I worked and finally finished late in the afternoon. Donald Hopson telephoned in the morning to say there were 'straws in the wind' indicating it may not be too long before somebody comes to see me. Ray Witney called to say he would not try to bring books because this might be construed as attempting consular access. BBC London news said the troubles in Wuhan were not finished. Radio Peking was quoted as saying there would be rehabilitation if the rebels laid down their arms. Later, London news reported troubles in Shantung province, where other opposition groups had seized people sent from the capital. One *New York Herald Tribune* arrived today.

Several people telephoned and I worked very hard, I suppose. At this moment the heat outside my bedroom door is incredible. There is no air conditioning out there as there is in here. The temperature is exactly 90 degrees in the dark at one o'clock in the morning!

The temperature of 90°F is equivalent to 32°C.

Thursday 3 August 1967

I rose at 10 am and worked on my Cultural Revolution file during the afternoon period and finished up to the end of March – my arrival here in China. There were no developments of interest. I received Chinese newspapers and one *Herald Tribune*. I got depressed at teatime and expressed depression on the phone to Jean Vincent and Noleen and Emerita. I played chess with John in the evening and lost. I started reading Edward Crankshaw's book *Moscow versus Peking*. The temperature at 12.30 am is 89 degrees. It has been incredibly hot these past few days. I had a beer and an iced whisky and soda in my bedroom tonight, standing the bottles next to the air conditioner. I am doing yoga breathing exercises every morning. I am sinking gently into a restless unease and I realise I shall have to assert a form of discipline soon.

Friday 4 August 1967

Two weeks today and God knows how much longer. Today a book from Noleen arrived in the post: Eric Ambler's thriller *A Kind of Anger*. I began reading at lunchtime and finished it at 11.30 pm. I just lay on my bed all day reading and drinking beer. BBC London news and Radio Japan said the Peking Revolutionary Committee had called for President Liu Shao-chi to be brought out of the Chung Nan Hai government compound by midnight on 5 August. Workers reportedly beat each other up in Shanghai, and there were helicopter landings at leftist headquarters in Hong Kong. Six cigars arrived from Emerita. I begin to feel extremely lazy and realise I must do something about it – or else.

Saturday 5 August 1967

I wrote letters to Shirley, Mother, Ed, Bob and Kim. I read some more of Crankshaw's *Moscow versus Peking* and received John Braine's *Room at the Top* from John Weston. Chinese Embassy staff are reported on the BBC to have opened fire on demonstrators in Indonesia. This was later found to be incorrect, I believe. There was more trouble at Lo Wu, the border point with Hong Kong, but the demonstrators were talked out of violence. There was a big rally at Tien An Men Square against Liu Shao-chi and some stories said land lines were set up between the meeting and the place where Liu lives, when he appeared at another meeting. China today rejected a protest from Sweden about correspondent Harald Munthe-Kaas and the incident involving their diplomat.

Kim Davenport is a lifelong friend from my days in Great Yarmouth on the Yarmouth Mercury.

Sunday 6 August 1967

An unremarkable day. I continued writing letters and there was an afternoon delivery of *Time* magazine and a Reuters pay slip from London and a letter from David Chipp, saying he had visited Mum and June. He said it was not clear to him whether I could file news. He also asked that his regards be given here 'to those who remembered him'. I later played John at chess and won, making it 3–2. I resolved to rise at 7.30 tomorrow to do a hard day's work. Tonight I read more of '*Moscow versus Peking*'.

Monday 7 August 1967

I rose around 7.50 and listened to the eight o'clock news for the first time in weeks.

I got down to sorting out my cuttings, then my file cuttings, which took all day. It was 92 degrees and was so humid that I dripped incessantly over my work. I have never known it so hot. I finished *Moscow versus Peking*. I received a set of Chinese chequers from Noleen and a novel. I am still feeling as I did yesterday, like sending a note to Long telling them they clearly don't understand the situation. But I will give it a couple of days. My spirits are now even and unchanging. I feel I have so much to do. Tomorrow I will sort out the New China News Agency file and follow that by feature writing for several days.

Gerald Long was general manager of Reuters.

Tuesday 8 August 1967

Up at 7.50 am and sorted out the file of copy of the New China News Agency, cleared up my desk and finally brought the Cultural Revolution file fully up to date. I had a letter from Angel, a short two-page affair. It came from Germany and it served to distance me a little from Shirley's image. Perhaps it was 'almost too hot to write', she said. Or maybe it was the way she said it was 'all fun here'. Lots of eating, concert going and life was one big social whirl. I just didn't appreciate it. 'Eating and concert going' seemed a little old for me. And I feel hard and joyless and disinterested. I tried on the phone to press John for information and did little to hide my annoyance at 'nothing having been done for 18 days'. I also received some books from John, but began reading *The Loser* by Peter Ustinov from the motley collection of books collected together here by previous correspondents.

Wednesday 9 August 1967

I am feeling very restless tonight. (I am writing this at 10.25 pm, long before thinking of going to bed. Since this diary is normally a tiresome task before turning in, it indicates my restlessness.) I slept today until 11.30 am, having woken in the middle of the night because of the heat. My air-conditioner was switched off because its plug got very hot and I feared a fire. I had breakfast on the roof, read a *Herald Tribune* and received several books from dear Emerita. I lunched off chopped meat, beans, rice and peaches with soup and beer. Then read *The Loser* all afternoon, finishing it at 10.15. It is very funny.

The 'masses' set fire to the car of the Mongolian Ambassador today and burnt it out, then they demonstrated at the embassy. I sat on the roof in the dusk, looking at the dark shape of the roofs of the Forbidden City, pondering without conclusion on this strange plight of mine. I looked over the parapet and watched a young girl wash herself sitting on a stool in the street below – a bowl between her legs, trousers rolled up and using a flannel. A few yards away, Chinese men in vests and rolled up trousers squatted in a circle on the pavement. The night is peaceful and orderly and not too hot. Light glittered in the moat and panpipes wailed somewhere in the darkness.

Thursday 10 August 1967

Donald Hopson called to say he was puzzled because there had been a firm indication that access would be allowed here in return for access in Hong Kong. But a trial was still going on and either the Foreign Ministry or the New China News Agency were preoccupied with several things or the outcome of the trial was being awaited. Otherwise apart from the arrival of some more books and *Times* newspapers, today was routine. There were an unusual number of callers, including Magnus the Swede, Vladimir the Russian, Milo the Yugoslav, Maria the Italian, Pat, Ann (England) and others. Jean Vincent hadn't had received any news of his visa which expired today. Harald Munthe-Kaas got his exit visa and was somewhat unctuous on the telephone, saying how right their complaints had been. I read Graham Greene's *The Quiet American* most of the day and turned to Carew-Hunt's *The Theory and Practice of Communism* at night. I am being terribly lazy again and achieving nothing. It has taken me two days to get myself together enough to plan two letters to David Chipp and Don Ferguson, the head of Visnews.

Friday 11 August 1967

I rose late, got on at last with writing the letters to David Chipp and Don and finished them by lunchtime. In the afternoon I read more *Theory and Practice of Communism,* cleared out my desk and squandered the evening reading and lazing. I went to bed with the chess book and board. Telephone calls came from many people. Jean Vincent's visa expired with no renewal in view. It is the three-week 'anniversary' of my house arrest today.

Saturday 12 August 1967

I rose late and worked out chess moves, read and worked out chess moves again at lunch, and continued afterwards. Later I read some more of *The Theory and Practice of Communism* with dinner. I also took photographs of Ming Ming 'playing chess' with one paw on my desk. Finally I played chess on the phone with John – and lost!

The news of the last two days is that Canton Radio is behaving strangely, just playing music instead of news. There were reports of fighting there. Peasants are said to be flooding into the city because their work points are not being worked out properly. Border incidents at Hong Kong, involving Chinese crossing over having difficulties with British police and Ghurkas. No serious injuries reported, although the Ghurkas reportedly drew their jungle knives. The Russians say one of their ships is being held in Dairen. Eleven sailors got off another ship in Canada rather than come to China with cargo. China has also accused Burma of border incursions. Meantime the anti-Mongolian demonstrations here in Peking are continuing. Oslo publicly announced the recall of Harald Munthe-Kaas. And so to bed. Many telephone callers again today.

Sunday 13 August 1967

Up at 10.45, breakfast, New China News Agency, newspapers – five new airmail copies of *The Times* – and *The Economist*. I had lunch with the papers and read the papers some more on the bed after lunch. Later I went on the roof with the chessboard. Read *The Economist* with dinner and had a second bottle of Medoc wine. Played chess with John and won a long game, on the endgame. I called John at eleven o'clock to check a New China News Agency report, which said two women reporters had been sentenced to one week in prison in Hong Kong. In fact the sentence was 50 dollars fine and prison if they didn't pay. The Minister rang with the same news. Erna of the Norwegian Embassy was among today's callers. Today the Hong Kong trial result was due. It seems that prospects may have improved for access and perhaps even release. I feel much better anyway. Today the formation of a new Revolutionary Committee in Shanghai was announced.

Erna, a lively and friendly girl, was a secretary at the embassy.

Monday 14 August 1967

Up at 6.45 am and followed roughly the new plan set out on the next page of this diary. I skipped for five minutes – killing it was! – and slipped behind with the schedule somewhat. The sunbathing was missed. But I produced two Reuters Situationer features although it should have been three. Stanislaus, the Polish news agency correspondent returned from Warsaw today and tried without success to visit me. Donald Hopson was called to the Foreign Ministry tonight, but he didn't call me so I assume it wasn't about me. Jean Vincent had to hand in his press card today, but didn't know why. I was so busy writing features today I didn't have time to think about my predicament.

Plan for week beginning 14 August 1967

6.45	Wake. Teeth, breathing, shave
7.00	News
7.15	Exercise and wash
7.30	Work
9.15	Skipping (5 mins, increasing 1 min. per day)
9.30	Breakfast: Hsin Hua news agency copy – read and file
10.00	Work
12.00	Sunbathing one hour
13.00	Lunch (sleep or read)
15.00	Work
16.00	Listen to radio news at desk
17.00	Listen to: news and editorial comment from London
17.30	Work

19.30   Dinner, reading, chess, bed before 11 pm
23.00   Bed and sleep
Write feature articles in 'Work' periods.

Tuesday 15 August 1967

Up at 6.40 am. Planned the army feature and got a page written before breakfast. Continued with my skipping. I finished my feature before lunch, sunbathed, had wine with my lunch, did a crossword, had a sleep, planned and wrote a feature on toys in Cultural Revolution China, while sitting in the sun on the roof and later read it through. I played John at chess and more than held my own in a game we decided to hold over. The East German correspondent for ADN, Herr Eckleben, Stanislaus the Pole and Jean Esmaine of the French Embassy were among today's callers. Jean Vincent's press card was renewed. The previously secret decision on former Defence Minister Peng Teh-huai's sacking in 1959 was published yesterday by the New China News Agency. No developments in my case. It turned out the British authorities in Hong Kong got money for the fine of one of the Chinese News Agency reporters and drove her out of prison, while the other one had to serve a week.

Wednesday 16 August 1967

Up at 6.45 am and wrote another feature about new Cultural Revolution plays before breakfast. Then wrote stories about the publication at last of the previously secret Central Committee decision on Peng Teh-huai and a Red Flag editorial linking President Liu Shao-chi with him. After breakfast I skipped for 7 mins. (161 skips in 2 mins. 10 seconds was my record!) I sunbathed, slept and read newspapers during the afternoon and wrote a schools feature in the evening. I beat John at chess. Ray Witney again called about the Hong Kong trials. He talked of there being another one starting on 21August, which plunged me into a helpless fury at the feeble British Government (continuing to accept the situation). Noleen had a pair of sunglasses refused today at the post office when she tried to send them to me. Alistair had a parcel refused yesterday. Emerita was also refused something the day before. Some cheroots arrived from Erna today and I had my first decent smoke.

I was writing the timeless Situationer features that Reuters correspondents all over the world wrote then, so that they could be routinely distributed to Features Editors worldwide by airmail from London if I was suddenly released. I was writing the harder news stories just to keep myself abreast of developments in the Cultural Revolution and for the office files, so that there would be no gap in Reuters local record.

Alistair Hunter was a trade diplomat at the British Mission.

Thursday 17 August 1967

I moved my total of written Situationer features up to eight today. I wrote an early-morning piece and a late-night piece on Chinese officers mending socks for their men! In between, I messed around reading the New China News Agency file from the basement printer, among other things. Then after lunch I slept and read the newspapers and magazines that arrived from Jean Esmaine of the French Embassy and the Dutch Chargé d'Affaires, Andreas Fokkema. I lost to John at chess in the evening. I also got a headache. In Hong Kong three newspapers were closed. In Peking, the Italian Trade Mission chief was dragged out of his office and put on mock trial by Red Guards for an hour because of a Chinese ship getting into trouble in a port in Italy, according to radio reports.

REFLECTIONS - 2
Friday 8 December 2006

At this point the diary was interrupted for a two-week period. On the night of Friday 18 August, a mob of around 200 yelling Red Guards smashed down the courtyard gate and invaded the Reuters house, cut my phone link, put me through a bizarre process, known as a 'struggle meeting' in Cultural Revolution parlance, and confined me under close guard from then on in a small room about eight-feet square on the ground floor of the house. Public Security Bureau officers from then on occupied the whole house, making their headquarters in my former dining room.

Miraculously, however, I was able to resume the diary two weeks later, writing it then secretly in shorthand so that it would hopefully be indecipherable by my guards if discovered. Until 17 August I had written the diary each day in ordinary legible longhand, since I was still in control of the inside of the house and did not fear it being inspected. Later I translated the first month's entries laboriously into shorthand, then carefully blacked out the original words.

3
THE INVASION

Thursday 31 August 1967

I obtained a pen without being noticed today, while getting the chequebook from upstairs under escort – and what a joy it was!

So here is an account of recent events: on 18 August at about 10.45 in the evening I was writing a feature at my desk. Ironically I was summarising all the anti-foreign demonstrations of recent weeks and months in Peking, when I heard sudden loud shouting from the street outside. Rushing to the bathroom, I looked out and saw a crowd and rushed back to telephone. But even as I dialled, I heard Red Guards shouting and banging their way up the stairs. I don't know whether the number of the British Office rang or not.

Three Red Guards burst in, snatched the phone from me and others crowded in behind them. I was dragged down into the yard where I was 'jet-planed'. Black paint was daubed on me, down my right side, and I was made to bend double. While I was in this position, a poster was pasted on my back. All the time there was shouting. Then I was dragged back up to the top of the steps and made to bend double again while various Red Guards proceeded to read out 'lists of crimes'. I couldn't hear most of what was said, although someone was translating.

Whenever I tried to straighten up to ease my back, which was becoming painful, I was hit in the stomach by one Red Guard, who was obviously in charge of keeping me in this position. He forced my head down while hitting me in the stomach – very effective. At this time the dead body of Ming Ming, my cat, was suddenly lowered on a rope from the roof or balcony above. His body was dangling in my face as I bent over on the front step. There had been cheering earlier and applause and I think this must have been as Ming Ming was strangled up above. This whole treatment lasted about three-quarters of an hour I think. I have no way of knowing exactly.

The only 'crimes' which I could make out were that I had 'drunk alcohol' in my home and had 'despised' the paper tiger hung outside. 'Even despised' I think was the exact wording. I believe there was also something about 'sneaking around' in my own house. I was referred to throughout as 'reactionary newsman Grey'. When the cat's body was lowered there were loud shouts of 'Hang Grey! Hang Grey!' After a time I was able to see the reflection of my face in a pool of sweat that had gathered on the step in front of me, dripping from my face, neck and shoulders. How big the crowd was I have no idea.

At the end, a four-point order was read out which said:

1 I must obey the guards.

2 I must remain in the scope designed by the masses.

3 I must respect the posters put up in the house.

4 I must await further notice from the government.

Organisers associated with this were: Red Guards and Revolutionary Rebels of the Peking Photo Machine Factory and the Red Guards of the city's primary and middle schools. One after another, while I was bent double, they read out long statements. Things I remember from them included: 'We could kill you, but … Hang Wilson! Hang Grey!' This I think was when the cat's body was lowered.

'You have unjustly arrested newsmen and today closed three newspapers,' they yelled at one point. Every few moments the crowd interrupted with new shouts against me. At the end, long quotations from Mao were read out. The whole situation was nightmarish. Whenever I bent one knee to ease my position, some bright Chang in the front of the crowd pointed this out to my 'keeper' who pushed it straight. When I rested my arm on my knee to take some strain, it was pushed away.

My hands were not held behind me after a while but when I tried to rub my back they were snatched away. Eventually, with my head almost between my knees, I managed to get my arms round in front and rest them on my thighs without anybody noticing. This saved my back considerably and I was pleased with this. Both arms were covered in black paint by this time. Steps were put up beside me and something – which I later discovered was a Mao portrait – was pasted over the door. I heard loud sounds of hammering with wood and nails above and around me, and cheering. This, I later discovered, was the doors and window of my 'cell' being secured.

At last, with my back seemingly breaking, I was allowed to stand up and led inside and up the stairs to be shown the handiwork of the 'masses'. At the bottom of the stairs was one of the most beautiful Chinese girls I had ever seen, a Red Guard, of course. But she wouldn't look at me as I went by, staring instead straight ahead with a shake of her pigtails. The walls of the stairs, the landing, the bedroom, the bathroom and even the sheets and blankets on my bed had been daubed with slogans and stuck with posters. The bath was painted black inside and one other fine detail was that the bristles of my toothbrush were also painted black, making it unusable.

The door of my office had been sealed with stickers across the doorjamb. I was told to take 'what I required for my daily needs' by an interpreter working with an impressive-looking Public Security Bureau man. I said I could not take it all at once and was told I could make two trips. From the bedroom I took bedding – with some paint on it – and spare shirts, shorts, pants, vests, handkerchiefs and pyjamas. There were four books in the room. They were Harry Golombek's *Chess, The Theory and Practice of Communism* by Carew-Hunt, *True Yoga* by William Zorn and Pasternak's *Doctor Zhivago*. They allowed me to take down all of them except *Zhivago*. The critical *Theory and Practice of Communism* passed muster because it had a big picture of Marx and a hammer and sickle on the front, I think. This made me reflect on the similarity in reverse of the case of William Shirer's *The Rise and Fall of the Third Reich*, which was confiscated from me by East German border guards at Checkpoint Charlie in East Berlin because it had a swastika on its cover. Interesting contrast. I also took my wallet and my manicure set. The alarm clock completed my possessions.

I asked for a pen, but was refused one. After a brief look in this book – my diary – it was passed. The whole episode upstairs was over in a few minutes.

Earlier, after a round of the house, I was taken down into the scullery and driver's room and read the Declaration of Four Points again. Photographers who had been present throughout taking pictures of me bent over, with flashguns, then took more pictures in the scullery. The crowd shouted to me to bow my head, but since they hadn't forced me, I glared at the cameras. But then they forced my head down again, so I relented and let them take them how they liked.

After that they left and it was about midnight. I was aching all over and out of breath, and didn't sit down for a long time.

On gathering my senses I washed some of the black paint off as best I could with a handkerchief. After a while I made up my bed in the driver's room and fell into an exhausted sleep.

The next day the pattern of my new life was soon established. Breakfast at 11, scrambled eggs and coffee. Lunch at one with meat and dinner at six o'clock, sometimes with meat. Three bottles of water were allowed each day. No butter and no fruit. The door of the scullery was to be kept open and the light left on all night, so the guards could see me at all times if I left my little room.

The guards set up an office in the dining room and after two days a phone was put in. A portrait of Mao was hung on the wall in a gold frame. In big daubed black English letters on one wall, a slogan said, 'Down with A. Grey!' The guard changed at nine o'clock, morning and night, with a loud gabble of Mao's quotations. Sometimes a guard came into the scullery to look at me. I was allowed to close the door to go to the toilet, but had to open it again afterwards. On the twelfth day I asked for some papers and got them – Chinese ones of course. My meals I have to eat sitting on the edge of my camp bed and eating from a chair on which the tray of food is placed.

The cell is interesting. It is about eight feet square. It was previously a room where my driver took a lunchtime nap. It was indescribably dirty and I had to clean it out myself. On the wall which I face when lying in the bed, the Chinese characters say, 'Long live Chairman Mao Tse-tung!' On the door and wall on the other side of it two slogans say, 'Down with British imperialism!' On the left wall is a portrait of Mao with the words in English 'Long live Chairman Mao!' On the other door and two walls are copies of the posters, again giving the Four Points.

Two large pink paper posters above my bed say, 'People of the world unite and defeat the US aggressors and all their running dogs.' And, 'Lifting a rock to drop it on one's own feet is a Chinese folk saying describing the behaviour of certain fools. Reactionaries of all countries are fools of this kind.'

More slogans against British imperialism are on the walls above my head and at the side. The east window is painted black and both windows and the outside door are nailed up. Both windows in the scullery are painted black and are nailed up. One small section at the top of one window was opened on the third day and this is my only air supply. At night I have the choice of sleeping with air and with the light of the scullery shining in, or in the dark without air. From one end of my cell to the other end of the scullery is eight and a half paces. I walk this frequently, estimating two miles an hour.

Today, 31 August was the first time I left the cell – to go upstairs to get the chequebook to pay the staff wages. I was pleased to see that although things were in a mess, apparently nothing had been stolen. I was refused permission to have my shortwave radio. Red Guards, apparently from the

Photo Machine Factory, came to break the seals on the office door to let me in, and crowded in with me to watch what I did.

On the wall alongside my bed in this cell in English in blue paint is the slogan, 'Those who oppose China will come to no good end.' The walls of the scullery are daubed with slogans too. The mirror was, at first, but they allowed me to clean that off. The lavatory seat was painted black, as well as the bowl of the toilet. The bath was painted completely black inside and I have made no attempt to clean it. Two more copies of the Four-Point order were pasted up in there – one at eye level beside the mirror. Two copies of the poster were stuck up in the scullery.

I can't clearly remember what I have done in the intervening days, but I have performed all kinds of memory feats to keep myself occupied. I have taken up yoga. I have thought about all my sporting achievements. I have recalled thoroughly my school days and all the names of members of my classes at all the schools I have ever attended. I have recalled where I was on certain days, going back years. I have gone through my life in the Air Force and my journalistic career in great detail, and even tried to recall all the pubs I have ever been in. I have read *The Theory and Practice of Communism* one-and-a-half times and am constantly reading the chess book.

I do yoga exercises in the morning and afternoon and sometimes three times a day. The only other piece of furniture in my cell, apart from the bed and the chair is a canvas fishing stool on which I keep my few belongings – shirt, pants, vests, socks and spare pair of shorts.

I have sometimes played a game of trying to look at the guard as I cross his line of vision without him seeing me looking. I have devised a points basis for this, calling the game Pass-Look and in my mind I pit international teams in pairs against each other. I wash some of my clothes and the first night had to wash myself with a handkerchief in the sink. I am under the impression that I can't clean out the bath and don't intend to anyway. Watchers gather on the roof to look in at the window of the scullery quite often.

REFLECTIONS - 3

Saturday 9 December 2006

I can still clearly remember today, without any memory-jogging from the 31 August diary entry I have just read, those dark jeering faces peering down from the low roof of the restaurant next door to 15 Nan Chihtze. Usually male and usually youths, my gleeful observers could see straight into my little eight-foot-square cell. I could swing my legs up onto the low broken-springed bunk and sit with my back to a wall to avoid their direct gaze – and usually did when they appeared. Yet I remember that, whenever they came on me unawares, pacing restlessly back and forth towards their window vantage point, I knew just how caged zoo animals must feel on being confined and gawped at from beyond the bars of their prison.

Mao Tse-tung had his invasion in Wuhan on Friday 21 July – and I had my own version exactly four weeks later on Friday 18 August. The circumstances of the two invasions and their outcomes were different – though they did have one thing in common. Mao, with the ever-faithful Chou En-lai's help, dodged his invaders and narrowly evaded death, it seems, at the hands of the mob of angry men with machine-guns and iron bars. My invaders came armed with rope and, to my dismay, Ming Ming became their token victim in my place. I remember too, as I straightened up to find the cat's body dangling in my face, doing my best to stare expressionlessly ahead above the heads of the baying mob. Much much later, in my office upstairs, I would find a pair of scissors encrusted with dried blood that had obviously been used to stab the cat in order to daub its blood on my sheets.

Mao escaped, Ming Ming and I didn't – but the common factor to both invasions was that there were two lots of 'jet-planing', that favourite sporting pastime of the Cultural Revolution. I was held bent double on my front steps for half an hour or more, receiving occasional additional blows, while the unfortunate General Chen, ex-commander of Wuhan's Peerless Million Soldiers, was dealt with similarly, as part of the agenda of a formal Politburo meeting nearby. In General Chen's case the head of China's Air Force, Wu Fa-hsien, led the beatings and kickings.

In retrospect on this winter's afternoon in December 2006 from the comfort of my home in Norfolk, I feel that perhaps I was very fortunate indeed to survive my invasion in one piece at such a wild time in the Cultural Revolution. According to Jung Chang in *Mao: The Unknown Story*, during his 27-year reign Mao was responsible for the deaths of 75 million Chinese. That I was not added to that staggering statistic now seems fairly miraculous in view of all the violence that was going on around me.

In any event, that night of 18 August marked the end of the journey to the beginning for me. It signalled the end of that strange 'phoney war' period of precisely four weeks living relatively at ease under house arrest, making and receiving telephone calls, reading newspapers from Britain, eating and drinking normally and listening to radio news from London and elsewhere. During that time I was in limbo, halfway between freedom and total captivity, in a kind of no man's land or purgatory, keeping away thoughts of how things might get worse by furiously writing feature articles that would never get published. As the mob broke down my gates, I was in fact typing the words, 'A long list of foreign embassies and residences have come under direct attack by China's "masses" in the last few months ...' I did not finish the sentence, because the next thing was the sound of the mob coming up the stairs to my office. By two weeks later, as August ended and September was beginning, I had become very much an out-and-out captive. The only bright spark in the darkness was that somehow I had obtained a pen without anyone noticing – and, after a two-week interval, I still remember feeling the most enormous sense of relief that I would be able to resume making entries in this sanity-saving diary.

4

THE EIGHT-FOOT-SQUARE CELL

Saturday 2 September 1967, 7.40 pm

Dinner at 6 pm was two fried eggs, two pieces of ham, a few chips, two pieces of dry toast, sliced cucumber, egg and potato and two bottles of water. Since then I have lain on the bed and wondered if there is any possibility of me ever getting out of here – and walked up and down for most of the rest of the time.

Today I rose around nine, cleaned my teeth, shaved, exercised and did yoga postures. For a quarter of an hour I walked, before breakfast arrived around 10.30 am. It was one slice of dry toast with some scrambled egg and a pot of coffee. After breakfast I walked again, then had a whole body wash using a screwed-up vest as a flannel. It was the third wash in 15 days – of its kind. The other two times have been with handkerchiefs. After this I changed into clean clothes. I wore for the first time since 18 August the yellow shirt that still has black paint on it. My white socks also have black paint on them. I washed my grey shirt and socks and after that I walked again until lunchtime.

Lunch, which was typical, was a plate of chips, three slices of bread, sliced cucumber and sliced potato and one bottle of water. After lunch I walked again for some time, then asked for some newspapers. They included the *People's Daily*, which had a statement by Mao, Lin and Chou on the front and I could see Britain mentioned although I don't know why. Around 4 pm in the afternoon two cadres of the Public Security Bureau arrived. They wore more faded jackets than my guards and looked tougher, more senior and more intelligent. One of them looked a particularly tough nut.

They looked around all over the house and set me speculating as to the reasons for their visit. Did Hsieh Fu-chih want a report? Could it mean some action? In a vague way I found it encouraging. I scratched my fifteenth nail mark on the wall today and for some reason I can't see more than four weeks going up there. My hopeful estimate is that something will turn up within two to three weeks – but most probably in around 12 days time.

My main logical reason for this, I suppose, is that my press card and visa run out on 21 September. Although this is no solid reason, it is a point in time of sorts. Also I think this ridiculous feeling that my saying many months ago that I would 'try to stay in China six months' may turn out to be true. (I meant then before taking a break in Hong Kong or somewhere outside.) It will be six months about 18 September. This, plus the fact that by then Hong Kong will have had time to settle their court problems and some kind of arrangement might be made. But of course this is all guesswork. I find myself thinking about going home and arriving there so much that it frightens me to think it may never happen.

I have prayed a lot, night and morning recently. My mood is kind of resigned to the reality of the situation and I am not depressed. Over the past few days I have managed to adopt a kind of resigned acceptance of the position. I know it doesn't help being extremely depressed, so I have tried to keep my mind level on another plane. I suppose I am doing well at it now but fear some deterioration of my position. God, how long is it to be?

Trying to remember how I have felt over the past 15 days in detail is difficult. The first few days were not too bad. I found that somehow I had four pages of *The Times* of May 1965 – two years old – in here and read a page of this a day for the first four days. Perhaps they had been used to wrap something. I adopted a system of reading parts of Carew-Hunt's *Theory and Practice of Communism* and doing some chess in the afternoons.

My thinking sessions have been devoted mainly to times when I am walking back and forth. I have gone over in detail my Royal Air Force days, my school days, my press career to date, all my different birthdays so far. I have also thought in great detail of all the girls I have had three kinds of 'relations' with and I have invented an ideal girl, Angeline, that I met imaginarily on the A11 road from London to Norwich, have made imaginary love to Pauline, a totally unknown girl, thought about many of my male and female friends in enormous detail – and in fact my memory is becoming so stimulated that it is bringing back all kinds of little cameo pictures of isolated incidents constantly now without any effort.

On about the seventh day I remember having bad depression and thinking this must be some kind of turning point – like the seven-year itch. Mostly in the early part of this spell I have despised the British Government for being so weak. But this has watered down in my present mood of resignation. It is quite amazing, really, how one adjusts to such a situation because there is simply nothing else one can do.

I have bitten the string that makes up the clothesline in the washroom to ease my anger sometimes and I have on a few occasions kicked out at something with my foot. But apart from this, my physical reactions have been controlled. My face has been in my hands only rarely. I've found this doesn't help. Occasionally I resort to muttering 'Oh God, please get me out of here!' Today I have watched ants on the floor of this cell doing amazing things.

One pulled a huge moth's wing ten times bigger than itself across the room to the ant-home in the corner under the wall. It was fascinating to watch. Later another pulled a crumb in the same fashion across the room. Lao Chiao asked for some overtime payment today. I suppose he is due something, since he was very good when he was working on his own without the cook, who didn't come for a few days for unknown reasons.

I have carved a small nude figure out of soap. It was coming along well until, while trying to make the arse too big, I broke off one of the legs. But the bust was quite good. Yes, I have been able to make myself laugh. I have recited four Morecambe and Wise sketches from their LP record and have often recalled funny incidents and laughed aloud or laughed at my own mental irony. Example, 'There might be a consular visit in 15 days' time, there's something really wonderful to look forward to!'

I have recalled the funniest things that have happened to me in my whole life to date and decided the funniest was falling in the lake in Regents Park while walking nonchalantly beside Shirley carrying a furled umbrella and wearing a new Austin Reed suit just before leaving to take my assignment in East Berlin. Splitting my shorts down the back on a private tennis court at Diss in front of many posh guests, and dropping my tie in my coffee while dining as a newcomer with the Foreign Press corps in Bucharest were second and third.

I have begun sleeping better these last 3–4 nights. It has been cooler and I have been sleeping under a sheet. The lumps made by broken springs in the bed make it difficult. For many nights I have had bad, restless nights. There have not been many signs of demonstrations, although there have been some. I have often not dared to sleep early because of the fear of Red Guards coming in again. But since they came peacefully to watch me get the chequebook, I have felt more assured. Once I shot up in the middle of a yoga session because I thought another 'invasion' was on.

'Cadres' were government or party officials, usually wearing 'proletarian' blue high-necked tunics with matching 'engine-driver' soft caps and trousers, rather than the khaki tunics and soft caps of the Public Security Bureau men who guarded me.

Hsieh Fu-chih was Minister for Public Security. He survived the dangerous visit to Wuhan with Wang Li. I imagined he was the minister ultimately responsible for my house arrest – along with the Foreign Ministry – under the overall direction of the small group of four leaders under Chiang Ching, Mao's wife, who ultimately did Mao's bidding. When disgraced around the time of Mao's death, they became known as the Gang of Four and Chiang Ching was later sentenced to death – accused of no less than thirty thousand murders!

During the first two weeks in the small cell, I scratched a mark on the wall each day to keep count of the days, not knowing whether I would discover any other way of knowing the date.

The edge of the lake in London's Regents Park has sloping stonework at its edge and I placed the point of my furled umbrella on the edge of the sloping stones and skidded down slowly into the water, up to waist deep, in the new grey chalk-stripe suit – to the uproarious laughter of many watching sunbathers, who continued laughing as I scrambled out and headed for the gates, accompanied by a helplessly giggling Shirley to change and dry out at her nearby flat.

Tuesday 5 September 1967, 3.45 pm

Today I rose around 9.15 and, after ablutions and exercises and yoga, I walked briefly until breakfast. Then after breakfast, for the first time, I sat and sang songs softly on the edge of my bunk. The songs were: 'Maria' from *West Side Story* and 'There's a Place for Us', plus 'If I Had a Hammer' by Trini Lopez – or is it called 'All Over This Land'? I'm not sure. Anyway I sang softly, melodically and well, I thought. It was a happy-making experience.

Then I walked for about two hours until lunch. I played an exciting game of Pass-Look on the guards, in which Denmark beat Canada 50:40. After lunch of chips, soup and cucumber slices, I read about Burma's Communist Party in the *Peking Review*. The *Peking Reviews* for three weeks were delivered on Saturday, with the unreadable Chinese newspapers, and were brought to me almost immediately to provide me with the first news of the outside world since 18 August. I found that the Chinese Government had protested to Britain on 20 August over the arrest of more newspaper people in Hong Kong and there had been a demonstration on 21 August at the British Office here. It also said some 34 workers of various Hong Kong papers had been arrested. This didn't help my case, I thought. But the simple gaining of knowledge after such a long time in the dark was encouraging.

The main Cultural Revolution trends to be found in the *Peking Reviews* were articles trying to whip up support for the army and for certain revolutionary cadres – and a huge new campaign – surprise, surprise – against Liu Shao-chi and Peng Teh-huai.

One interesting fact that emerged was that on 18 August a celebration of the first anniversary of the first Red Guard parade in Tien An Men was held. So it seemed that my invasion came immediately after the rally in the Great Hall of the People. Quite an honour really, I suppose!

On Monday (yesterday) I became very depressed and did a lot of head-in-hands stuff. I knelt at the side of my bed and prayed for help. One of the reasons for this may have been that in the morning, while doing yoga, I started swallowing and couldn't stop. This may have undermined my nervous well being for the day. Anyway in mid-afternoon it became very bad and I was in the deepest depression of the six weeks. Today it is six weeks and four days.

Last night I spent an enjoyable evening thinking in great detail about Janet and Elizabeth and put into perspective all four of my main girlfriends. And also lining up Pauline, Carol and Doris in East Berlin as 'second strings'. I realised how Janet, Elizabeth, Mary and Shirley had all followed relatively quickly after one another and marked stages in my development. Interesting. I carried on along these lines until after midnight.

Last week, when I felt the need to do something to keep up my morale, I began each day naming the days. Monday was the Day of Optimism, Tuesday the Day of Possibility, Wednesday the Day of Hope, Thursday the Day of Expectation, Friday the Day of Probability, Saturday the Day of Indomitable Will and Sunday the Day of Inexhaustible Confidence. Monday, yesterday, became the Day of Imperturbable Optimism; today is the Day of Distinct Possibility. This all helps a little.

The guards all changed on Sunday night and the new set are very keen and keep coming in and looking at me more often. One came into the scullery today to find a place to put a second Mao quotation board.

The Peking Review, *published each week in English, carried translated articles from the wider Chinese press and was the main international propaganda tool of China's Government, circulated worldwide.*

Janet, I'd met when I was 17 at the Lido, one of Norwich's two fairly rough-and-ready Saturday-night dance halls in the pre-disco era. Vivacious and uncomplicated, she worked in one of Norwich's many shoe factories. She lied about her age, saying she was 17 when she was 18 and I lied about my age, saying I was 18 when I was 17. We were together for a couple of years very happily before and during the time I was doing National Service in the Royal Air Force. Got engaged briefly then parted amicably. Memorably warm and loving and my first real 'grown-up' girlfriend.

Elizabeth was a lovely-looking impeccably smart secretary at a Norwich insurance company. We met at the smaller more upmarket Gala ballroom in Norwich. She lived in the countryside near the North Norfolk coast and we met shortly after I had become a very new junior reporter on the Eastern Daily Press. *Had to buy my first second-hand car, a Flying Standard, to drive her home. A lovely friendship lasted two years then ended for reasons that now escape me.*

Mary (full name Mary Ewington-Cooper) was London-based, more sophisticated, Catholic, convent-educated, the daughter of an RAF Squadron Leader and very very glamorous – coming from a flat-share with three other equally sophisticated girls at Clapham Common in London. Mary was quite like the Julie Christie character in the famous contemporary film Darling. *Met her while she was demonstrating Remington electric razors in a shop next to the Yarmouth Mercury office in Great Yarmouth during a national tour she was making of such shops. She entered local beauty contests for fun while extending her stays in Norfolk to be with me and became Miss Anglia TV. We got engaged on a rock on a Jersey beach in the Channel Islands and Mary helped me – still then generally a bit of a provincial greenhorn – make the smooth transition to Reuters and life in London. Somehow we fell apart later.*

I had met Shirley in the language laboratory at Westminster College when I was brushing up my German. I thought at first sight that she was a 'resting' actress moonlighting. A Yorkshire-born Oxford MA from Somerville College, she loved opera and classical music, about which I then knew very little – and to pass the difficult time while I was a hostage and London reporters were plaguing her constantly at home and at college, and wrongly making her my fiancée, she quietly studied for an MSc in International Relations and learned to drive.

Friday 8 September 1967, 3.30 pm

Today I have named 'The Day of Constant Probability'. Yesterday was the Day of Increasing Expectation and Wednesday was the Day of Undiminished Hope. Today in the afternoon I have been quite depressed again, but not so much as on Tuesday. A feeling of hopelessness came over me then. It is exactly seven weeks today, 50 days in fact. Hell, that is a long time! And not the slightest sign of anything at all coming along to help me. Have again felt furious with the worse-than-useless British Government who are clearly doing nothing to help me. What a bunch of faint-hearted twits!

Today I rose, washed, did exercises and yoga then walked briefly and after breakfast I sang hymns, quietly sitting on my bunk. I managed ten. The main ones were: 'O God Our Help in Ages Past', 'Jerusalem', 'The Lord is my Shepherd', 'Eternal Father' (had to make do with only two choruses), 'Hark the Herald Angels Sing' and 'Once in Royal David's City'.

I have spent a lot of time in the past two days thinking about life with Mary in great detail. This has been a time-consuming and not unpleasant experience. She was really extraordinary. I also spent time thinking about memorable meals. The newspapers, which I ask for each day, haven't seemed to contain much about England or Hong Kong. Lunch today had a new ingredient – lettuce! Wasn't bad: chips, cucumber, egg, potato. Last two night's dinner has been good with lots of chopped meat. Have eaten my fill. Today Lao Chiao bought me new spearmint-flavour toothpaste and six shampoos and six toilet papers. Hope I don't use all of them!

My prediction for getting out of here, which I may have already noted, is by 20 September. Heavens above, it does seem to get more difficult to stand this. Exactly three weeks of sitting in this cell isn't unendurable, but it is very hard indeed and lazy-making. At this moment I can't envisage release at all. I pray very hard on my knees, night and morning, for release.

I am so much wanting to get home to England and Shirley, and to see Mother and June again. It seems literally ages since I was put under arrest – almost like eternity. What can I do to pass the time? I walk and romance and read very little. I have nothing to read anyway. I have nearly finished Carew-Hunt's book for the second time. I often wonder whether I am on the verge of beginning to have nervous trouble, but so far I think I have kept up rather well.

People staring in at the top window have lessened a little. Frequently they come to look every night and the guards do nothing to stop them. The guards pulled up one of the armchairs into their open doorway last night to sit in and watch me.

Oh, how I need a grain of encouragement! But my general expectation is that it will be very difficult for any kind of arrangement to be reached, because of the situation in Hong Kong, with the arrested press people, Chinese intransigence and the desire of the British Government not to 'spoil' relations with China by doing anything 'tough'. It does seem a hopeless position and England seems to be on another planet. I am so desolate and miserable.

Monday 11 September 1967, 3.30 pm

Feeling not bad today. Rose at nine, washed, shaved etc. Did exercises and yoga. Named today the 'Day of Unshakeable Optimism'. (Sunday was the 'Day of Inexhaustible Confidence in the Future', Saturday was the 'Day of Permanently Indomitable Will', Friday was the 'Day of Constant Probability'.) After breakfast I walked and played Pass-Look, which Denmark won 50:47 in the second game of a three-game final. After lunch I read the boring portions of *Peking Review* and walked until 3.30 pm.

The arrival yesterday of the *Peking Review* gave me my second dose of information since I was put into solitary confinement. It revealed that on 22 August Red Guards 'took strong action against the British Office' after a demonstration, and that on 29 August three newspaper publishers in Hong Kong were each sentenced to three years in prison. The most interesting news was from London, where it turned out that those pictures I had seen earlier in the papers were of the London Office of the Chinese Chargé d'Affaires in Portland Place and the report talked of attacks by British police and guards on the building! It also said certain limitations and restrictions had been placed on Chinese diplomats and their press and commercial people.

Another item showed that on 30 August, China had protested about the incidents of 29 August – police had been there from at least 27 August and it seemed possible they were there from about the time of the 22 August attack on the British Office here. China has forbidden any British diplomats to leave China and confined all their activities to the office, their respective homes and the route between the two as from 30 August. While this was some illumination from the overall relations' point of view, I found some encouragement in the fact that at least my case would receive some attention through the association of the London branch of the New China News Agency with the affair. Perhaps it might in general help to speed my release. I was somewhat comforted by the fact that at least something had been done at last by the British Government.

Last night I found a pleasant way of spending some time, going to sleep by imagining a perfect day with Shirley. This was a snowy Sunday in England, waking, bath, put on clean crisp white sheets, drawing curtains, having delicious breakfast with lots of hot toast, bacon and eggs and coffee, then getting back into bed for two hours, then getting up and walking to the village pub for port-and-brandies and drinks and laughter, then back with the newspapers for lunch and reading, perhaps a book – possibly *A Short History of the World* by H.G. Wells, which I have always wanted to read) and so on until dinner at the Golf Club in the evening. I imagined this in great detail and went off to sleep doing it. It lasted perhaps several hours. The beauty of the scenes was the creative aspect of it all.

It is now getting colder. After a fierce storm on Friday night, the temperature has dropped and yesterday the guards came in and asked if I had any long trousers. I said, 'Upstairs.' I am now having to wear my dressing-gown to keep warm. I must ask for more clothing soon. Until three weeks ago it was too hot to sleep!

My current thinking is that perhaps the Chinese Foreign Ministry will use the opportunity of my expiring visa and perhaps agree to expel me then – and so start to straighten out some of the current London–Peking mess. I am aware it could well be several months, possibly running up to December or January, before anything is done. But I feel that the difficulties regarding the Chinese Chargé d'Affaires' Office in London will make the authorities here anxious not to hold me indefinitely. I hope I am right. I still pray night and morning after yoga.

Lunch today was onions and peppers, and some gravy, cucumber, tomato (after a break of about a week), eggs and lettuce. Soup and rice and water completed the bill of fare. Meals have been better recently. Dinners have been good and last night was ample, with fish and warm bread. I enjoyed eating dinner and reading. I completed yesterday Carew-Hunt's book on communism for the second time.

Quotations from Mao are put up periodically – about once a week – on blackboards propped on chairs in the adjoining room where I can see them. I have just learned them for something to do. The first one says, 'Make trouble, fail … Make trouble again, fail again … Until their doom, this is the logic of the imperialists and reactionaries of all countries in dealing with the People's cause and they will never escape this logic. This is a Marxist law.'

The second week was, 'The enemy will not perish of himself. Neither the Chinese reactionaries nor the aggressive forces of United States' imperialism in China will step down from the stage of history of their own accord.'

The third week (the present one, put up a little late) was, 'Mao Tse-tung's Thought is Marxism–Leninism in an era when imperialism is heading for total collapse and socialism is advancing to worldwide victory. It is a powerful ideological weapon for opposing imperialism and for opposing revisionism and dogmatism. Mao Tse-tung's Thought is the guiding principle for all the work of the Party of the country and of the army.'

Another board, put up for the third week, reiterated another one already in my room about 'Lifting a rock only to drop it on one's own feet …'

I spied my name today in the writing on the scullery wall and also picked it out in the poster (there are three altogether in different places) in there. But I have no idea what these posters say. In a dream last night I dreamed that John Weston came in and they took my bed away. Very strange. Always dreaming about John.

Wednesday 13 September 1967, 9.45 pm

Today another visit from the Red Guards who 'look after' me. This time to grant my request for warmer clothes.

I was taken upstairs to my bedroom and allowed to choose some shirts, jackets and my sheepskin overcoat. I also asked for some books, namely Mao's books in the lounge, and was allowed to get them. I also managed to get Stuart Schramm's biography of Mao from my office, and this was the first time my poor three books had been supplemented in 26 days. I also got Mao's *Little Red Book* of quotations. This I have read with interest this evening, realising how lazy I am with my reading of Mao in normal times.

Five volumes of Mao are also sitting on the windowsill now and I estimate they will last me about a month. Some consolation! The presence of my leather jacket on the door with my grey suit and sports trousers, and two pairs of shoes on the floor somehow give this little cell a more homely appearance and are rather cheering. Funny how little things that are familiar and part of everyday life bring comfort. The lack of hostility in the Red Guards was also again noticeable – and this was also vaguely encouraging.

My bedroom was a total mess, with the walls smothered with paint and the wardrobe too. Lao Chiao collected two blankets for me and carried down some clothes. I had a tie and top of pyjamas and some socks. Lao Chiao also picked up the *Little Red Book* for me. I got my sheepskin coat from the wardrobe on the landing and two tins of coffee. I noticed the novel *Dr Zhivago* was still lying on my bed. In the lounge the mess was greater. Paint had been daubed on the furniture, I noticed; particularly on the yellow covers of the chairs, and my Berlin picture lay smashed on the floor. My records were strewn all over the floor and books were tumbled down there too. My one and only Chinese scroll painting that I had bought in the antique market was doubled up on the sofa. The rubber plant was broken and dead.

In the office, paint and glue were everywhere. Chessmen and the board were all over the floor, the radio was on the floor with the typewriter; pictures of Mao alongside the Stuart Schramm book had been reverently stood up on the windowsill.

The doors of the office had been re-sealed since my last visit on 31 August. One learned-looking Red Guard with glasses looked carefully into the Mao books before 'passing' them. I was refused permission for any other books. I asked to be allowed to go outside and get some air, and they laughed. But when I said I had no fresh air, it was arranged a window should be opened tomorrow. The lack of hostility was again very striking and a little strange.

Twice the chief Red Guard tried to open the bedroom door and the wardrobe door for me but I had to do it because they were both stiff and they stuck. Downstairs I asked how long I would be kept and a Public Security Bureau man said, 'I don't know.'

The visit was stimulating. I found a trace of happiness in seeing my familiar clothes again and it is always refreshing to go out of this tiny room. The lack of hostility was comforting, although this of course doesn't promise anything for the future!

Lao Chiao 'translated' in his very limited 'pidgin' English and the exchanges were unfruitful. Having some books does ease the worry of occupying my mind for a few weeks. Today I rose around nine, did my exercises and yoga and had breakfast. For the second day running I got two extra pieces of toast and enjoyed them as though they were the best food on earth. Sat in the sun on the bunk really enjoying them. I spent the morning imagining a golf round with Shirley on holiday in Scotland with big breakfasts and sheltering from the rain in a little hut, with the rain drumming on the roof while we had Marmite sandwiches and drank coffee from a flask.

Port and brandies play a big place in these dreams, and draught Guinness with avocado pears and shrimps, and sex and rosé wine. Grand way of passing the time in fact. Then there was darts in the bar of the Golf Club and reading by the fire in the hotel and more drinking, etc. Oh, and yes, visits to bookshops!

I am enjoying my food tremendously these days. Today Lao Chiao cooked dinner, which was chopped meat and beans plus cucumber, tomatoes, egg and rice and soup. Small but tasty. I am pinning my faith somewhat now on some action around 21 September. But the obtaining of the books eases the problem a little. Recently I made some predictions during an afternoon's 'Thought' session. They were:

1 Nixon would win next year's presidential election on a ticket of loosening America's ties to Vietnam

2 Britain would get a Conservative–Liberal coalition in 1970, and

3 Mao would die in 1969, de Gaulle in 1970 and Bolivia would be the next communist country in 1970. Guinea would be the first African communist country in 1975.

All these predictions have been made with the supreme confidence of absolute ignorance!

Saturday 16 September 1967, 10.00 pm

What a way to spend Saturday night! Today the pattern was: rose at 9 am, did yoga and exercises and had breakfast at ten-thirty. Walked and stood at the window looking at the sunshine. Had lunch, read Mao's biography by Schramm until 3.15 pm, walked, read the *Peking Review*, which arrived early, did yoga exercises again, prayed and walked some more. Then had dinner – fried pork, eggs, potatoes, lettuce, cucumber, tomatoes, dry toast.

Read the *Peking Review* again after dinner. It carried a big critique of Tao Chu that was very long. Then there was interesting stuff at the end about 'opposition elements' sneaking around Peking in the silent night and hints that important decisions were taken concerning personnel at the Eleventh Plenum of the Central Committee in August last year. Afterwards I walked for an hour, then rested and began writing this diary.

The points I want to record are as follows: yesterday was the twenty-eighth day and it was marked by the opening of one of my nailed-up windows. This allowed me my first direct breath of fresh air in a month and I stood submerged in it for a full hour drinking in the beauty and the closeness of the air. The sun shone and leaves blew around the courtyard, two birds wheeled in the sun and two green trees were visible. Sounds were louder with the window open and looking back into the cell and scullery they looked black.

The other thing was that the day before, on Thursday 14 September, I put on trousers for the first time. Seemed strange after nearly two months in shorts. I think I was much slimmer and my hips seemed straighter than they have ever been before and the formal 'putting on of trousers' was a strangely outstanding event. Yesterday I also thought of some things, which are now clearly more important to me than they seemed to be before this arrest. They were:

1 Liberty
2 God
3 Mother, family and Shirley
4 Books
5 Experience
6 Radio news
7 Old friends
8 Exercises
9 Mind
10 Patience

The weakness and helplessness of the individual alone has been brought home very forcibly to me. I pray twice every day for deliverance. Things which I have decided are not so important overall, are: dodging around after birds, and fame and success. Food and drink themselves are entirely subordinate. I have subsisted quite well on minimum food. In the last two days I have been 'thinking' a walk that will go the length and breadth of Britain. I have so far covered six days going through Exeter and Bristol, stopping at hotels and Bed and Breakfast boarding houses, imagining all kinds of feasts and fucks, mainly fucks.

It is amazing how much pleasure can be obtained from thinking about drinking pints of Guinness, eating toast and steaks and imagining love affairs. The walk is becoming quite real. Tonight I fell to wondering whether I shall be here for Christmas. I have almost reconciled myself to being here for the four weeks to 1 October. I think every day about release in every respect, but find it difficult to imagine: 1 because I want it so much and have thought so much of being home with my loved ones, and: 2 because it seems so impossible in the current political climate.

The Chinese hardly seem likely to give me up without gaining anything, and the British are clearly intransigent. The Chinese newspapers seem to indicate another arrest of a New China News Agency man this week. The *Peking Review* carried nothing on Hong Kong. After one month of solitary confinement, I suppose I am still as sane as I was before and suppose I can hold out for a long time. But it does give me desperate moments, the terrible interminable aspect of things. I still fly up at the slightest sound outside, dreading another break-in by Red Guards. But there is no sign of anything reaching me. Heaven knows what is happening to the British Office.

Wednesday 20 September 1967, 10.45 pm

Today was a red-letter day! With the morning paper, a letter from Shirley was handed to me by Lao Chiao, containing photographs of my angel. Dated 25 August, this was my first contact with the outside world since solitary confinement began, 33 days ago. The letter itself was brief and a little depressing. It seemed scrappy and funny and seemed to indicate that no idea of my predicament was known to the world. Shirley didn't seem unduly worried and that was good – but she did seem somewhat offended by my cut-off state, about which I can do nothing. But the letter in itself was heartening and the sight of the pictures of my angel was a joy, although I did harbour some unpleasant thoughts about her lack of sympathy for me.

The reasons for this sudden delivery were difficult to arrive at. I eventually concluded that it was a sign at least that somebody somewhere had decided on some position, perhaps with a view to keeping me from suicidal depression. It was not a good sign that release was near necessarily, but it did seem to indicate another watering down of the severity of my confinement. Perhaps they don't want to appear too harsh after my release. Whether there would be more, it was impossible to guess.

The letter came at an interesting time, as I began to feel I would never be released. Hopelessness had been growing recently. Much depression and praying a lot. I had – and in fact I still have – begun to see my imprisonment in terms of perhaps six months. I can't see how the position will be resolved. I don't know whether the British here are still under restriction and have no idea of any moves to help me. The Chinese newspapers seem to indicate that another New China News Agency reporter has been arrested in Hong Kong, so what the hell can happen to me?

Reading in Stuart Schramm's biography of Mao that Chiang Kai-shek is still keeping the leader of the 'Sian Incident' under house arrest on Taiwan after all these years and that Westerners were put in iron shackles here in the early fifties didn't help. Lao Chiao has bought me six more toilet rolls and six shampoos! Four weeks and five days, it is now.

Looking back in this diary book to 8 September, I see my despair clearly showing and there seems nothing in view. Ten days later, of course, the misery was not that great, so perhaps I begin to see the perspective. There just seems no hope of release, even on the distant horizon, at the moment.

Today I stood at the open window for an hour, as has been my practice every morning since it has been allowed open. The autumn is truly beautiful in Peking. The sun shines, the skies are clear crystal blue, and there is a crisp breeze, but it is warm and the birds wheel high in the sky. Standing at the window is quite beautiful, watching the leaves blowing round the courtyard. Yesterday afternoon new loudspeakers right outside the house opened up suddenly with a strange mixture of opera and invective. It continued today in the morning and afternoon, sounding like a new propaganda style. I think I can pick out 'Ying Kuo' (the words for England or Britain), but it was not addressed at me as far as I could make out.

Tonight I began reading the *Selected Works of Mao* and found them very interesting. His *Class Analysis and Study of the Peasant Movement in Hunan* were both very readable and informative, and especially the section which told of parading landlords in the 1930s in paper dunces' hats and other such Cultural Revolution habits. I formed the impression that some of the present movement's methods have been modelled on such things.

Today I rose at nine, did exercises and yoga, had breakfast, walked and stood at the window until lunchtime. Today's thinking was centred on my decision to take up journalism and how I pursued this. I was admiring my drive and enthusiasm. This subject followed on naturally from my analysis of my education yesterday, which led me to the conclusion that my education was just about to start when I stopped it and left school at 16. My leaning was clearly towards languages and English and history. I must read more if and when I get my freedom.

After lunch I continued to think along these lines, after reading the conclusion of Stuart Schramm's book. I am now more or less decided to write a book myself, with chapters on Mao, on his various 'Rectification Movements', on the Chung Nan Hai government compound adjoining the Forbidden City – I will include how I sat on my roof, having that magnificent vantage-point watching the swallows dip over the roofs and wishing I could see what they saw. I will include my train journey here from Hong Kong, driving in the capital, its restaurants, the reasons for the

Cultural Revolution and other experiences and how we worked under very difficult conditions to report on it. And how we couldn't speak Chinese and about the devilish Chinese drink, *mao tai* and its fierce properties. I will do my train journey, because that was the only glimpse I had of China outside Peking almost. And of course I will write about my solitary confinement.

This afternoon I walked again, thinking about my career to date, then had dinner, which was three slices of fish and potatoes, cucumber, radishes, tomatoes and lettuce with toast and soup. I began reading Mao's works. Today I named the day the 'Day of Real Hope'. Yesterday was the Day of Clearer Possibility, Monday was the Day of Refreshing Optimism, Sunday was the Day of Inexhaustible Confidence in Deliverance, and Saturday was the Day of Indomitable Will to Prevail.

In my book also I want to mention the extraordinary street noises, the way *'Mao Chu hsi'* (Chairman Mao) is always uttered so unctuously all the time, echoing and re-echoing constantly, everywhere. Tonight in reading the *Selected Works* it turns out that *'Wan Suî'*, meaning 'long live' or more literally translated as 'ten thousand years', is also a synonym for 'emperor'.

Two nights ago, I learned the two latest quotations on the blackboards. They are, 'The socialist system will eventually replace the capitalist system – this is an objective law independent of man's will. No matter how much the reactionaries try to hold back the wheel of history, revolution will sooner or later take place and will eventually triumph.' (NB Should it really read, I wonder, 'revisionism will surely ultimately triumph'?)

And, 'I have said that all apparently powerful reactionaries are paper tigers. The reason is that they are divorced from the people. Look! Wasn't Hitler a paper tiger? Was Hitler not overcome? US imperialism has not yet been overcome and it has the atom bomb. I believe it will also be overcome. It, too, is a paper tiger.'

Today one of the guards opened the door of my room while I was praying on my knees. But generally they are not too bad, if you don't count the spitting that goes on all the time. They have hung up their blackboards today with new quotations on.

They have set up their office in the lounge. They have beds there and two sleep while one watches me. They have a telephone, which rings frequently. A big rattling tea-can is carried in periodically. Three days ago I began doing advanced yoga postures, which is making me quite stiff. (I have to keep covering this up with the *Peking Review* as I write, in case one of the guards comes in and finds me writing.)

The Sian Incident was an event in China's Civil War that took place in 1939.

I remember reading with a sinking feeling that hated landlords after capture had been habitually kept locked up in sheds for a long time before being taken out and executed 'so that they really suffered and became desperate and nervy, jumping at every sound' before their lives were finally taken. But I probably chose not to write this in my diary for obvious reasons.

Friday 22 September 1967, 3 pm

Today I decided on a new attitude. After doing nothing the whole day yesterday except reflect about my journalistic career in detail and choosing the best stories I have ever obtained and written etc., I thought that it was about time to be more constructive. So on the anniversary of the ninth week in captivity – 63 days, one day over two months and exactly five weeks in solitary confinement – I decided that the 21 September having come and gone unsuccessfully, the fact had to be faced that it looked like 'a long job'. So I decided I should try to take a long-term view of things. I cleaned my room, washed, put on a white shirt and my hard black shoes and worked out my first '23-day Plan'.

I did this simply because 15 October appears to me as a day to work towards. I decided not to think so much about quick release, but to make the next 23 days a period of the study of the *Selected Works of Mao.*

I summed up the likely happenings as follows:

1   Release and deportation from China under guard – with violence
2   Release and expulsion – without violence
3   Release and refusal of permission to leave China, possibly being ordered into the Hsin Chiao Hotel or being ordered to clean up this house
4   Put on mass trial and imprisoned properly
5   Imprisoned without trial
6   Sent to Sinkiang for years simply as a reprisal and revenge
7   Held for a long period here

Reviewing what I know of the situation, the seventh option seems most likely. But I can expect a Red Guard intrusion at any time, I suppose. There is not much planning I can do against it. If it is sudden and violent, I am helpless. I think the worst thought of all is that something dreadful might happen in Hong Kong and I might be the object of vengeance of the utmost kind.

So thinking about a six-month term puts my thoughts as far as January. And that is how I have decided to look at things while still hoping, of course, that something will turn up. But it seems two months is not very long if you say it quickly and clearly. The British Government is either unwilling or unable – or both – to do anything.

After 15 October I shall review situation and make fresh plan. Today's review amounted to this:

18 August   Confinement began

31 August   First break in terrible confinement; got pen by subterfuge

2 September   Public Security Bureau cadre's visit

3 September   Three Peking Reviews were delivered

13 September Granted warmer clothes; allowed Mao's works and Stuart Schramm

15 September Window opened

20 September A letter from Shirley

Today I signed a cheque for September wages for Sao Kao and Lao Chiao. The guards have begun to peep into this cell at me – from the courtyard standing on a chair – when I do my yoga exercises lying on the stone tiled floor. Quite stupid really! Sleeping is reasonable these days. I go to bed about 11.30 pm and sleep soundly until about 6 am, I think. Then I doze and get up at 9 am. Food, I fancy, is better than at first, with a lot of eggplant this week. For the third day today, lorries have roared by with drums beating and gongs sounding. I believe it is because petitions of support are being presented to the Central Committee. Big event today! I cut my hair for the first time and funnily enough after two snips at the ends of both sides I looked much better. So there, the new tone is set.

Wednesday 27 September 1967

Tonight I have enjoyed reading the third volume of Mao's *Works*. Today I asked Lao Chiao if he could go out to buy the Chinese Volume Three, which he did. It cost 1.80 yuan. Tonight's enjoyment came after a particularly bad spell of depression that lasted two or three days. I have been terribly low and pessimistic and defeatist. I have been unable to think of anything good and have imagined things like being kept here all my life, or for several years. Today it is 40 days in this cell and 68 altogether. At one point today I just keeled over on my bed in despair. Very difficult to shake off depression this deep. It really does look like at least six months now, and this really is a horrifying thought!

Tonight I enjoyed particularly Mao's article *The Chinese Revolution and the Chinese Communist Party*, which seemingly gives good factual information on history. Details of the Italian aggression against Abyssinia and the Spanish Civil War and Germany's experience helped put China into perspective. Imperial overtures to China in the last century were also well set out.

I decided to try yet another new attitude tonight after these terribly depressing days – of thinking only of future release. But really I have so little to go on for optimism. In the last few minutes I have just re-read for the first time the news agency copy of the Foreign Ministry Order on me and the *Peoples Daily* leader of the next day – both of them in reprinted in the *Peking Review*. 'He must await further notice,' they both say. Well, I am doing that all right!

Tonight is quiet for the first time for several nights. Loudspeakers booming from Tien An Men Square and marching crowds going by have been regular features of life since last Sunday. I presume they are practising for the 1 October National Day celebration parades, because today's papers show that the Albanian premier arrived yesterday to a big welcome. Loudspeakers went on last night until after midnight – and very vicious and aggressive they sounded too! The marching crowds have drums and cymbals, and both boys and girls shout marching songs. Lao Chiao tonight cooked meatballs for me, which was the first new dish for weeks. Sao Kao has been dishing up some bad pork in the past few days, disgusting, with tomatoes, etc. and it upset my stomach. Cabbage has returned to the salad and I see this as things coming full circle, just like when I arrived. A good sign!

The *Peking Review* on Sunday contained only one interesting item – the expulsion of three Japanese correspondents. Otherwise it was mostly India and the border incident. I broke my watch two days ago and this didn't help my mood.

Depression takes the form of getting up at 9 am and having no energy then to wash, and the day seems heavy and dead. Outlook seems hopeless and prayers are almost lunatic. I have been doing more advanced yoga postures and seeing some improvement now. But the Lotus posture is impossible for me and my bandy legs. I have been thinking increasingly about marriage to Shirley and how nice it would be. I have worried a lot about her becoming disenchanted recently. I worry about my dear mum, too. I do hope she's all right. Heavens, home does seem remote and impossible. I pray I shall be allowed to return some day.

Yesterday I learned Mao's poem 'Snow' and enjoyed doing it. I also learned two new quotations put up on the blackboards, 'If the United States' monopoly capitalists persist in pursuing their aggressive policies of war, the day is bound to come when they will be hanged by the people of the whole world. The same fate awaits the accomplices of the United States.' (Implication? Grey is US accomplice and watch out he doesn't get himself hanged?)

The other one was, 'They (the diehards) always have many schemes in hand, schemes for profiting at others' expense or double dealing and so on. But they always get the opposite of what they want. They invariably start by doing others harm and end by ruining themselves.'

I added another quotation, learned from memory from the *Red Book* to make my list up to ten. It is, 'What we need is an enthusiastic but calm state of mind and intense but orderly work.' My head has been itching furiously now for two or three days. That doesn't help either. What I need is something that helps!

The overwhelming need to write this diary tonight was to try to convey the feeling of depression of the past two days. But it really is difficult to remember depression after it evaporates. And today I have started having headaches.

I decided that if it appears I am going to be here through the winter, I should ask the Foreign Ministry for a move, on the grounds that it is cold and unhealthy here and I am likely to catch a disease. Today was cold and stormy and it rained very hard – the first day the sun hasn't been seen for a long time.

Albania at this time was isolated, China's one firm ally. Albania, being perhaps the smallest communist state in Europe, if not the world, it was a curious 'elephant and flea' union.

Saturday 30 September 1967, 11.00 pm

I am sat in my cell on the chair opposite tomorrow's breakfast and dinner. Cold meat, cheese, bread, tomato, cucumber with mustard. On Thursday 28 September I received a postcard from Shirley, which she had posted on 26 August, apparently at the airport in London. It said, 'Love you, my darling', which was encouraging, and it also gave details of the Beatles taking up deep meditation. How funny and coincidental!

The reason my two meals for tomorrow are already here is that Sao Kao, the cook, says there will be too many people tomorrow for him to come to do them, tomorrow being National Day. Tonight I have read Mao's *Works* again and walked back and forth considering the latest information to reach me today in the *Peking Review*. This was that another Hsin Hua (New China) News Agency correspondent and four other reporters were sentenced to three years' imprisonment in Hong Kong on 13 September. I feel this would have made it clear to the Chinese that they were going to gain nothing by holding me. But might that mean my release is imminent? It is imponderable.

I am in a flat reconciled mood at the moment, unable to get very depressed about what seems bound to be a very long period of imprisonment – perhaps six months or a year even. Yesterday, however, produced some good signs. I noticed that four of the six toilet rolls bought for me had disappeared. I dropped my watch in deliberate desperation and it started after several days of inactivity and my constant fiddling with it. For dinner last night I was given shish kebab on knitting needles for the first time with sauce. All these things seemed good omens. But are they?

Yesterday was also marked by a 'window' incident, whereby I was told to limit it to one hour and Lao Chiao was ordered to put a lock on the outside. The guards showed it to me to tell me this. Today, as on many others recently, singing crowds of marchers have gone by the house. There was also much loudspeaker-play today outside with lots of attacks again on Tao Chu and much playing of 'The East is Red' and so on. Papers are full of pictures of banquets and talks with visiting groups.

Two days ago it became cold enough to have to wear a jacket when walking back and forth. This is a complete change from the early days in here, when it was sweltering.

Tao Chu, a southern Politburo Standing Committee member, was under constant attack in the slogans yelled by marchers at this phase of the Cultural Revolution, along with President Liu Shao-chi (Liu Shao-qi) and General Secretary Teng Hsiao-ping (Deng Xiao-ping). Unlike Teng, who survived to become a supreme leader for several years after Mao's passing, Tao Chu seems never to have recovered his position.

Tuesday 3 October 1967, 6.30 pm

I am writing this sitting propped up on my 'bed', wearing my dressing gown after eating a meal of boiled fish. I am feeling a little recovered after more than a day of illness – of violent diarrhoea and stomach trouble.

This afternoon and evening I have been overcome with despair. Moans like, 'This is hell on earth!' and, 'A living death!' have escaped my lips. It seems I will never get out of this terrible, awful prison. I feel helpless and desperate, and at times as though I am on the verge of going crazy.

The illness began about 3.30 pm yesterday. Then after a violent session on the toilet, I lay on my bed for a time and there followed several other sessions. I had almost nothing of my dinner except soup and one slice of toast, and it stood all night on the chair. I just fell on the bed and dashed to the toilet throughout the evening. The climax was a terrible moment when I stood before the toilet not knowing whether I was going to be sick or shit myself – or both! I went to bed in my dressing gown with an extra blanket and got up twice in the night.

Sao Kao had asked if I wanted 'to go look-look', meaning, I suppose, to the hospital. I said, 'Tomorrow.' (Frantically hid my diary and pen at this point because I heard guard coming – but it was a false alarm.)

Today I haven't walked at all and the smallness of the cell became almost unbearable in the afternoon. I have lain on my bed reading and thinking, and the time has gone very slowly.

What is to become of me? Also, I have found it particularly difficult to keep my pledge not to be annoyed by the hawking and spitting of the guards. The noise they make outside is quite disgusting, today particularly so. It is a matter of fighting back the revulsion. In addition to the sickness, I also have a stiff neck to make matters worse. Today Sao Kao was (almost) kind and considerate. He lifted the chair over to the bed and seemed more polite. The window was left open all day by the guards, seemingly as a concession.

The slogans in the cell hit me afresh last night during my period of overheated brain. At my feet, 'Long Live Chairman Mao'. At my side, 'Those who oppose China will come to no good end.' To my left, 'Down with British imperialism' and, 'Long Live Mao Tse-tung' in English under his portrait. The pink posters with the four declarations above my head and also the slogans, 'Down with Grey!' and, 'Down with British imperialism!' on the back walls. How disgusting and trite and stupid! This is persecution of the most mindless kind!

National Day, 1 October, was not too interesting. Noise of columns marching began very early and at about 10 am a thrill of screaming ran among through the crowd in the Square of Heavenly Peace, as the loudspeakers proclaimed that Mao was on the gate. Lin Piao's thin whining voice rang out for about half an hour, then lots of playing of 'Sailing the Seas Depends on the Helmsman', as the crowds marched by.

In the evening I watched the fireworks from my window. (Remembering how I idly thought, back in August, whether I should be here for them, I idly wondered this time whether I should be here for next year's National Day or even for May Day 1968!) Some of the time I lay with great laziness on my bed, watching with the aid of my shaving mirror. The papers on October 1 had contained pictures of an H-bomb test with idiots waving Mao's *Little Red Books* at the explosion!

Mao looked well in the papers on both days. Today I began Volume Four of Mao's *Selected Works* and reckon on finishing them within a week. They are fascinating historically, but sometimes a bit of a grind to get through. Oh Heaven, please smile down on me and hasten my release! Yesterday and today I did no yoga exercises for the first time because of my illness.

Sunday 7 October 1967, 11.45 pm

Today is the fiftieth day of solitary confinement! No celebration was held, at the request of the prisoner!

The high point of the day was perhaps the worst-yet depression, brought on by the delivery of a bill for three months' rent up to December. I refused to pay it and afterwards wondered whether this was wise. Then I was hit by the realisation that it meant another three months at least. When the bill was brought to the gate two days ago it was held by the guards, I think, and there was a lot of telephoning and I thought I even heard the name of the Public Security Minister himself mentioned. So I had the feeling the delivery today of the bill represented a decision, making clear I was to be held for at least three more months and probably more. I keeled over on my bed in absolute despair, with all strength gone at one point. I couldn't even find it in me to walk. I have begun to force out mutters of, 'You fucking bastards!' between my teeth recently to relieve my feelings.

But today, even when I managed to start walking again, the despair and dispiritedness overwhelmed me and I was reduced to begging for help from God, standing with my head hung backwards and my eyes closed, feeling absolutely lost, miserable and hopeless. I tried to pull myself together and be more 'positive' and fortunately managed it.

This evening I finished reading the *Works of Mao*, Volume Four. They have been very interesting and I have finished them in 18 days. But I still have some more material to read, because yesterday I got Lao Chiao to buy a new edition of *Selected Readings from Mao*, which contains eight previously unpublished articles. Some 100 pages will keep me busy a little longer.

Yesterday was also remarkable, because I got a new refill for my pen. Lao Chiao left his pen behind by accident after I wrote the name of the new book for him and I changed the refill in it, which was absolutely new, for my old one in this pen which incredibly was on the point of running out. I've felt elated all day about this!

Looking back I see that the last time I wrote was on the day I was ill. The next day that I was able to return to walking it was such a welcome relief. Just walking up and down is very important. It was also like welcoming back an old friend to start doing yoga exercises again. My thinking on release is becoming really reconciled to the long term. It seems not impossible that I will be held for a year or even more. Six months seem almost certain. It is only two and something months to Christmas and I find it impossible to imagine release before then – and very far into next year.

The guards went over to a new system of 24-hour shifts from last Sunday and now stay round the clock from 9 am. Two or three mornings ago the bell rang and Sao Kao had to go in for the date stamp. This excited me, thinking it was a cable, but it turned out to be a bill for the car licence.

Last week's *Peking Review* gave details of the sentencing on 13 September of five more Chinese correspondents in Hong Kong for three years each – including one New China News Agency man. They had waited 45 days for their sentences. It also said four other Hsin Hua (New China News Agency) personnel had been arrested, so that also doesn't help. The story was about a protest from Chinese journalists in Peking and it demanded that all sentences be made null and void. My position seems really hopeless!

My prayers are more fervent than ever these days. I do worry about my lovely mum and hope she will be all right. I have been unable to convey the despair I feel today because I am tired now. But it was terrible. Tonight I resolved to take the next seven days 'like a man!' (Trying to shock myself into resistance!)

I could make eight and a half walking paces by starting with my back to the nailed up outside door of the little cell and walking towards the window across the scullery, through which youths and other were able to peer down from the low roof of the adjoining restaurant. The rhythm of the movement was in itself soothing and was extremely helpful always in stabilising my mood. I took to ignoring the rubber-neckers until they got bored with watching me.

Wednesday 11 October 1967, 10.30 pm

Today has not been remarkable in itself, but was part of a wave of optimism which I have been sustaining since I wrote the last entry on 7 October. The big event since then was the arrival on Monday of a really good letter from Shirley. This was a six-page letter written on 24 and 25 August and contained the first real details of events, unlike the previous two communications which were devoid of anything interesting.

This letter (which arrived on the fifty-second day – which is divisible by 13, my lucky number) gave me an enormous boost in morale. I'd had the strongest premonition that something was going to happen on Monday before it came. The newspaper was early and there was no *Peking Review* with it. I was anxious to see *Peking Review* for National Day. Then after breakfast, one of the guards called Sao Kao and he brought the *Peking Review* and the lovely letter. I had prayed in so many words before its arrival that I really needed a morale booster and this is exactly what it was. It gave details of press coverage of my predicament and of a gossip-column piece about me in *The Times*. It also said how much Shirley loved me and missed me, and told me lots of little details about her life and brought me closer to her than for many, many weeks.

I feel this letter was a sign that the worst was over, that the turning point had been reached – perhaps some time ago – and this was confirmation. I was elated by the letter and felt splendid for a time. The mood brought on by the letter, plus the determination to be more positive this week, have resulted in four better days. Two days ago I asked Sao Kao for milk, cheese, butter and fruit and he said that the Red Guards had written down what I shouldn't have. All these things were mentioned.

Today I rose at nine, did yoga, had breakfast of beautiful thick toast, made and brought by Lao Chiao. Then I walked for an hour.

Yesterday I began reading a slim book called *The Sino-Indian Boundary Question* and I continued this over lunch today. Lunch was chips and breadcrumbs! I read after lunch, walked for an hour, then did my accounts for the period 3–9–67 to 11–10–67 and then did yoga. With dinner, Lao Chiao's now familiar stew – which was very good – I continued the 'boundary dispute' book and eventually finished it. I walked again for an hour after dinner.

I am telling myself now that there are several good days to come. They are Friday 13 October (13 again being my lucky number) and 15 October, which was the end of my current 23-day plan, plus the fact that the three months' anniversary comes on 21 October, and 22 October is 13 days on from 9 October when I got the good letter (I have noticed that multiples of 13 days have almost always been 'good' days); 31 August was the first Red Guard (peaceful) visit, 13 September their second; 26 September was nothing (nothing bad!) and 9 October was the letter. So with these four days to come, things are promising.

I also was encouraged to note that in *Peking Review* the reports on Hong Kong always mention the Hsin Hua News Agency Hong Kong Office in capitals, as if they were conscious of the fact that these chaps haven't been sent from Peking and were making the distinction. I hope this is so.

The report on National Day included few surprises. Only Hsiao Hua and Tan Chen-lin were missing from the rostrum, as far as I could see. The main speech was poor; quoting Mao as saying everybody should, 'Combat selfishness and oppose revisionism'. Chen Yi was on the rostrum, but not present at any meeting with delegations. Different forms of warmth for greetings (at the airport) were interesting. There was also a clear line against peace talks over Vietnam, but this is nothing new.

I finished reading Mao's *Selected Readings* two days ago. *On the Correct Handling of Contradictions Among the People* was interesting. Details of strikes in China in 1956 and a few other questions were new to me.

I washed yesterday; five days after my last 'cleanse', and cut my fingernails. I am becoming a little restless now for the first time and also attribute this to the possibility of something happening. I speculate that possibly a month after the cleaning up of the last Hong Kong court mess (if the four other 'journalists' were not held for long), there might have been time for some negotiations. But then I shall probably be looking back to these outlines in a month's time and smiling to myself at my optimism!

I still pray very hard three times a day! Heaven above only knows how long it will be! I hope my prediction about a month's time is wrong. Getting back to Angel's letter, although she mentioned a report about me in *The Times* on Monday, she didn't say what it said, so I still don't know what the world knows about me. It seems letters still arrive in order – but all about 6 weeks late.

Goodnight diary!

Friday 13 October 1967, 9.30 pm

I want to record in summary my optimism. I allowed myself to believe today that release would take place some time within one month. That is, on or before 12 November. This is a kind of prediction within the larger framework of a more certain belief that the whole period can't possibly last more than 160 days, beyond 28 December. This is based on the evidence of the arrival of Shirley's letter on the 9 October, making it clear that the halfway stage had already passed on, at the most the 80-day mark.

I sustained my natural optimism with the view that Britain holds the cards with two big New China News Agency offices in Hong Kong and London and this must in the end prevail. Today it is 12 weeks all told and I calculate that enough time has now passed for China to 'save face' and to allow some kind of negotiations to take place. Eight weeks are marked on my wall in nail scratches. I do hope release is near. (If all these predictions and expectations are wrong, it will be clear I have no future as a fortune-teller!)

Another supporting factor is that, since long ago, for some reason I have imagined myself arriving in London on a dark November night – with rain blowing in the wind!

I remember often repeating to myself this last expression 'on a dark November night, with rain blowing in the wind' because I liked the poetic ring of it. Pure imagination, yet somehow comforting.

Tuesday 17 October 1967, 9.30 pm

Today another postcard from Shirley. Therefore recent arrivals of mail have come in on 17, 16 and 12 October – all postcards – two of them from 16 September in Bath and one from 9 September in Brighton. Thus, since 9 October, within eight days no less than four communications have arrived. This seems to indicate some kind of relaxation perhaps – but of course it is not very strong proof.

Today I washed and changed my clothes. I had washed my hair last

Thursday, 12 October, but today it is itching furiously again and my thoughts often turn to approaching baldness. But I hope this is not so. On Angel's card today she said, 'When you come home, perhaps we can stay with Jean and Neil.' What an angel she is, and how lucky I am to have her loving me.

Today I re-read the preface of *The Theory and Practice of Communism* again at dinner, having yesterday finished Stuart Schramm's biography of Mao for the third time. This is also the third reading of Carew-Hunt's book. Tonight the bulb in the light in the scullery went out. I don't know why I write this, apart from the fact that it is a fact. This morning I asked for extra toast and enjoyed five whole pieces (dry). What luxury! Today I also cleaned out my room, which was filthy.

The guard told me to close the wire part of the window. In all, the guards have kept themselves far from me recently, taking little or no notice and not peeping much, although they sometimes watch me doing my exercises from the steps outside the door. Apart from last night, which was four small pieces of ham, three fried eggs and potatoes, recent dinners have been fine, with a succession of pork in batter, delicious fried fish and Lao Chiao's stewing steak. The latest *Peking Review* is long overdue and I don't know why.

My trousers have been returned from the cleaners in good shape, despite the many food marks that were on them. Yesterday the guard told me to open the window myself when it was not opened by the staff. These are many disconnected facts which I am recording, I know, but I have taken to regarding this diary as an historical document of some kind. Anyway, today I am able to mark up ten days of consecutive optimism. Since that terrible depression of 7 October, I have managed to keep my spirits up. At present I am keeping them that way without too much difficulty, with my eyes firmly fixed on the weekend.

The weekend in fact contains a remarkable series of 'lucky days'. First of all 20 October is the thirteenth-week anniversary, 21 October is the three months' anniversary, and 22 October is the multiple of 13 on which good things have happened. Because of this, I have put back formulating the new 23-day Plan until 23 October. If these days pass without anything happening, I shall buckle down again to long-term planning.

But it isn't all easy, naïve happiness. Tonight I got out an old *Peking Review* and read for the first time in solitary confinement the statement of the Foreign Ministry. It says, of course, the Chinese Government has decided to restrict the freedom of movement of Grey in view of the persecution of Chinese correspondents in Hong Kong. In all reasoning, of course, this means that I am going to be here until they get some satisfaction. The cold hard print is a bit of a jolt to the senses, but the fact seems to be that I must prepare for a long stay here yet. What hope really is there of release?

I think the fact is that I am becoming really adjusted to the horror now. No doubt many sour depressions lie ahead, but the past ten days have shown how I can adjust. I do think each day now that 'perhaps something will happen today'. But of course it doesn't happen. But being depressed makes things so much harder to bear.

Today is the sixtieth day. I reported this to myself aloud several times this morning because it sounded incredible – 60 days in this cell, 88 days altogether. Will it never end? I pray now three times a day and hope fervently for deliverance.

The moon tonight is full and bright through the scullery window. As I write this, one of the guards has just spat water so noisily three times outside the window that I had to stop writing. The guards have gone back to 12-hour shifts now. Most of them spend their time writing new slogans on their little blackboards, obviously conscious of the fact they are writing. Today I wrote the chronology in the front of this book, putting into perspective the various events up to date. When will it end, I wonder?

I have learned two more Mao boards in the last three days. That seems to be all the day's facts for the moment. Goodnight diary.

After walking for a while I thought of three other things to mention:

1   Today was marked by a huge shit after some eight days of constipation.
2   A crowd grinned and clapped at the window today.
3   I have thought a lot about my 'book' recently.

Jean and Neil Merritt were close friends of Shirley.

Thursday 19 October 1967, 11.00 pm

Not long ago the guards 'gave me my medicine'! I had the doctor tonight after a second and more severe bout of stomach trouble. It began yesterday morning – and got rapidly worse during the day. The night, in which I didn't sleep at all after about 12.30 am, was terrible! I ran to the toilet and back again and again, and couldn't even become comfortable in bed.

It was a restless and enervating night. I slept only a few minutes after it got light. During the night through the very top of the window, I suddenly saw a star for the first time for two months and wished very hard on it for release and recovery. The night, however, was one of the longest I have ever known and one of the most unpleasant.

Today I ate only dry toast and soup until evening, when I had some vegetable stew. The doctor came after Lao Chiao asked me if I wanted one. He arrived about 9.15 am with a tall English-speaking cadre from the Public Security Bureau. The tall cadre first addressed me in Chinese, then went into English. He had a strong American accent. He also had a moustache and bi-focal spectacles.

The doctor was a nice-seeming little man who peered at me over his spectacles in the worldwide manner of doctors. He was quite unaggressive and gave me a thorough examination without a word, giving instructions through the interpreter. At the end I said, '*Hsieh-hsieh*' (thank you), and he smiled a very pleasant little smile. He didn't let his gaze rest very long on the slogans when he came in, since he was obviously, I thought, used to behaving in a way necessary for his own survival.

After the examination the interpreter came back and said the doctor wanted to see some shit, but I couldn't oblige. About 90 minutes later, the guards came in with a little bag of pills and a bottle of yellow liquid. A guard I call 'Charles', because he reminds me physically of a great friend from my schooldays with that nickname, shook out two green pills and one little yellow one and poured some of the liquid into the glass I was holding. Neither tasted bad.

Then 'Charles' and the other two guards went off, giggling and laughing like schoolgirls apparently at the amazing idea of young 'Charles' doctoring the foreigner! I didn't shave or wash. Very lazy. Became very depressed in the afternoon, the worst for a long time, and felt I couldn't see release happening in a year again. I pulled out of this depression in the evening, however, and had an hour's sleep on the bed.

'Charles': real name Robin Brown. With Brian Middleton, Robin Brown was my closest friend at the City of Norwich Grammar School. In that era we greatly admired American comics filled with gangster stories and we went to watch gangster movies in Norwich at the weekends, starring the likes of James Cagney and Steve Cochrane. We gave each other American Irish–Italian gangster names, which seemed much 'slicker' and more glamorous than our real English 1950s names. Robin Brown became 'Charles Mancini,' Brian Middleton became 'Eddie Mandelli' or 'Ed' and I was 'Slim Moran'. The two nicknames stuck for a lifetime for Charles and Ed. For some reason my nickname, 'Slim' never took hold. I was disappointed. So that's how unknowingly one of my guards was briefly named after an imaginary American gangster.

Saturday 21 October 1967, 11.15 pm

I am sitting on my bed writing this to 'celebrate' exactly three months under house arrest. Friday 21 July seems years ago now. Today has seen my gradual recovery from my illness, which has lasted four days. I have been drinking hot water from a flask for two days and have not shit now for 36 hours. Today in the afternoon I felt nervy and edgy, and thought again about the possibility of having nervous trouble. But prayer helped me overcome this. I thought about religion in some depth today and decided I believed in God, mainly because I want to. From this, all else follows in my case. Trying to find a rational explanation for belief is difficult.

Lao Chiao said today that the doctor said, 'WC was good.' He went off across the courtyard yesterday carrying a tiny box of my shit to the hospital for examination.

Today I have been eating broth and scrambled eggs for lunch and dinner. I have eaten very little in the past few days, but have no hunger. Tonight for the first time for four days I enjoyed eating again. Yesterday it seemed I would never enjoy eating anything ever again.

Tonight I finished composing my own first ever made-up crossword puzzle on a piece of paper. I also got on with the third reading of Carew-Hunt. I promised I would prevail today in a very strong prayer. This followed immediately on my deep depression and nerviness, and made me feel better. The possibility of a year is becoming very real now and I am not saying this simply because I hope that it won't follow. (I hope it won't follow, but a year seems really very possible now! After all, I have done a quarter already.) This afternoon I was terribly strongly struck by the incomprehensibility of this whole situation. Why am I here? What purpose does it serve? How long shall I be here? Where in the world is the end of it to be?

There have been several more pieces in the paper in the last few days about Hong Kong which, although I can't really understand them, have depressed me.

Tuesday 24 October 1967

New 23-day Plan

Plan is divided into seven different parts. Its title is, 'Determination not Dejection'.

1   Determination-not-dejection creed is to be referred to regularly and certainly whenever depression comes.

2   Attempt to get upstairs to get the following: Peking Reviews and as many books as possible; chess set; stomach tablets and other medicaments; wool shirts and suits and towels etc.; garage keys; coffee and marmalade.

3   If above unsuccessful, try to buy book from Foreign Languages Press through Lao Chaio (or if above only partly successful).

4 Plan book, both chapter-wise and jot down other thoughts.
5 Closer study of yoga, doing it an extra hour per day for concentration and other practice, read again and develop other advanced postures and generally tighten up approach.
6 If both the efforts to get upstairs and bookshop efforts fail, re-read important Mao works.
7 Innovate where possible, try to be busy and not extremely lazy for days on end.

New creed

I know that I shall prevail and one day get out of here. Every day that passes is one day nearer release. Dejection can only do harm, not good. Therefore it must be resolutely repulsed by determination to remain optimistic and calm. The Chinese authorities have nothing to gain by keeping you here and they know this.

Days and weeks seem long, but governments work slowly to save their faces. Be patient, try to keep busy and think only of preparing yourself for the future.

Nothing but good can befall you! Peace, happiness and contentment lie ahead. Prepare yourself for happier climes with a calm untroubled mind, free from worry or fear. You have a good future; your fate is in God's hands. God will deliver you. Something good is coming.

This plan expires 17 November 1967.

Thursday 26 October 1967, 7.30 pm

Will they never let me out of here? This plaintive question has passed my lips several times today – a day of bad depression. It became acute this afternoon while I was walking and led me to drop to my knees in prayer at my bedside. I read for the first time since I wrote it, my 'creed' of 'Determination not Dejection', but it was not all-powerful.

Today there have been five or more guards on at one time, which I don't understand. It has been a very hard day of very big depression. I have just finished a dinner of liver, carrots, chips, soup and vegetables. This morning I had another stomach upset, but I am hoping it will not be severe.

Yesterday I launched my new 'plan', but up to the moment I have had no reaction from a request to Lao Chiao for me to go upstairs. I have been reading yoga and doing exercises for two days. On Sunday 22 October I got a postcard from Shirley in which she said, 'Damn, damn, damn! That you are not here!' and threatened to 'visit' me 'soon'.

The next day I received a letter from her telling me nothing important, but giving large details about driving lessons she is taking for the first time. It was the third letter from Shirley. Since Monday there has been no mail and I have been despondent each day when the papers have come. I am still reading Carew-Hunt's book for the third time and am still finding it very interesting! Today I made out – I should say I was allowed to make out – cheques for the wages and for the rent and car licence and electricity. I had a long tussle with myself about whether or not to pay the rent and still feel a little weak for not withholding it. But it wouldn't get me out of here, I don't suppose.

There has been no sign for me to grab or cling to and my morale today appeared to be getting rather low. I pray tremendously hard but sometimes feel there is no God. I try to fight this. It has become so cold now that this morning I had to put on a sweater over my cardigan and then put a jacket on and walk about with the collar turned up. Winter is going to be hell in this cell.

The staff today asked for an extra 40 yuan for their winter uniforms. How long will this hell on earth go on? I do so long for some encouragement. I am very low in spirits.

Saturday 28 October 1967, 7.00 pm

I have just eaten, with delirious enjoyment, an apple. I have smelled it like an idiot, caressed it, washed it, polished it and almost made love to it. Then I cut it in half and ate it and have just been asking my stomach out loud what it thought of that after 71 days. The shattering arrival of a big yellow apple and a square of butter came on my dinner tray this evening. For 71 days since I was put into this room, I have been denied milk, butter, fruit and cheese. I have asked many times for them, only to be told that the Red Guards had said 'no'. Tonight Sao Kao explained that the people who wrote the slogans had said 'yes', and from now on I would get fruit and butter.

The thrill of eating an apple was unimaginable. The smell was delicious and I couldn't take it away from my nose. It tasted splendid. I ate it in a semi-daze. The butter on the toast was great too, although not so strong in impact as the apple. The butter was very small, but to eat toast with it on again was tremendous. These two things I have found have made me almost happy. My mood, which this afternoon was very pessimistic and bad, has changed to an almost elated one. I believe that these small quantitative changes are paving the way for eventual release.

This morning there were several strange incidents. A fat Public Security Bureau cadre I had never seen before arrived at 8.30 with a three-buzz ringing of the bell. In the next hour the bell was rung twice. On each occasion with three long – unusually long – rings, and a lengthy conference followed with the police and Lao Chiao taking part. Lao Chiao said only when I asked, 'It was police.'

The fat cadre stayed all morning and nothing happened. Strange. I thought it could be some kind of rehearsal. The activity was somewhat exciting.

Sunday 29 October 1967, 22.00 hours

The wind is howling outside very strongly as I write. Watched fascinated and with great excitement, over a quite a good spell of time, as a long strip of poster gradually tore itself free from outside my window on the street side of the cell. I was urging it to go, silently, all the time I was watching it. Eventually it flew off into the wind. I saw it symbolically as an act of my winning freedom.

Today was the hundredth day of house arrest overall. I had an apple at breakfast, pear at lunch and apple at dinner to complete a *very fruitful day!* I also had cheese and butter with toast at dinner, which was good roasted pork.

Another noteworthy thing today was that I noticed that a new slogan had been written in chalk above the kitchen window facing the courtyard saying, 'Down with British imperialism!' This was strange, since it must have been written during the night. Why I can't say, unless it confirms my theory that preparations are being made for consular access – which I coined last night. This would explain the rehearsal mode of yesterday, with the three-buzz ringing of the bell, if this is planned to be to be held in the yard. Otherwise, I have new hope, in the wake of the arrival of fruit and butter on my tray after all the misery of recent days. (There was also butter in the eggs for breakfast.)

It has been cold tonight and I had to put on two sweaters to keep warm and turn up my collar as I walked up and down.

Tuesday 31 October 1967, 22.00 hours

Well, well, well! Today another visit from the Red Guards – or, more exactly, 'my proletarian friends'. Clearly this was the object of the Saturday rehearsals; around 11 am they came in, in a gaggle, and this threw me into a dither of excitement. They didn't come to my cell, but after a while went upstairs and clumped around. Then they came down to me, looked around then, making my pulse race, went outside and broke the seals on my door.

My heart beat faster and I sat and prayed on my bed, and thought about getting *The Times*, being allowed back upstairs, having a bath, reading and writing and living again. I thought, 'Perhaps 74 days in this cell is not too bad after all.' But alas! I was a bloody pathetic twit. Not only was I not allowed back upstairs, but was told by Lao Chiao that he could bring nothing down for me.

I finally saw that the house was 'unsealed' simply because the heating had to be turned on today. What I first saw, after my first disappointment, as at least a small concession was in fact no concession at all and was not even the slightest help to me.

On the contrary, it was evidence of a long-term step. I believed it for about an hour. When realisation dawned, I was in despair even deeper than before. After lunch, when I found I could have nothing from upstairs, it was worse. But after this passed, I think somehow it has strengthened my resolve, by making absolutely clear that I am again settling down to a long term. Christmas is eight weeks ahead less one day. To make it a better Day of Disasters, in the middle of all the activity Lao Chiao brought me a letter which fell to the floor and at first it looked like my mother's writing.

However it was not from my mother, but from Emerita. I do so admire her initiative in getting a letter to me via London. Very persistent and kind. Today's events were very frustrating, but the whole thing about seals and the ultimate 'control' by the Red Guards is worth noting in my 'book' whenever it gets written.

I recognised several of the same Red Guard faces from the two previous visits, but they wore capes and winter jackets this time and it was more difficult to identify them. Some of them looked new. They stared at me through the window as they trooped out afterwards. Not a word was spoken this time. This led me at once to think it was an issue about which they had nothing to say. The heat being turned on today has turned my room into a much warmer place. The radiators are very efficient.

The thrice-rung bell routine practised on Saturday was messed up today when whoever had the job rang once, then tried to recover quickly and rang three more. The fat cadre was here with them. The big rehearsal on Saturday made it all rather ridiculous. What a bloody visit!

I remember praying over and over again, 'Please, God, it looks good, please make it absolutely good!' I cursed myself for being such a fool afterwards. Tonight Sao Kao asked me, on advice of the police chief, whether I wanted a haircut.

I said, 'Where? At the hotel?' And Sao Kao said, 'He says here.' So I said no.

Dinner tonight was ham with four eggs and carrots, and four pieces of toast, cheese, butter, an apple, cabbage, tomatoes, cucumber and egg and good soup. The food has improved very much recently and is now good and eatable. Last night and this morning I had bananas. Yesterday Sao Kao asked for more money for the rent, since it was a fine to pay a day late. This served to emphasise my abject dependence on them here and sent me plunging into another fit of misery, when I had to give him an extra 20 yuan from the money-box.

I dropped my plan to try to get books bought today, because of all the excitement. So ends the month of October 1967. Goodbye October, you were one of the worst months of my life!

Wednesday 1 November 1967, 23.00 hours

Today I succeeded in keeping a calm mind all day and feel I have at last grasped the essentials of yoga. Tonight in fact I decided today would be the first day of a 'Calm to Christmas' campaign. Today I washed myself full length and cleaned the room. During the night I had a funny dream about being held in a house in England, 'escaping' for a few hours to have a meal with a few British friends here – including Theo Peters – then returning to find my two guards, British police, had found out and said it would be the last chance I got for a year. I asked if they really thought that I should be held for a year and one said, 'Well for eight months.' I thought this worth recording just in case it is a prophetic dream. I sincerely hope it isn't.

Theo Peters was, if my memory serves me correctly, commercial counsellor under Donald Hopson at the British Mission. Urbane, charming and affable, he left a pleasant impression in my memory and that is perhaps why he had a walk-on part in this faintly pleasurable dream.

Thursday 2 November 1967, 09.30 hours

This unusually early diary is being written as Lao Chiao and Mrs Hou, the Amah, are cleaning the scullery next door. It is a good point to record the mess. The windows in there and here were covered so thickly with black paint that the paint is still wet after 11 weeks. The inside of the bath was totally sloshed with paint, as were the toilet seat and bowl, the mirror, windowsills and doors. Paint ran down the walls from the slogans on either side. It was extremely dirty and unhygienic. Wood was nailed up. Posters and paint were also stuck up on the walls and under the towel rack. I was allowed to clean off the mirror, but nothing else.

I never had any intention of cleaning the black paint from inside the bath and didn't ask to do so. The clean-up appears to be the direct effect of the visit of the Red Guards. I wonder what else will follow, if anything? I feel this is a sort of an admission of the inadvisability of carrying on this treatment, at least, if not relieving the extreme severity of it. I feel a noble victim this morning while they are despicable oppressors!

(Part II, 23.15 hours)

The clean-up covered the bath, lavatory and sink. The slogans remain. There was quite a pathetic touch. Two daubs of paint across one wall which meant nothing at all, but were just a mess, as one splashed slogan dribbled across into another, were left obviously on instructions as they seemed to have been dubbed 'sacred writings' of the masses. The pink posters about me also remained. The bath can't be got clean.

I tried to get more Mao books today, but the shop had none of the five in stock. The paper arrived in mid-afternoon without any mail and I was ruefully saying to myself that it wasn't my day, when the bell rang and after a while it turned out to be a cable from Angel saying, 'Love you, darling.' This was the first cable of the whole 15 weeks, and was clearly a decision of the Foreign Ministry Information Department. Not anything fantastic in itself, but another small pointer to concessions. I was thrilled.

In this era, long before Islamist terrorist groups began vengefully and horrifyingly executing foreign hostages publicly via video cameras and the Internet, I believe the presiding understanding was that a dead hostage was not a good hostage because he or she was the bargaining counter. This applied more particularly to a government-held hostage rather than to terrorist groups. I believe my circumstances were improved, as winter drew on, chiefly to preserve me as a viable hostage in good health. The next comparable situation to my own would come in 1979–81, when a whole embassy-full of American diplomats would be taken hostage in Teheran for over a year. President Carter launched a Special Forces helicopter mission to rescue them, but it foundered in the desert storms and the helicopters all crashed or crash-landed with sand jammed rotors, far short of their target.

Friday 3 November 1967, 23.45 hours

(I am writing this sat on the closed lid of the loo.)

Today I was 'moved' into the former translator's office next to the scullery. Without warning, after lunch I was asked to sit in the scullery while office equipment was moved into it from there and eventually into my little cell. All three Chinese staff – Sao Kao, Lao Chiao and Amah – helped move a proper single bed down from upstairs and cleaned up and prepared the room. The 'cell' was filled with furniture and locked. I don't know why it happened. It appears to be a result of the Red Guards' visit and I trace everything, including fruit and meat at mealtimes, back to the Saturday visit of the fat cadre a week ago. Anyway, I have a new bed and I am somewhat unsettled. I have just done an hour's unsatisfactory yoga session in the dark and have not yet found a new pattern.

Walking tonight was strange, going right up to the guards as they sat watching me across the entrance hall from their chairs inside the dining room. I am now making a slightly longer L-shaped walk, from beneath the scullery window beside the loo and round into the former office and up to the open door facing the guards and back. In general I find the change encouraging. I had asked in my prayer this morning for a sign of encouragement and I think this was one. I was almost totally indifferent at first to the change, but some two or three hours afterwards I feel tremendously relieved to be out of that small cell after exactly 11 weeks. I'll write more about this tomorrow; my impressions are still a little confused.

Reflections · 4
Monday 11 December 2006

'My impressions are still a little confused,' I wrote finally in that diary entry of 3 November 1967, and this morning, thirty-nine years later, I awoke at my home in the Norfolk countryside just outside Norwich with a different feeling of confusion – left by a dream. Re-reading the diary entries to this point has produced very mixed feelings and on waking I immediately felt there was a connection between those uncomfortable feelings and the very contemporary dream.

In the dream I found myself looking into the faces of seeming British building workers on a mundane building site in the UK. Yet, on looking more closely, I found I was looking at stylised flatter, broader faces, in fact Asiatic faces with heavy-lidded, downcast eyes like those of serene Bodhisattvas.

These finely-wrought faces and bodies, I saw then, were formed from pale gold sand and I was walking confusedly among them on their building site, close to a snarled-up suburban traffic jam on a roundabout, possibly beside London's North Circular Road. I had just been forced off the road in my car by impatient hooting fellow motorists who were being made more impatient by my uncertainty about which direction to take off the roundabout.

So unable to make up my mind, I had pulled over and got out to try to find my bearings. Then I noticed the trenched ground, across which I was idly picking my way, was more like a partly excavated historical dig than a building site. The ground itself was composed of the same pale golden sand as the building workers' faces and bodies. Shapes, big and small, identifiable in the sandy trenches were strictly geometrical, precise and intriguing. What were they, what did they mean?

No ready answers were immediately available and, before I could get back to my car, I woke up. Then a bit later, puzzling over the dream, I realised that the sandy faces on these otherwise mundane British builders resembled the impassive lifeless features of some of China's impressive archaeological army of thousands of Terracotta Warriors, discovered by farmers digging a well in 1974 near the ancient imperial capital of Sian. They form a unique martial bodyguard for Emperor Qin Shi Huang (259–210 BC), the first emperor of the Qin Dynasty and founder of China's first empire. In his lifetime he built a real-life army of one million soldiers and started construction of China's Great Wall. Archaeologists had initially found 1800 out of a possible 6000 warriors, including cavalry, infantry and charioteers, making this one of the most extraordinary archaeological discoveries of the twentieth or any other century.

If there was any meaning in my dream, I decided, perhaps it was that revisiting and reviewing my China experience through this diary was similarly a process of excavation and rediscovery that might have some value and could point out new directions. Possibly the snarled up traffic roundabout and my uncertainty about which exit to take symbolised some hesitancy in myself about this review process. And the intriguing mathematical and geometric shapes in the sand were symbols of things still hidden, still to be investigated and understood.

So looking back at my description from outside it, of the locked door of that suddenly impenetrable eight-foot-square cell, I wonder now how I existed for 11 weeks in that horribly confined space, without outside exercise or any idea of what was to become of me.

I obviously felt, first and foremost, an obscure sense of relief. I'd twice become acutely unwell because of the spartan, dirty and unhygienic conditions which had been imposed on me deliberately to humiliate and discomfit my representative 'British imperialist' body and mind. Also, for the first time in my life, I had come face to face with a sometimes frightening and debilitating depression that threatened to engulf me. I was glad then to be out of there, yet looking back from the safety of my home this mid-December day in the year 2006, I see those first 11 weeks of enforced isolation as profoundly significant.

The struggle was not over by any means and in fact was due, mentally and psychologically, to become much more acute in the months to follow. Yet the days in the eight-foot-square cell marked a clear turning point in my life. Heavily disguised at the time beneath a thick veneer of often seemingly unendurable mental anguish and fear, without my being aware of it, seeds of great positivity I sincerely believe had been sown deep inside me.

After being a rouseabout reporter, happy until then to rush hither and thither every single day of my working life, first in Britain and then abroad, looking for new exciting scoops, I had been stopped dead in my tracks. Almost without warning, I had crashed into immovable buffers. I suddenly had the time to analyse my life, my career and personal relationships, review my past and my beliefs, search and re-search my memory and ponder about the world and China's history and how it was interwoven with that of an aggressive, arrogantly colonising British Empire, which I then figuratively represented thirty years before the return to China of the colony of Hong Kong.

I had literally for the first time been personally caught up in history, and was paying painfully for past British high handedness on Chinese soil over more than a century of time. Almost certainly in those 77 days, without knowing it, I was being turned from a foreign correspondent into an historical novelist, more interested in discovering and revealing historical insights that might lead to some enlightenment, rather than grabbing fleeting contemporary 'scoops'.

The actions of the Chinese against me and the Peking British diplomatic mission and its personnel might have seemed outrageous at that time on the face of it. Yet we British had left our tiny European island in the nineteenth century to come to a vast, then backward, country to exploit it mercilessly through the Opium Wars. China could not snatch any British territory in revenge, at that time in 1967. If they could have taken over, say, the Isle of Wight and turned it into a thriving, economically booming bit of China, they could perhaps have really got even with us for our continued holding of Hong Kong well beyond the demise of the full-force, colonial era in the 1950s and early 1960s.

In the absence of that, one thing they could certainly do, was thoroughly 'colonise' a British journalist in his Chinese house in the heart of their own capital. And a week or so later, burn down a bit of Britain and nastily frighten and rough up a few British diplomats in the process a few miles away in the Peking diplomatic quarter. Historically, and given the generally vengeful and unforgiving matrix of human nature to date, there really was not much room for complaint by Harold Wilson and Donald Hopson, or Gerald Long and Reuters and myself.

More important than all that, however, it is clearer than ever to me today that I had also begun that vital internal reflective journey in search of greater enlightenment, which is still continuing and will continue always, so long as consciousness remains. Whatever else is true, I am obviously much further along that road than I might have been without my experience in China.

All this was figuratively kick-started in that cell in those seminal 11 weeks. I hadn't suddenly begun meditating consciously in the little cell – in fact quite the reverse. I deliberately avoided anything that smacked of pure meditation. I knew nothing of this vital subject then and the very idea of going inward frankly frightened me. My chief concern was to preserve my sanity, and my ignorance of everything to do with meditation made me feel that drifting off indefinitely into some kind of mental void or reverie might be a sure-fire route to losing my reason altogether.

So I deliberately adopted what I saw as a thoroughly British policy of 'muddling through' as best I could. I would use the yoga book I so fortuitously had in my cell, to teach myself purely physical exercises, as I thought. I had always been blessed with a relatively athletic physique and had always loved sport and played football, cricket and tennis, and ran and jumped and thrown things in my school sports with huge enthusiasm. I had even had a trial for Norwich City FC at Carrow Road (admittedly unsuccessful) when I was 17. So yoga, according to my lights then, was OK because it was mainly physical. What I was not so aware of was that it was the beginning for me of meditation 'through the back door', so to speak.

The yoga book in question I had bought on my last day in Hong Kong, because I had thought that politically turbulent China would be a barren social desert. I wrote in my original account about this experience, *Hostage in Peking*, that I felt a guardian angel had propelled me into the Hong Kong bookshop on that last day before departure for China proper, so vital was the book to my eventual survival and well being. I am even more sure today that it helped save me mentally, psychologically and physically.

Yet in addition to the very physical Hatha yoga exercises, which led me through quiet exertion into unknowing meditative states, the book also suggested closing one's eyes and, in order to still one's thoughts, visualise a rose or summon a memory of a beautiful landscape to that internal cinema we all have. So I would conjure up a favourite visual picture of the sunlit sea and cliffs at Sheringham in North Norfolk where, for a year before leaving to join Reuters, I had worked as the solo regional reporter for the Eastern Daily Press. And whenever I did that, feelings of peace and calmness invariably stole over me.

At one point in the diary I notice, I said that I had become very conscious of 'The weakness and helplessness of the individual alone …'. And, yes that was partly true. Yet paradoxically in that tiny cell at the same time, I was being forced to understand and become aware of a new form of self-sovereignty and self-dependence, which was also to be life-changing. There's much more to say on this subject, but for the moment it is enough to relate that on re-reading these sections of my diary for the first time in nearly four decades, I am more aware than ever before of how fundamental were the changes which took place during those first 11 weeks in 'solitary'. The twenty-nine-year-old man who emerged from that cell on 4 November to be quartered in only slightly improved new circumstances a few paces away, was already radically different to the one who had been dragged in there with his paint-and-blood-daubed bedding on the night of 18

August. Another phase was over – phase two perhaps – phase one having been the 'phoney war' period from 21 July to 17 August. Phase three was beginning and it would eventually embrace the biggest effort up to then to exert and sustain self-control over a long period.

5
CALM TO CHRISTMAS

Saturday 4 November 1967, 10.00 pm

(My second successive diary sitting on the loo, because I don't feel the room so close to the guards' position is secure enough to write in.)

I am now more settled in the new environment. Today has been a pattern-setter. The morning was dramatic. I was doing my yoga, when the guard I call in my head 'Loud Lout' flung open the door in his typical quiet way. I got up angrily from my postures and closed it. He threw it open again and I charged back and closed it again, saying, 'Not until I am dressed!'

Miraculously it stayed closed until ten o'clock. I completed a rather scrappy set of exercises, during which I couldn't quite calm down. After that it was my first breakfast at a table for 11 weeks (my translator's utility desk). I walked back and forth and stood at the window and did yogic breathing until lunch, and put my clothes in the drawers of the desk after lining them with newspapers – an event in itself after 11 weeks.

The door remained closed during breakfast for half an hour and during lunch for an hour. The afternoon was spent walking back and forth again and thinking, and I decided on a regular yoga session at 5.30 pm on the floor of the toilet.

This was more successful and I spent 50 minutes at it. After praying at the bedside, came dinner and afterwards more lolling on the bed, walking, breathing and time-wasting. I have read nothing since finishing Carew-Hunt's book. Somehow the day has seemed longer than most. The room has three slogans against me personally and two against British imperialism. Two signboards on which quotations are chalked have been set up inside the room facing my bed.

The window has been open all day. On the wall behind my bed in

English it says, 'Down with all reactionaries' – a counterpart of the English slogan in the 'cell'. (My name, daubed in two Chinese characters, is 'Ger-Lai'. My walk overall is now ten paces, so it is two paces longer! Today the guards decided not to face me; the chair of the 'lookout' man was set to one side, so that I didn't stare into his face at every step. I found a ten yuan banknote in a drawer of the desk.

My need continues to be a completely calm and detached mind. I am very proud of my new control. The one encouraging event of the day was that my chequebook was given back into my control by Sao Kao. This was very small, but was a gesture that was sufficient to keep up the tempo of little improvements away from humiliation. The chequebook not being in my control was a humiliation. He handed this back after giving me Lao Wang's receipts and statement.

I slept very badly in my new comfortable bed and was awake at seven and didn't sleep again. It's so very English. My bigger view of life from the bigger window in here didn't produce anything startling. The larger size of the room is pleasing, but the overall impact of the change is not great. The toilet, as I write, seems small and my old 'cell', now closed up and locked does look terribly small, however.

I am happy for the continuation of the concession trend. Today Lao Chiao and Mrs Hou were cleaning and banging upstairs. I saw Hou go out with some Red Guard paper seals in a dustpan, having obviously swept them up. They were in the bathroom and all over the upper house, but I have no idea what it means, if anything. It could well be that the concession and developments have finished now for a long spell. But of course I am hoping, as ever, for the best.

Today was another multiple of 13 and the chequebook saved it from being barren. I have put a towel over the mirror, because it is too depressing seeing myself walking towards it for a few paces each time as I go up and down. I look pale, thin and sickly and it isn't good for my morale to see that all the time.

Monday 6 November 1967
(Written 7 November at 9 am.)

After three days the new accommodation is becoming as oppressive as the old. The feeling that it was part of a string of concessions is forming. Today I tried through Sao Kao to get some reading materials from upstairs. The interesting thing was that he and the nice guard admitted that they had rung the Foreign Ministry and had received no reply. This was the first admission that the Foreign Ministry controls me again. But the lack of a reply indicated a negative response and I decided tomorrow to begin a second reading of Mao's works. Otherwise Monday had a quiet and almost unnatural hush and uneventfulness.

I learned the two boards of Mao's quotations in my room headed 'Class Struggle' and 'Class Society'. They are hereby added in my memory bank to the other 16 quotations, which are:

Make trouble ...; The enemy will not perish ...; Mao's thought is ...; Lifting a rock ...; People of the world ...; The socialist system will ...; Paper tigers ...; Monopoly capitalists ...; Die-hards ...; What we need ...; Raging tide ...; East wind ...; Communism is ...; The world is bright ...; National struggle ...; Revolutions ....

On Sunday my guard 'Charles', the bright lad, decided to fasten up the window (as of old) and I almost got angry. But it was not properly closed until Lao Chiao went home. It had sprung open again on its own, symbolically, I thought. 'Charles' also ordered me to close the screens, which I had opened. Reflecting on this yesterday, I decided that in future I would not obey these people. This time I showed some resistance. I also considered going upstairs both by stealth and openly as a form of protest ... going on a hunger strike for something to read ... breaking into the little cell. (Is that an irony or what!)

In this new room are two portraits of Mao, one small and another large one above the door. I am still waking early from my sleep in the new bed, although it is an improvement over the low bunk with broken springs. I have managed to sleep straight through the last two nights without getting up to pee. This I have done by drinking nothing after 8 pm. The overall impression of the last three days in the new cell is one of settling down and back to a terrible empty routine. But I have maintained my calm absolutely and intend to continue to do so. Mrs Hou is continuing to clean upstairs as I write this. I have watched her carry out more sweepings up of the old seals and an empty inkbottle. This of course indicates nothing. I fear that the move was an end in itself, and not part of a bigger movement.

Good morning, Diary!

(On Saturday night I became convinced that I had been seen writing this diary by a guard, through the lavatory window. I worried and prayed about this. Since then I have hidden my pen in my slipper. I am writing this sitting on the blanket on the lavatory. I have settled down to my yoga sessions in the loo here now at the old times.)

Wednesday 8 November 1967, 16.00 hours

This has been one of the happiest days, because this morning I got a letter from dear Mother after 82 days! It was so wonderful, I was so happy to hear from her. I had asked in the morning for encouragement and this was it. She told me how David Chipp had been to see her and about everybody I had been mentioning in my prayers.

I do so love my dear mum and will help her more when I get home. The happiness of this event has filled the whole day. Lunch was delicious curry. Yesterday's only remarkable occurrence was that Lao Chiao cleaned this room in the morning. A small thing, but I think significant. It was the first time since 18 August that my room had been cleaned. There is still no answer from the Foreign Ministry on my request. Clearly the answer is 'No'. I spoke to the 'Nice Fellow' guard last night; he suggested I read Mao again!

I have almost lost the ability to reason out the chances of release since I have received no *Peking Reviews* for nearly three weeks. But my calm state of mind leads me not to worry about this. Looking up the stairs it looks like a nightmare. 'Long live Chairman Mao!' and 'Down with Grey!' are splattered everywhere in thick black paint. (An 'honour' perhaps for me to be so juxtaposed?) In the lounge the big pink poster in English on the window says, 'All reactionaries are paper tigers!' Yesterday I washed all over. Today is very windy and I like the wind, which strikes me as a freeing force.

Saturday 11 November 1967, 12.40 hours

Today the first snow fell. It was only slight. Yesterday I got a pencil from Lao Chiao due to his absent-mindedness. On 7 November I didn't shave for the first time and today, after four days, something of a stubble has appeared on my face. It can't yet be called a beard.

The room is cleaned every day now by Lao Chiao. Last night I washed my hair, losing a great chunk in the process. Reading the twenty copies of *Peking Review* brought down for me on 9 November by Sao Kao has been interesting. The May Circular of the Central Committee and the famous Literature and Art Forum summary and Lin Piao's article on 'Long Live People's War' have all been interesting.

I also found a piece about myself from 21 July, but I long for newspapers and books without Mao in them! The daily newspapers have begun now to put Mao's picture on the front, and sometimes every other page too, with the rays of the sun coming out of him. It gets crazier and crazier. Otherwise the days are flat and quiet and long and seem to bear little encouragement.

My mood is still absolutely calm and my thinking wavers between believing the Chinese must release me around the six months' mark or realise they will endanger press relations between countries generally – and feeling that the move into the new quarters and all the other 'concessions' were only to make it permanent and they are determined to keep me until they get some joy.

But I feel I have lost the power to reason things out now, without information of any kind. Oh, how I long for newspapers and books and magazines above all else. I have been worrying a bit about my mother since getting her letter and wish I could get home to help her sort things out. I prayed today more fervently than ever before for release.

Tuesday 14 November 1967, 22.30 hours

(My pen broke yesterday and I am writing this in pencil.)

In fact the appearance of this pencil, a few days ago, must have been an act of providence. I have spent a very worried afternoon after declining to have my hair cut this afternoon. I have cursed myself for my foolishness and know not what tomorrow will bring in the way of reprisal. Today I was allowed out into the yard for half an hour! It was so marvellous to feel the wind and see the sky and the trees. This followed a big event yesterday, when an English-speaking cadre visited in the afternoon. He came in with the four guards of the Stone-Faced shift and asked me to get out my *Red Book*. I dodged this and listened as they read two quotations, 'The enemy will not perish of himself' and 'The socialist system will eventually replace the capitalist system'. (I resisted saying that I knew them off by heart already among my memory-training 16 quotations!)

Then we sat down and he said he had 'some points'. He looked frequently into his notebook. The 'points' were:

1   You must obey the guards. (He referred here to the incident of 4 November when a guard opened my door in the morning and I leapt up and closed it!)
2   You must have your hair cut.
3   You must keep yourself clean.
4   You will be allowed outside soon.
5   You must ask the guards first if you want anything.

I said I could cut my hair, I didn't need reminding about washing, and anyway the bath was covered with paint. I should wash it once myself, they said. Asked if I had any questions, I asked how long I was to be held and he said, 'I have not been told.'

I asked for things from the bathroom upstairs, for more warm clothes, books, to send a cable to my mother, to do my accounts, and to have the Hsin Hua News Agency printer switched on and to be allowed upstairs. They said they would check up on some of these things. The four guards didn't want to let me do my accounts or to have anything to read except the *Peking Review*.

I was so excited I could not eat my dinner of curry – the second time there had been curry in one day. I saw the visit as an excuse to give me concessions and they had started with a 'reprimand' to make it look good for them. This is why I now feel so miserable about my stupidity about my hair. I shall never get my other requests now.

I have thought I might be beaten up again by the Red Guards, taken to the Police Headquarters or otherwise punished for disobeying a Government Order to have my hair cut. The barber who came was very nice and was absolutely worried about my refusal and kept saying the Government had sent him. He said he knew how to cut it and would only give me a trim.

I should have accepted this. I really have had the feeling back again tonight that I never shall get out of here. The barber said he had been ordered to come every ten days. I cut my hair tonight. Earlier I had washed myself and put on my new suit. Yesterday the activities occurred on a double 13 – the thirteenth of November in the thirteenth week. It was the first visit of its kind since 31 July.

On Sunday, delivery of the Peking Review was resumed after three weeks and another letter from Emerita arrived, telling me that some captured foreign pilots somewhere had been released and that David Oancia was back for the *Toronto Globe* and *Mail*. I had been saying every day, 'Something good is coming', since last week and sure enough something good did come. I wonder what is coming now. I am a fool!

Immediately after yesterday's visit I was allowed upstairs with Sao Kao to get all the bathroom things and my suits. The rooms had been cleaned, but the slogans were still there. I noticed many pink posters about me were plastered about and didn't think they were there before. I wonder whether this meant that I was to go upstairs some time. Later in the afternoon the guards took away my Anadin tablets. This must mean that they thought I would commit suicide. Then they took my Coldrex and I began to get annoyed. I was refused permission for cough sweets, but it was nice to get Nivea cream and combs and everything.

Monday 20 November 1967, 9.15 pm

In bed. I start this new week with some hope of something good coming, but feel an awareness of the realities of the situation. In the past week I have become fully adjusted to the idea of being here for Christmas. I have also become adjusted to having to stay here for six months and more, perhaps up to a year, even over a year. The timeless inevitability of the situation became very clear to me during last week.

(Now it is eleven o'clock, sitting on the loo because I fear for the security of this diary writing in bed. I try to keep my optimism up, but at the same time I am thoroughly aware of the smallness of the possibilities.)

It is a week since I last wrote in this diary and this is for two reasons. I was very uneasy over the haircut visit and the security aspect. Anyway, on Wednesday at 4 pm I apologised for not having my hair cut. They had closed off the fresh air and not allowed me to go out to walk in the courtyard. It was clear that it would get me nowhere refusing any further. My mind was much easier afterwards. On Thursday I was allowed outside to walk again.

Outside I was able to see that the door of my cell and the windows had all been nailed up with wood from the outside. I have quickly come to enjoy the trips outside. On Friday 17 November a letter from Angel fell through the letterbox of the gate while I was out there. This was the first letter from her since 23 October. It told me she knew of my 'visitation'. (Well put!) On the same day I went upstairs to get the cashbox. Sao Kao asked for money for medicine and after a short delay I was allowed up there. The tidy nature of the office struck me and I wondered if it had been cleaned.

So I was twice up there in one week, which was as many times as in the whole of the time from the invasion night of 18 August. On Saturday 18 November the guards were all changed except one. This led to a few new teething troubles, which are not over yet. I write this diary very much on edge these days, not being sure enough of my security with it.

Now the morning of 21 November 1967

(In bed.)

Last night I realised it was exactly five weeks to Christmas! I looked back over each of the past five weeks and found they all had fairly noticeable changes. I wondered how things would seem when I looked back on the coming five-week period from Christmas Day. Angel's depression in her latest letter and her talk about coming for Christmas, although it was written in September, made me think about how clear it must be to the outside world, and how hopeless my hopes of release are.

Last week the haircut affair made me worry and depression set in, and I said many desperate prayers. Now I am determined to be practical again, reading in the periods that I am not walking, and working away at the task of getting five weeks passed up to Christmas. I have decided to wait until Friday 24 November to see if I get an answer to my 'requests' to the Foreign Ministry. Today it began to look unlikely.

Yesterday one of the new guards inexplicably told me to close my window soon after it was opened. I didn't understand and still don't. But yesterday's walk in the courtyard was beautiful, with the gilded roof of the Forbidden City Corner Temple visible in the sunlight above the wall and the sky blue and the red berries on the trees and the cold crisp air. I have bought winter uniforms for the staff, had the office jacket cleaned and yesterday washed and put on my red wool shirt. Today is the anniversary of four months! Good morning, you blasted Diary!

Sunday 26 November 1967, 13.30 hours

(Sitting on the loo with the lid down.)

I want to record my complete feeling of emptiness at the moment. The past 17 days have been almost entirely without incident. Only on Thursday 23 November did I go upstairs for two minutes to get the keys to the garage, which were needed for something obscure. Also the old office jacket turned up. Otherwise the week was barren and as I often said in my prayers, kneeling at the side of the bath, 'This is the vacuum of hell.'

I pray frequently now and have come to look on Sundays as a special day and one from which to review the past week and look forward to the next week. Most disappointing thing about this week has been the complete lack of letters. The last one was from Shirley on Friday 17 November. Thus it is now nine days. Only once before, from 28 September to 9 October, has there been such a long gap. This coincides with the new 'guard' arriving last Saturday and I wonder whether my mail has been stopped. Each morning I have hoped and been disappointed.

At the moment I am not unduly depressed. I have somehow developed a dead feeling, which makes it hard for me to make my mind do anything active. In some moments I am seized with despair, but most of the time I can contemplate long weeks ahead as empty as this without any feeling at all.

It now seems as if I shall never get out of here. Life seems to be totally concerned with being a prisoner now. Today it is four weeks to Christmas Eve. I have hope that Christmas will bring some concession, but don't know what. I so want even the smallest thing to happen now to break the monotony that even any incident seems impossible. I plan to put on a good suit at Christmas and some after-shave and clean my shoes to make it special. I shall pray a lot. I think a sense of martyrdom helps me to look forward to Christmas.

My days now are: rise around 9.15 am, do yoga, shave, dress, go back into the bathroom and pray, have breakfast, walk, be allowed out into the courtyard, walk inside, lunch, read or lie on the bed thinking, walk, read or think, pray, dinner, lie on bed, walk, read or think, yoga at 23.00 and bed.

This week I have been reading *Peking Reviews* from upstairs, sorting through them for the least vestige of interest. It is becoming increasingly difficult to remain enthusiastic about yoga – or anything else for that matter. I vaguely hope that when I have done six months, there might seem to be more hope of release. But considering Chinese intransigence, however, that seems wishful thinking. I worry about my mother, think a lot about Angel, and pray for them all the time.

The new guards are settling in now. Some watch me like hawks as I walk outside, while others are less enthusiastic. They generally sit at the table under the Mao portrait and the blackboards bearing blue and red inscriptions, reading or smoking their pipes or doing nothing. My life seems becalmed in a flat sea, never to become mobile again.

Yesterday I was struck by the great length of time I have been under house arrest – from the heat of July to the freezing days in the courtyard of the present. I try to tell myself that in the future you will look back on this with a smile – but it is very difficult to see that now!*

I often wonder if I shall ever lead a normal life again, and ask God to help me face with courage any terrible happening. Concessions seem out of the question now and I am puzzled by the fact that no haircut has taken place. I am completely unable to read the Chinese mind. I have dreamed of throwing my arms around Mother in reunion and having interviews with Chen Yi. My sleep is not bad, but is always interrupted every night. One of the guards sits right outside my door, so that I can hear every move he makes. Oh please, Heaven, bring me some encouragement, I am so disheartened.

I smile broadly as I read this, on Thursday 14 December 2006, to finally fulfil my own prophecy.

Thursday 30 November 1967, 23.00 hours

Today, although a multiple of 13, was almost empty. In view of the fact that I was allowed to walk for one hour for the first time saved it from being completely so. Since the last diary entry, nothing at all has happened. The days have grown colder. The guards now wear fur hats and today the temperature was 27 degrees Fahrenheit, I could see from the thermometer on the wall by the gate. My mood is nondescript. Today I have worked out the third 23-day Plan and hope to remain calm to Christmas. I have noticed that since the move into the new room, I have become more accustomed to the likelihood of long-term imprisonment. On Monday 27 November I got new *Peking Reviews* and have been enjoying reading them – one per day since. I am looking forward to Christmas, but mostly because it will be more time past.

Yesterday I cut out paper dolls from the newspaper, and the day before 'maintained' or oiled the innards of the clock with mouthwash! Yesterday I also exercised my mind by converting my thermometer scale from Fahrenheit to Centigrade. This is a tremendously empty period. But the thought suddenly occurred to me a little while ago, 'Why not enjoy it?' and this is what I shall try to do.

The guards became more friendly today. One actually smiled at me. Tonight water started coming through the ceiling from upstairs. Life is very dull and I miss Shirley tremendously. There have been no letters since 17 November – 13 days. It is difficult to guess why they have stopped. The only thing I can think is that the reason is the same as for the *Peking Review*'s cessation. I am glad to see November go. It failed to fulfil early promise.

So here is my third 23-day Plan. Its title is: 'Calm to Christmas – Dominate Circumstances and Endure Emptiness'.

1   The main method is yoga. Complete, absolute control for 23 days is the target.

2   Pray to God. Your fate is in his hands. Be your own encouragement. Be more disciplined; allow no daily 'hopes and expectations'. Ignore the arrival of the Chinese newspapers.

3   Material targets: suit, shoes, brush, scarf and gloves, chess set.

4   Enjoy yourself!

5   Neutralise relations with the guards.

6   Innovate where possible. New intensive study of yoga and practice.

7   Don't swear or have bad thoughts.

Good luck, old boy!

Wednesday 6 December 1967, 09.00 hours

(In bed, as the reading of Mao's quotations are ringing out in the room next door!)

On Monday 4 December at 4 pm, Sao Kao returned from his shopping with an English Carlsberg lager box on the back of his bike. He carried it into the guards' room and they closed the door. I tried to contain my excitement and guess what was in it. After a lot of telephoning and checking by them, I was handed letters from Sally, John, Emerita and Noleen!

The letters were followed by the box, containing ten books, cheroots, chocolate, sweets, toothbrush and a screwed up *Spectator* and half the

Daily Telegraph! My joy was immense! It was Christmas come early! This is what I had been praying for and never expected from outside.

After examining my gifts, I went to pray and give thanks in the bathroom. The box had been sent on 15 November. It appeared as a reward for my determination in the new 23-day Plan. Soon I was hiding the books and newspapers, in case there was a change of mind and I lost my new treasures. Its arrival came as a tremendous relief after so long with an empty mind.

The afternoon sped by as I read the prefaces etc. to the books and reviewed my treasure. Perhaps the most exciting things were the bits of newspaper and magazine. I spent all yesterday reading almost every word in them. New drink tests had been introduced in England with breathalysers, there had been a Cabinet reshuffle and all the beauty and greatness of Britain flowed back to me as I read the Spectator reviews of books and plays. I can't thank God enough for this tremendous development! I asked him to bless Sally and John, and I more or less decided not to touch the things until Christmas in case nothing else came: and also as an act of will.

This was something I thought would never happen. Whether it means I can have other books remains to be seen. On the day they arrived I was still trying to make one *Peking Review* last each day. But this had become very monotonous.

On Monday morning I was allowed marmalade with breakfast for the first time. It however was not an enormous experience. My desire for pleasure is not great – only for freedom. Also yesterday the *Peoples' Daily* was taken away by the deliveryman not long after he brought it. It contained pictures of Mao and Lin. Can't guess why it was necessary to recall it. My 'Calm to Christmas' campaign is going well. No lapses yet. Last night a guard opened the door of the washroom while I was exercising on the floor. I asked, 'What do you want?' He said nothing. He did knock.

Saturday 9 December 1967, 19.00 hours

Since the last diary entry I have had a haircut. On the afternoon of 6 December a different man came along and gave me a very neat haircut for one yuan. I washed my hair that night and was so very pleased indeed to have it done. A very pleasant guy, he also asked me if I wanted a shave. This week has been quite different to the others.

Been spending my days reading George Mikes' *How to be an Alien* (Wednesday 6 December), doing two crosswords and also reading Dennis Wheatley's *Mediterranean Nights* (Thursday and Friday). I have been indulging in the luxury of reading in bed at nights. It has given me quite a different feeling and I rarely think of release now, as my mind is able to turn to other things. First impressions of Dennis Wheatley's writings were very poor – but to have them to read is important. The weather is tremendously cold with temperatures yesterday and the day before of 19 and 20 degrees Fahrenheit. I sat on the bed wrapped in an old coat to keep warm. Having books is a sheer luxury and I only hope I can get more.

Mikes' book deals with being an 'alien' in the Second-World-War sense of being a non-British subject of possibly suspicious non-British loyalties, yet resident in war-xenophobic Britain.

Monday 18 December 1967, 13.50 hours

Today, a week before Christmas Day, I am remaining calm. A bank statement came with an early ring on the bell. Yesterday the Peking Review was delivered for the third week running. On Saturday a telegram from my Angel was delivered at around 5.30 pm saying, 'Love you, Darling. Shirley.' On 14 December I was allowed upstairs, at my request, to get clothes, scarf, suit, shoes and shoe brushes to prepare for Christmas. Since then I have been daily 'buffing' up my brown shoes to a high shine.

Halfway through last week the guards started singing 'The Helmsman' and 'The East is Red' morning and night, standing in front of the framed portrait of Mao. They also seemed to have new small *Red Books* from which they read at lunch. Caught a reference to Britain and imperialism, which I know are in the *Red Book*. Yesterday's *Peking Review* reported the latest Chinese protest over Hong Kong, which I found encouraging, because its language was comparatively mild and it talked of improving relations. This was the first real confirmation that I was not alone in the persecution.

A few days ago I came out of a kind of euphoria after reading my new books for more than a week. This week I didn't think much about my predicament. Now again I have begun thinking about it and realising just how bad my position is. But I can only wait and see.

Yesterday's *Peking Review* raised my hopes more than anything for some time. But I am not unduly optimistic about it. Last week new posters were put up everywhere. The big one in the guard's room goes, 'Oppose revisionism, fight self!' The appearance of posters in my room didn't cheer me up at all. All my thoughts are directed to Christmas now and afterwards I must think of a new plan. All in all things are not too badly depressing. I can read; the guards are not too unpleasant; some have been almost friendly. One of the first four is very friendly, smiling at times. Today I had a 50-minute walk. The other night one came into the room and asked if I was reading. It seemed friendly rather than intrusive. Sao Kao is friendlier too.

Christmas Eve, Sunday 24 December 1967, 13.00 hours

Yesterday about five o'clock, I received two cables from Reuters. These were the first ever cables from Reuters. They came from Long and Underhill. The latter I liked, but Long's was dead funny. The day before I received a card from Angel with two elephants on its front - one coy, shy, female with long eyelashes and obviously flirtatious, the other clearly masculine yet receptive to the female's advances. Yesterday the guards refused to allow me upstairs to get throat sweets. On Wednesday 20 December they introduced new rules about not closing the doors when I washed and not reading in bed. This has stopped my second yoga session and made necessary stealthy movement in the morning to wash in peace.

My mood on Christmas Eve is calm. I believe the 23-day 'Calm to Christmas' Plan has been successful. Today I plan to wash my hair and body, and clean my shoes ready for the big day tomorrow. There is no sign of any development and yesterday's cables do little for my morale.

Gerald Long was Reuters general manager, whom I did not know well and who had seemed gruff and distant during our brief meeting in his seventh-floor office in Fleet Street before I left for China. I can't remember now why I found his cable 'dead funny' - possibly it seemed stilted and formal at that time, on the face of it lacking any real heartfelt content. However after my arrival home I was touched in retrospect by how deeply Gerald Long and everybody at 85 Fleet Street had obviously been concerned about me and my plight. I was shown a letter to the then-Foreign secretary Michael Stewart in which Gerald Long admitted that he felt personally responsible for sending me to China, and he obviously worked unstintingly though for so long with no marked success, to try to do something to help and bring about my release.

Stuart Underhill, Canadian editor in chief of Reuters when I left London, was a likeable, warm, friendly and more evidently caring man who had invited me to his West End flat for supper in London before I left for Peking.

Boxing Day, Tuesday 26 December 1967, 13.00 hours

(Standing in the washroom.)

Christmas Day 1967 was not unpleasant. I rose at 9 am, getting into the bathroom under cover of the chanting and singing of the guards. After doing yoga and washing and shaving, I dressed in my suit for the first time for five months and put on a tie. When I appeared the guards, who were having a nine-man meeting, looked suitably impressed. *[Pun intended!]* For my part, I felt magnificent!

Breakfast was normal then, after a walk outside, I sucked a polo mint to begin my treat. Coal was delivered during breakfast and I thought this was lucky. I had to shorten my walk because of coal in the yard. It was bright and sunny.

For lunch Sao Kao made a flower from an orange for dessert. I read and laughed a lot at George Mikes' *How to be Inimitable*. I continued this after lunch, then opened a bar of chocolate and had a cheroot. This was also great. Afterwards I walked again for one-and-a-half hours. I offered Sao Kao a cheroot and he refused, as did the guards, whom he asked on my behalf. (Shades of World War One in the trenches, when a curious Germany v England football match was arranged spontaneously – and normal hostilities resumed next day?)

I then completed the *Daily Telegraph* crossword in one hour and seven minutes and was immensely proud of this. Dinner was a big surprise. I got a dish of beef and a dish of fish, as a treat without any explanation. With dinner I again read George Mikes, laughing a lot. This, and some quiet reflection, carried me up to walking time around 8.45 pm. I smoked one of my bigger cheroots during this time, but it didn't seem to impress the guards much!

After this I sat down to read the sad and sentimental opening of Somerset Maugham's famous novel, *Of Human Bondage*. This carried me quietly up to bedtime at 11.30 pm. I prayed about five times, asking for Christmas happiness for my mother and relations and friends, and for release soon for myself. I whistled and sang some carols during my walks – to myself, softly – and knew a quiet kind of joy.

The 'martyrdom' aspect wasn't permanent. The chocolate and butterscotch tasted good, but I didn't eat much of either. I sat all day on the chair for the first time. I didn't feel like taking to the bed in my suit. This morning Lao Chiao asked in the bathroom, 'Was yesterday all right?' And added 'Christmas?' in a quiet reflective way. He told me only very quietly when I asked what Christmas was in Chinese, presumably because of the guards listening.

On Christmas Eve, about 4.30 pm, as I was coming out of the toilet after praying, Lao Chiao came to me and said I could send cables. I wrote three to my mother, Shirley and to Reuters. They were sent to the Foreign Ministry and I have not heard any more of them. This seemed to be in answer to my prayer of minutes before. Later in the afternoon I washed my hair with the door open and succeeded in washing myself with the door closed. This was a great victory for me.

One of the amusing points: when I said that I wanted to send a cable to my mother, the guard grinned in a shy way. I sent the Reuters cable to the Foreign Ministry with the Rhinanthus telegraph office payment card.

On Christmas Eve, just before I was told I could send a cable, the signboards were changed. One said, 'Imperialism will not last long because it always does evil things.' The other one said, 'All reactionaries are paper tigers. In appearance the reactionaries are terrifying but in reality they are not so powerful. From a long-term point of view it isn't the reactionaries but the people who are really powerful.'

I had half expected them to say, 'A Happy Christmas to all Readers!'

Sunday 31 December 1967, 12.30 pm

(The last diary entry of the bad year of 1967!)

Today a bad year of my life will pass away and I am hopeful that 1968 will bring better days. But I am also aware my ordeal may not be over by a long way.

Since Christmas I have been reading Maugham's *Of Human Bondage* with great interest. It is a very stimulating book and I find myself comparing my emotions with the writer's. Yesterday I got my tiny electric fire going and I was able for the first time to abandon my heavy coat in the afternoons as a means of warmth. This has made my life a little more comfortable.

More importantly, yesterday was the request for books. At first the guard said, 'No', but I managed to get the chief guard to ask the Foreign Ministry, by referring to the books from the British Office. I am now waiting for an answer, but fear it will be negative. It is so important to my peace of mind to be able to read.

Recently I have finished two *Guardian* crosswords and feel pleased with my progress in this direction. I have this minute just finished sharpening this pencil in the lavatory with a razor blade. My state of mind at this time is calm. This is becoming a habit now I think. Perhaps good result of the plans. I hardly dare think about when I might be released.

But the events of the past week – the decision to allow cables in and out here and also reading in the *Peking Review* a reference in the report on the Canton Trade Fair only to British 'violence' and how to 'stand up to British imperialism', convinced me that the Chinese attitude is softening. This is not to say, of course, that my release will follow. How I hope for some improvement. Yesterday I received a cable from the guys on the Reuters World Desk in London sending me, 'Best wishes for 1968'. This was a nice surprise. The cables from Mother and Shirley were a relief on 29 December. That Mother was now living in Perth in Scotland was a big surprise and I feel a little sad at the end of Norwich as my real home city.

I was very struck by the use of the word 'desperately' by Angel in her cable (as in the expression 'desperately missing you'). I can't think that January will bring anything new. Each day now has little meaning and I have grown used to the monotony. I am sleeping better, but still getting up in the middle of the night to pee. Two days ago Sao Kao began helping me to lift the table out for dinner after bringing the tray up from the kitchen – a tiny sign? I also got a clean white tablecloth and table napkin two days ago. I paid the double wages two days ago and went upstairs under escort to get the accounts file from which I could study the last account, which will enable me to do the accounts up to date.

As I sit here on this last day of 1967, two boards face me from the opposite wall. One talks of 'Imperialism not lasting because it always does evil things'. The other says, 'All reactionaries are paper tigers'. On the windowsill are a bottle of cold water and a flask of hot water. A useless telephone instrument which doesn't work and a pile of unreadable newspapers lie there too. Also the dishes from lunch are on the chair in the corner and my little electric heater is purring away.

On the bed are piled my blankets and sheets. On top a fur-collared jacket. Slogans are daubed all over the walls. Furniture is a bare desk, two chairs and, in the corner, clean and dirty washing and old *Peking Reviews* are piled on the empty Carlsberg-lager box from the British Office. On the windowsill are Mao's works, other books and a Black Magic tin of money, and a tin of butterscotch and an empty cigar box. The scene is bare, but not somehow unduly depressing.

Mao's portrait is on the wall and there are notices in Chinese too. The windows are sealed up with paper to keep out the draughts. One pane is broken. Two books are hidden under the mattress to escape detection in case I am raided. The sun shines in through the window. Almost every day is bright with sun, although the temperature has been as low as 15 degrees. A few clothes hang on the back of the door – I have nothing to keep my clothes in. In this room, I shall see in 1968. I hope I shall be out of it soon during 1968 and not see 1969 in here. Writing this is extremely difficult. I have to keep putting it aside and hiding it in case the guards come in. Now I am sitting in the toilet – soon to clean my shoes. This is my final diary entry for the year.

My sister June acquired the lease of a small hotel in Perth, Scotland with her husband Ric, and my mother went to Scotland to help them run it for a year or two. She then returned to live in her Norwich home again – so false alarm about losing my Norwich connection! Even better, Agnes met and fell in love with the chef at the hotel, Geoffrey Maw, and they became devoted partners for the rest of her life, returning to live together in Norwich. Geoffrey lovingly supported her from then on, which was a great relief to me, and shared the burdens of handling constant media attention and liaising with the Foreign Office and Reuters. Dear Geoffrey died in 2008, by a strange coincidence on Saturday 4 October, the precise anniversary of my release.

Appendix: My guards at 31 December 1967

At nine o'clock each morning and nine o'clock each night, they gather before their 'shrine' portrait of Mao, placed high up on the wall. Under it is a blood-red poster with white characters saying in Chinese, 'Down with revisionism, fight selfishness!' Standing reverently and looking up at the portrait and poster, they shout twice, '*Wan shou wu chiang*' (Life without end.) Then they sing 'The East is Red' or 'The Helmsman'. Then after the leader shouts, '*Wei ta te ling hsiu, wei ta te tao shih, wei ta te t'ung shih, wei ta te tuo shou!* (Our Great Leader, Great Teacher, Great Supreme Commander, Great Helmsman), they launch into their quotations. They have recently started using a small diary-sized *Red Book*, which seems to have quotations against imperialism and Britain in it.

My guards are pipe-and-cigarette smokers and all spit loudly the whole day long. Yesterday I conducted a conversation with one about getting more books and he told me quite seriously that I should read Mao's works ten times. The day before, I disobeyed the young nervous guard for a short time when he told me to come in from the yard. He flew into a rage waving his arms wildly to get me in – but I suspect it is due to his nervousness. They all have different ways of treating letters and cables; some hand them to me themselves, others go to elaborate lengths to hide them and give them to me late. I notice that when they read the paper, the first four printed pages are cast aside in about two minutes and the main time is spent on the foreign news pages.

They had several meetings early this week, but nothing came out of them except my being allowed two walks outside in the yard each day instead of just one – which is great. Sometimes, on giving me the daily Chinese newspaper, they hold it low around their knee level to make me bend for it. They have no authority to do anything except the smallest detail and must ring for advice to headquarters. Some are friendly. The one I call in my mind 'Idiot' often smiles bizarrely. His chief asked me yesterday if the fire was on. I suppose they could be much worse. One sent me out to walk a few minutes after I had been brought in early through a misunderstanding and he smiled with embarrassment. During the night of 1 January one of them – I sense it was 'Idiot'- came into the room and I woke suddenly at the sound to see the door closing quietly as he left.

REFLECTIONS - 5
Saturday 23 December 2006

That incident of waking and finding the seemingly unstable guard in my room by my bed in the dark disturbed me much more than the pages of the diary reveal. The possibility that he might do something unpredictable and insane, like try to strangle me while I slept, was at that time an intense fear – yet I now discover to my surprise that I wrote nothing of it.

But I recall clearly that every night after that, before getting into bed, I carefully and silently placed an empty water bottle on the floor next to the door. I did this so that if he or any other guard tried to open the unlocked door silently while I slept, I would at least be wakened by the clatter and have a chance to protect myself.

I did not write of it because, on reading this section of the journal for the first time in many years I recalled suddenly that then, and later, I consciously withheld some of my worst fears from the diary. I felt if I wrote down fully everything I feared, I might somehow encourage such fears to become reality and help them materialise. Glancing quickly ahead at the next two months that followed the end of 1967, before writing these reflections, I saw that this was about to become much more acute.

However, before moving on to that, I feel there are a couple of other similar points worth highlighting about the latter months of the year. I was surprised first to discover two other complete omissions from the diary. The first concerned the ants that occupied my empty mind in my first days in that eight-foot-square cell. I read with great interest of my noticing for the first time, the ants on the stone-tiled floor twirling the wing of a dead moth slowly across to the corner where a hole led to their nest.

And I described also another ant tugging a single tiny flake of bread crust painstakingly back to the nest, up hill and down dale over cracks and divisions between the tiles. Yet I wrote nothing of the way that these discoveries led me to organise 'ant races' each morning for a while, by deliberately placing five or six tiny flakes of crust from my dry bread in a line across the side of the cell furthermost from their corner nest.

Then when they began spreading out from the corner, scavenging and searching for things of interest, they would invariably come across the flakes and begin the Herculean task of dragging them home as fast as possible. I crouched on the side of my bunk fascinated by this. It occupied my distracted mind. After a while, I began trying to judge which was the fastest, strongest and most agile of the five or six ants involved and most likely to arrive at the nest first with his crumb. I even began placing mental bets on them daily and fancied I could even recognise the most 'athletic' ant each day.

However on one fateful morning, an ant that I had picked out as my 'favourite' seemed to get himself repeatedly into a muddle, hauling his bread flake awkwardly and repeatedly back into a crevice and so falling way behind his competitors. To my later horror, I became suddenly irritated by this and, standing up quickly, I squashed the offending ant to death with my foot.

Instant remorse grew very quickly until it knew no bounds, since I suddenly felt that because I had shown so little compassion and understanding for the ant's difficulties, I had somehow morally jeopardised and forfeited my own chances of being released from my awful predicament of confinement. Perhaps it was because of this abiding remorse and shame that I failed to record anything in detailed shorthand symbols about these ant 'races' – which would, after my release, become one of the two things, along with the hanging of Ming Ming the cat, that most people remembered about the ordeal.

I also wrote nothing, I now realise, after scrutinising again the entries for the last four months of 1967 about another survival device which helped me through the endless-seeming hours and days in those confined spaces. Reflecting as I walked backward and forwards across my eight-and-a-half paces how I was caught fast in a conflict between capitalism and communism, I felt no absolute respect for either political philosophy – and decided, although I was a representative of the capitalist camp, I really needed a newly formulated and tailor-made philosophy of my own to help me survive this unique situation.

After some thought I concluded that if everything was all right in the given moment as I paced back and forth – I was still in one piece, apparently sane, receiving enough nourishment to go on and enough air to breathe – then everything very simply was 'all right' and I should do no more than relish and appreciate that moment. Searching for a name for this new challenge to the world's two major conflicting political philosophies, I came up with a very simple and half-jokey name – and called it, tongue in cheek, 'Momentism'.

And I – perhaps the world's first self-confessed Momentist – practised it with as much fervour as any communist or capitalist. It really did work, certainly for a while in the little cell, so I was surprised to find no reference to it in the diary. Perhaps I felt it was too silly or ludicrous to formulate into writing – but I remembered it again in recent years when reading with enthusiasm the books of the outstanding German spiritual writer, Eckhart Tolle, whose most famous title is *The Power of Now*. His lucid exposition of the profound importance for all of us of living consciously in the moment has made *The Power of Now* and other titles like *Stillness Speaks* and *Practicing the Power of Now* worldwide bestsellers, translated into many languages and with sales running into millions. Unknowingly it seems I had stumbled across – or muddled my way to – the beginnings of some deep spiritual truths. This feeling is reflected in my short poem, written in February 2004, that begins 'Seek the stillness, Quiet of the moment...' which I have set at the front of this book.

None of my devices or 'discoveries' up to this point, however, proved to be invariably successful. Nor did they make me impervious to falling back into spells of despair and depression. What they did do was give me 'weapons' and tactics of a kind to help me fight these unfamiliar battles.

One reference first coined as part of a larger 'new creed' was written on Tuesday 24 October in that year of 1967 at the end of the new '23-day Plan'. It was headed overall 'Determination not Dejection,' and it is worth repeating and emphasising here because it became a vital core part of my psychological self-encouragement throughout the rest of my time as a hostage, which I learned and recited to myself very regularly. Usually I did this when assuming a particular yoga posture called 'The Thunderbolt'. This is a simple posture where the practitioner sits straight-backed and very still on his heels with eyes closed and his hands resting gently on the top of his thighs. In this position for some reason, whilst remaining very still, I fell into the habit of repeating the last third of the 'new creed', which said:

Nothing but good can befall you! Peace, happiness and contentment lie ahead. Prepare yourself for happier climes with a calm, untroubled mind, free from worry or fear. You have a good future. Your fate is in God's hands. God will deliver you. Something good is coming!

I can still remember the words verbatim quite effortlessly. I believe I coined them originally as a mantra, as recommended by my yoga book, although I believe these sentences are rather too long to be regarded as a genuine yogic mantra. The wider 'creed' grew out of that intention. Again a bit of British 'muddling through' was thrown in possibly.

There are a couple of points worth commenting on regarding this 'mantra'. First some of the words have a slightly archaic ring, particularly 'befall', 'climes' and 'deliver'. Secondly, although the first paragraph of the 'creed' is couched in the first person with the word 'I' being used, in this third 'mantra' paragraph there is a sudden switch to the second person with the words addressing themselves to me as 'you', as though an outside voice was speaking to me. I have often puzzled over these points, without reaching any conclusion. Both perhaps have the tendency to make the whole statement more sonorous and memorable – and that is perhaps why my subconscious mind devised those particular words in the way it did.

'Nothing but good can befall you' and the uncompromisingly positive words that followed through to the very assertive closing sentence, 'Something good is coming!' became a silent inward watchword chant practised almost daily from 24 October onwards – and sometimes more than once a day if the going got particularly hard. It lives on very vividly in my memory even today, like a highly valued companion who shared hard times.

Writing this the day before Christmas Eve in 2006, after venturing into the afternoon mêlée of Norwich's city-centre shopping arcades, I found the annual commercial frenzy building to its accustomed climax. As I walked amid the coloured lights and decorations and crowds toting multiple plastic bags, I wondered whether perhaps 'Calm to Christmas' might with some benefit be adopted as a universal national slogan for this characteristic annual period, where a headlong stampede of food-and-gift-buying moves inexorably from October on towards its inevitable climax. But then I suppose the nation's shopkeepers and manufacturers would not like that very much!

My own personal 'Calm to Christmas' plan in China worked very well, back in that 1967 cell. It marked the arrival at a certain point of endurance. It put a flag in the sand on my route across a personal desert or on one of the lower peaks of the high metaphorical mountain range I was then climbing. Yet, although I could not see it on 1 January 1968, the onset of the New Year was about to throw up new challenges, which would reach another new and frightening climax before too long.

*Outside slogan-daubed 15 Nan Chihzte,
Peking, in mid June 1967 before it
became my prison.*

*Inset: my official press accreditation with
China's Foreign Ministry that would
normally have afforded some protection.*

Ming Ming playing chess a few days before the fateful Red Guard invasion.

Sao Kao, cook, (left) and Lao Chiao in calmer times, on the steps under the balcony where the Red Guard mob hanged Ming Ming on the night of 18 August. Inset: My official Central Telegraph Office cable card.

Pictures I took from my flat roof of the view towards (top) the golden-tiled Gate of Heavenly Peace and the distant modern lines of the Great Hall of the People... and (bottom) the nearer walls, roofs and corner temple of the Forbidden City.

Undiplomatic behaviour: China's diplomats in London emerge unexpectedly to launch their contrived 'Battle of Portland Place' against placid, unsuspecting, British Bobbies and passers-by, while Red Guards were setting fire to the British diplomatic mission in Beijing with staff and families inside.

112

Charred external ruins (top) of the British diplomatic mission in Peking that was fired by a mob of ten thousand male and female Red Guards ... and how the gutted interior was left after British diplomats and their families escaped through the flames.

PART TWO

1968

THE YEAR
OF
THE MONKEY

6
SEVEN-MONTHS-PLUS DETERMINATION

Monday 1 January 1968, 13.00 hours
Fourth 23-day Plan

'Endure doggedly and refine your calm.'

Be prepared for the worst and hope for the best.

1   Improve the quality of morning yoga sessions with advanced postures (rise before chanting starts).
2   If books refused, ask to send note to British Office.
3   Ask for pencil.
4   If books don't come, continue Peking Review reading.
5   Refine neutral relationship with guards (no staring).
6   No retaliation if books refused.
7   Innovate where possible.

Tuesday 9 January 1968, 13.00 hours

Today I write one of the most miserable diaries of this whole period of imprisonment. Since writing the above entry on New Year's Day, I have been battling continually with misery. I have been very depressed and reduced to falling on my knees and beseeching God to help me. I have doubted the existence of God and sometimes angrily ask if there is any point in prayer. I am now without hope of anything coming soon. An unpleasant two-line beginning to a poem has been coming unbidden into my mind recently. It had felt so ominous that I have not until now been able to write it down. It says:

Each day crouches huge and menacing at the window
And only at midnight steals reluctantly away.

Now I am without new books since last night, when I finished the last of the 4 December consignment in the lager box. I have more or less decided to read Mao's works again. My request for more books on 31 December has been ignored, with the infuriating contempt that makes me hate the Chinese Foreign Ministry. I swear and curse frequently. I have not been calm as planned. I have been giving way to despair and abject despondency. My life seems worthless and the prospect of getting out of here seems as far away as ever. How much longer is it to be?

It seems as if my whole life will be spent here. My mind now has grasped the fact that I am here until March. Who knows, it could be a year more, even longer. There seems no faint gleam of hope in anything at all. I am completely miserable and filled with despair.

There is little or nothing to say about David Chipp's cable or the five pieces of mail of 2 and 4 January. I find it impossible to make any sense of the stupid Chinese policy on my mail. Yesterday another card arrived – from Roland Flamini. The day before, two *Peking Reviews* and a handout from an American not personally known to me, Robert Williams. This fired in me a desire to write a story and it was almost a pleasant sensation for a while. Lao Chiao wished me a Happy New Year on the morning of 2 January and shook hands out of line-of-sight of the guards. But I am empty and feeling hopeless now. This is the most awful life of torture. Heaven help me soon, or I shall go mad.

Roland Flamini was a senior Time magazine correspondent in Europe, whom I had met in Romania on assignments. Dapper, bronzed, always beautifully suited in dark pinstripe and bright tie, and with a gleaming smile, Roland Flamini was a humorous, life-and-soul-of-the-party friend, and his card and the visual memory of him lifted my spirits.

Generally the Chinese attitude towards my mail was incomprehensible. When British newspapers urged their readers to send me Christmas cards or postcards from their holidays, they seemingly arrived in Peking in their hundreds and thousands, and were reportedly burned by the sack-load. (Thank you again everyone! That was wonderful!) I knew nothing of them until after I was released. Yet occasionally I would receive something like this isolated 'handout' from a total stranger, Robert Williams, which was inconsistent and to me inexplicable. Although they constantly delayed mail deliberately from my nearest and dearest, it must have been necessary to filter it out carefully from other voluminous arrivals.

Tuesday 16 January 1968, 3.30 pm

Today is a day as meaningless as yesterday and tomorrow. I have stomach trouble again, but not too bad so far. I am listless and despondent, but not desperately. An upturn in my mood occurred on 12 January, when I managed to get a marvellous book from upstairs secretly under the noses of my guards – and received two up-to-date letters from Shirley. This ended a very bad and monotonous depression, in force since the New Year. I was greatly excited in fact by 'capturing' the book, *Doctor Zhivago*, from its place in my old upstairs bedroom.

I had practised a ruse all morning, picking up a book from a chair out of sight in the scullery and putting it quickly away inside my jacket without breaking stride as I walked. I calculated how much lead up the stairs I would need to do this in my bedroom and prepared for all eventualities – even falling over upstairs. I emptied one pocket of my jacket to put the book into. I was worried about the effect of discovery if I fell.

I thought of putting it off and did, then in a slightly desperate mood I decided to go ahead. In the event, it was much easier than expected. The guard was tremendously slow when I made my request and I was bounding up the stairs and into the bedroom, almost before he had his cap on in the dining room doorway. I made a perfect 'snatch' pick-up and put *Zhivago* away inside my jacket perfectly, then went smoothly on to collect paper handkerchiefs and sheets from the ironing room.

I was exultant when I came down, with it hidden inside the jacket under one arm. Not least because it was thick and over 400 pages long, so would fill more time! The novel is truly tremendous and I have read it at the rate of 50 pages a night, saving it until then and savouring the prospect during each day. This has made all the difference to my morale. Wonderful!

It now appears that my mail might be arriving direct, because yesterday I had a card from Mark posted on 8 January, which is only seven days ago. On Sunday I received *Peking Reviews*, on Saturday a note from Emerita, on Friday two letters from Angel, quite up-to-date – posted at the end of December and early January – and the day before a card from Annelise.

Thus it seems local and foreign mail is being handled quickly. But although finding this encouraging, I realise it is not a firm indication of anything. The days are still as empty and meaningless as ever otherwise. Lao Chiao is alone, both Sao Kao and Hou have been away ill for a week now. Shirley's letters were beautifully loving and caught at my heart.

With one week today to the six months' anniversary, I desperately want a sign that something will happen. Emerita said in her note she was 'very optimistic' for 1968. I wonder if she knows something I don't. I still pray several times a day and hope fervently that something will happen soon. But I am now feeling that eight months is the earliest I can expect release. Every time I come near to an anticipated release date, it creeps back further.

Mark Meredith was a Canadian-born fellow Reuters correspondent and great personal friend who joined the agency at the same time as myself and succeeded me in East Berlin. Later he reported for the Financial Times *from Scotland and still teaches journalism in Edinburgh.*

Annelise worked at the Danish Embassy. During the weeks and months when the British diplomatic staff were confined and restricted in Peking, romance blossomed between Annelise and Donald Hopson. They later married and, after Donald was knighted, Annelise became Lady Hopson.

Friday 19 January 1968, 1.30 pm

Today is the anniversary of 11 weeks in this room – a total of 26 weeks altogether since 21 July. Half a year! I feel more than usually miserable. Yesterday afternoon I thought with horror of how likely it seemed that I would be here for perhaps one, two or even three years. I am so miserable and hopeless. Heaven knows how I manage to keep going. It is only because there is no alternative except killing myself, which is unthinkable. I love life too much.

Immediately after writing the last entry in this diary, trouble occurred. I refused to obey the orders of the guards immediately while outside. This was because in the morning I had not come in immediately when one young idiot lifted his chin at me in an annoying manner. Then in the afternoon the officious 'Little Caesar' guard decided on his own ingenious plan. He got his other man to step out in front of me. To their amazement I side-stepped and walked by him and as he came after me saying fierce words, I walked by him again and came in. 'Little Caesar' stamped in and stood glaring fiercely at me, rushed down to get Lao Chiao, then came back again, crashing back the door. The conversation that followed was ridiculous and he immediately reported by telephone. Next morning there was a big meeting about it in the dining room with lots of shouting – and all day on the 17 January I was not allowed outside at all.

Despite my efforts not to, I became depressed and was feeling very low and not like eating when, just before going home, Lao Chiao knocked on the door to bring in two letters – one from Ed and one from Emerita. This cheered me up a lot. Outside walking was resumed yesterday and today 'Little Caesar' brought me in quite quickly, before the usual time was up.

I am reading Mao's works again and am now halfway through the second book. *Doctor Zhivago* is well past the 300-page mark. Mrs Hou, who began seven days' sick leave a week ago, will be off for a month; this was conveyed to me on the 17 January on Sao Kao's return.

My love for Shirley overflowed in a torrent after receiving her two letters. They were both very loving. Then I dreamed of her – only that she stood waiting for me as I talked to three girls and she wouldn't draw near. This, typical of my Angel, suddenly made me love her more clearly than at most other times in this imprisonment.

My dreams continue to be vivid and strong. Two nights ago, for instance, I dreamed of Barry Midforth, about whom I haven't thought once since last seeing him many years ago, and he was never a particular friend of mine.

It hardly seems possible that six months of my life have been wasted here. What is to become of me?

Barry Midforth was a distant Norwich schooldays friend.

Thursday 25 January 1968, 13.00 hours

Things have changed greatly since my last diary. One of the biggest events of the whole house arrest came unexpectedly on 23 January. I had decided to try to send a note to John Weston asking for books and a Bible, with the idea that even if it didn't get through, it would convey my mood to the Foreign Ministry. ('Each day is difficult to get through,' I was going to say.)

As a preliminary I thought I would ask again for my own books from upstairs. I decided this sitting on the lavatory in the morning. I asked Lao Chiao after lunch without any hope at all of getting them. To my amazement after a telephone call and a reply, the guard clumped off downstairs, Lao Chiao came up and said OK. I still didn't really believe it and went upstairs to get an armful of books from the lounge. I could take that many and change them later, the guard said. I brought them down and immediately began making elaborate preparations to hide some in case there was a change of mind – in my bed and in the bathroom.

I waited for another call to hear that it had been a mistake. But no, I still have them two days later. On that day I was to read the final epilogue to *Doctor Zhivago* – one of the most splendid books I have ever read. Stimulating, beautifully tragic and tremendously encouraging in the face of the mindlessness of communism.

I finished *Zhivago* after reviewing my treasures and finding I had 16 completely new books and others I had wanted to read again and with parts I had read. This act of God came at a very desperate time. I was just beginning to feel a very serious danger of having a nervous breakdown. I was fighting it almost every minute of the day. This had been heightened by a clash with the guards during the night of 21 and 22 January. I was feeling nervous and couldn't sleep and outside the door a guard was scraping and rubbing something incessantly, sandpapering the stem of his pipe, I think. After a while I couldn't stand it any longer. I flung out of bed, tore open the door, and yelled at him to stop at the top of my voice, something like, 'Stop that bloody noise!'

I got back into bed and he came into the room and stared at me furiously in the darkness. Then he turned on the light and stared. Then he told me to put the light out and walked out, leaving the door open. I did nothing and he came back in again and repeated this and went out closing the door.

I put it out then and, shaking and with heart pounding, I tried to calm down. I didn't sleep much and next morning the new shift called an 'inquest', with Sao Kao hopelessly inadequate as translator. They produced fantastic explanations of noise from a window upstairs and policeman outside. I think the guard making the noise didn't admit his true role.

'You no good last night,' said Sao Kao. When he came in and said, 'At quarter to one today ...' I thought for a moment it meant I was to go to the Foreign Ministry. But alas, no. So then I developed indigestion over breakfast, could eat almost no lunch and felt wretched. I lay my head on my hands on the table and felt completely desperate. Then I prayed more desperately than ever before and determined to have a ten-day practice period of absolute calm until the new plan.

There was no mail, but I had the conclusion of *Zhivago* to read in the evening, which helped. Then next day came books, which helped immensely and encouraged me a lot. However, perhaps a small aftermath – I have a nervous indication at the moment of being conscious quite ridiculously of my heart as though there was something wrong with it. This will pass, I expect.

But the feeling of difficulty with myself was very strong before the books came. Yesterday I dipped in and out of *Sexus* (by Henry Miller), reading bits here and there but not being as interested by it as I thought I would be. I also read again Yuri Zhivago's poems, set out at the back of the novel, and found them awakening, I think, a first real interest in me in poetry.

Yesterday I received a cable from Shirley saying she had passed her driving test, which pleased me immensely. I have just asked if I might send a reply. I calculate I have enough books for two months or so. But I am now fairly well accustomed to the fact that the prospect of release is still very remote and it now looks like being a year or so perhaps.

I have more or less decided now that I will ask Shirley to marry me. It came as a result, I think, of reading *Zhivago*. Somehow my perspective on life and love as a whole has been heightened by the novel and I realise how important Shirley's love is to me and that my crazy ideas of remaining a bachelor are not necessarily right. I have often thought what it would be like to marry her in the last two or three days. This morning I thought how we might live together in her flat, using all of it. I do love her so much.

Last night the guards began *saluting* the portrait of Mao at their little gatherings!

Wednesday 31 January 1968, 4.30 pm

Have just completed a cold walk under blue skies with the temperature about 26 degrees. Before I was reading *Red Star over China* and enjoying it for the second time. Last night I began *Room at the Top* by John Braine and enjoyed the opening immensely – especially the part describing the munching of crisps and swigging of beer! The previous night I finished *Mandingo* after five nights' reading. And enjoyed it greatly.

The arrival on 23 January of permission to get books from upstairs has changed everything. Today I am preparing to begin a 28-day Plan of reading. Having passed the six months' mark, my mood is now one of acceptance of the inevitability of a long stay. I can almost say that all hope, apart from that hope that remains with life itself, but all real hope of early release has left me.

It now seems certain that the Chinese are calmly planning to hold me until they get someone released in return. I have enough books and other materials upstairs, I think, for about three months anyway, and perhaps by that time things will have improved sufficiently for further things to have begun arriving from outside.

On 25 January I sent a cable to the Foreign Office for vetting, but it hasn't been returned and looks a write-off. I see no encouragement in the granting of books, only confirmation that the intention is that of a long stay. The books have made possible my recovery from the terrible depression of a week or so ago. Letters from Kim (Davenport) and Angel a couple of days ago were nice.

January has been remarkable for the prompt arrival of letters. The last two were within five days and one from Shirley on the nineteenth arrived in four days. The January 23-day Plan was a huge failure apart from the books' success. I did bad things with the guards, so that part of the plan misfired. But I got one book by subterfuge and a host of others openly. Quite a month!

But now it is difficult to imagine February bringing anything at all. This morning I washed my socks and handkerchiefs. Sunday's first bath down here was beautiful and life, in comparison with a few weeks back, is not bad. But I still pray desperately for help.

At long last I had relented on my stubborn long-term decision not to remove from the bath the final traces of the Red Guard black paint, put there on the night of the invasion five months before on 18 August. I got down on my knees with scouring powder and cleaned away the last traces of paint from inside the bath. After filling it with really hot water, I lowered myself into my first bath for five months with a sigh of ecstasy and a sense of sensuous delight that I can remember clearly to this day, nearly four decades later! The delayed action compromise was truly worthwhile and unforgettable!

Thursday 1 February 1968, 13.00 hours

23-day Plan for February

Title: 'Read and Bath'.

Plan is very loose and meant to contrast with the strictness of former ones.

1 Read fact during the day and fiction at night. Study.

2 Bathe regularly.

3 Remain calm and do everything guards say.

Enjoy February!

Saturday 10 February 1968, 5.15 pm

Today I was able to send off a cable to Shirley. I had long written it off, but it returned today after 16 days. Two days ago I asked about it, but didn't think this had much to do with it. Just construed it as the usual awkwardness. Last night came two letters from Shirley – one a Valentine poem, which touched me deeply.

If you think I'll forget,
Just remember my pet,
We were both glad we waited
Although long separated
For our rare,
Love affair.

The other letter was long, but I got a strong aversion to the fact that Shirley never indicates any sympathy and seems to think this is half my fault at least. I desperately long for her to say that she appreciates how hard it is for me. On 5 February a letter from Shirley and an invitation to Frank Gordon's wedding arrived by separate delivery at breakfast time. Here Shirley said, 'Wonder how you must have changed and hope I can make it up to you.' Love her for this.

I have been fairly calm now since 22 January, although sometimes worrying about going mad. Have had two difficult nights not sleeping, with the guards sniffing, coughing, hawking and farting outside my door. I have a fairly solid acceptance of the fact that I must now look to the year mark as the next one in view. This is a terribly depressing prospect and sometimes seems unbearable. It is only bearable because it must be borne. I have known some very difficult moments recently, but have overcome them. Last night I finished the Lemmy Caution novel. Before that I read *Sober as a Judge* after finishing *Room at the Top*, which was brilliant and left a great impression on me. *The Doors of Perception* by Aldous Huxley helped me dwell on mental illness and at times I came out in a sweat about this subject. (NB My palms sweated as I read.) But I think I have it taped now. I also read a CBS TV book on television reporting American-style, which didn't leave much impression.

At present I have nearly finished a very good history of China, which has kindled a love of knowledge and learning in me very strongly. For the past eight days I have learned a page of the *Atlas of World Affairs* each day. This, plus the reading of it, has given me the feeling of a new understanding of the world.

I feel this is important for me. Emerita's letter on 8 February spoke of Len sending books and I hope that this means a new parcel soon. How can I say what is in my mind? (NB I really fear to express my fears!) I yearn with every fibre for freedom. I think I have a nearer understanding of the possibilities of life after death after reading Huxley's book. (NB Dare not read conclusion due to mental state.) My perception of the whole of life is more appreciative with my recent reading of Pasternak's *Doctor Zhivago* and Maugham's *Of Human Bondage*, among others.

My big progress, I think, is of an overall perspective of my own life and the important things in it, very especially Shirley. I want only to be home and married to her now. But it seems as if a genuine miracle is required to get me out of here. This I pray for. I feel it will be 18 months before I get out, since that might be the time when the British would perhaps release some of the Hong Kong journalists. Prospects are grim.

When wishing to send a cable I had to give it to the guards to submit to the Foreign Ministry and it was held in this process for arbitrarily long periods before being returned to the house for despatch to London by Lao Chiao, who would take it to the central Telegraph Office along with the Reuters transmission card.

Frank Gordon, a fellow junior reporter on the Eastern Daily Press, *married his wife Maggie around this time. A lifelong friend with a wonderful sense of humour, honed during our early twenties along with another humorous EDP cub reporter, Mike Farman. We all developed our sense of humour in general and satire in particular, inspired by the then ground-breaking 'Beyond the Fringe' team of Jonathan Miller, Alan Bennett, Peter Cook and Dudley Moore. Frank lived up to his reputation with this nice touch of humour – a formal wedding invitation card to a fellow humorist being held hostage in solitary on the other side of the world!*

Len Appleyard was a Russian-and Chinese-speaking second secretary at the British Mission in Peking, who later served there as our ambassador.

Lemmy Caution was a wisecracking hard-bitten American private eye character created by British thriller writer, Peter Cheney. The book I was reading was Never a Dull Moment. *Caution was a kind of upmarket Hank Janson-type character. The name Hank Janson was the pseudonym of writer Stephen D. Frances, and his hero, rendered in the first person, was also a very hard-bitten American private eye. Author and his main character became pulp-fiction giants of the fifties and sixties, not least because of the sexually titillating tough-egg descriptions of lust in the shadowy crime world genre.*

Thursday 15 February 1968, 2.00 pm

Just a brief note to record the first hints of spring in the past three days. Today seems very mild and I shed one sweater. Yesterday I got new books from upstairs, including a dictionary, and was well pleased with my discoveries. Yesterday also saw what appeared to be a high-level cadre making an investigation visit. It cheered me a little, but I knew I should probably look back from a few months hence on these notes, if I interpreted it to mean early release.

On Monday night and Tuesday I was ill with what I think was food poisoning with a temperature and backache, etc. On Monday I had a long-held letter from Mum which again worried me a little and on Sunday a lovely cable from Shirley, which came back in reply to mine in very quick time. Spring hints, the slightly fresh feeling of taking off a heavy sweater, and the cadre's visit have all served, along with the new books, to make me feel a little better than usual. Hope is undying.

Thursday 22 February 1968, 5.30 pm

Today I am slightly melancholy. Yesterday and today depression has been threatening to descend, but I have been fighting it. It keeps occurring to me how long it still might be and my mind wanders to the difficulty of holding out. It's a strange anxiety, hard to pin down and hard to shake off. This morning I felt a strong need just to see and talk to somebody. The pressure of solitude was felt more than before. But I expect this to be a temporary feeling. (NB Whistling in the dark, dare not write without adding positive inflection.)

I keep telling myself that I shall undoubtedly manage to pull through. Last night I started reading *Archie and Mehitabel*. The night before I finished Priestley's *Good Companions* after ten days of enjoyable reading. During the day I am reading Kazantzakis' *China and Japan*, which is interesting. Four days ago I finished the *Party and Army* book on China and found it very instructive indeed and wished I had read it before. Previously I had read the novel *Never a Dull Moment*, to add to *Sober as a Judge, Room at the Top* and *Mandingo*. Of course, like everything else, after one month books are not really enough. I want something else! The dictionary is proving very useful, especially with the crosswords. I have been doing the crosswords received in a 'parcel' letter from Emerita. This was a small victory and I enjoyed the 'Peter Simple' columns she enclosed from the *Daily Telegraph*. Sleeping has been better in recent nights although last night was not too good with the 'Closed Door' guard on duty. But in all I feel well enough. (NB Whistling.)

During a dream last night I vividly remember being with Shirley and while walking I suddenly cupped my hand round her left breast. Gosh, I do love and miss her so much! I still pray fervently and hope against hope that something will come before too long. But my mind is really orientated to one year in a hopeless sort of way. By then I suppose I feel there is some chance of releases of journalism prisoners in Hong Kong. It now seems impossible that I shall get out without something happening there.

New chalked boards bearing quotations starting, 'If the countrywide victory of the Chinese Revolution ...' were put up on the chairs in here on 16 February. A life of solitude is a miserable thing, but I am determined to see it through! Then life will seem wonderful again. Cold weather with temperatures at 18 degrees and in the low 20s returned three days ago, forcing me back into my sweater.

'Closed Door' was a banal nickname for a guard who gave me a lot of hassle about when to open and close the door of my room.

Saturday 24 February 1968, 12.45 pm

This morning the depression of the last two or three days reached huge proportions. The theme has been that I am unable to stand this any more because my nerve has given out. Thoughts of pleading for a doctor and asking to be allowed to go upstairs flooded through my mind and I felt absolutely desolate. At breakfast, for the second day running, I felt like eating nothing. Yesterday I had told Lao Chiao I felt very bad. He was very kind during the day. Then after praying in the toilet with a hopeless desperation, I suddenly decided that what I needed was: 'Fight!'

I came back into the room and forced down my breakfast, which I still didn't want, and swore at myself desperately in four-letter words, 'Fight, you bastard! Fight! Fuck you! Fuck you! Fight!'

During my walk outside in beautiful sunshine with the temperature at 32 degrees and blue sky overhead I 'discovered' the new ingredient that I required to help me on from here: 'SEVEN-MONTHS-PLUS DETERMINATION!'

This new super ingredient, I decided, is the answer to things. I told myself that if I wanted to avoid the personal disgrace of a nervous collapse and the consequent admission of failure, this was the answer. I am absolutely determined not to give in, but to see this damned thing through to the end, successfully standing firmly and strongly on my own two legs.

So this day has distinguished itself as the day on which 'Seven-Months-Plus Determination' came into tangible being. Outside, while I was walking,

I heard the first sounds of the Cultural Revolution that I had heard for a long time. A group of men or Red Guards marched by singing: '*Ta tao, tao, tao, tao, tao Liu Shao-chi!* and I could only walk back and forth muttering, 'Incredible!' But it did something to revive my interest.

I remember abusing myself aloud with great vehemence over and over again, while standing in the corner of the room by the chair on which I had placed the tray bearing my untouched breakfast, ready for later collection by the cook or Lao Chiao. I felt a desperate anger wash through me. I picked up a couple of slices of toast covered in yellow scrambled egg one after the other and pushed them roughly into my mouth with great energy, effectively force-feeding myself. This stark memory has remained with me ever since as a climactic moment and turning point of the entire two year and two months period of isolation.

'*Ta tao*' *meant 'Down with' and this renewed, ludicrous prolonged repetition of the words in song before the President of China's name, which had been mud in the streets for around a year by then, seemed strangely farcical to my ears after so long.*

Thursday 29 February 1968, 7 pm

Have just finished reading a lovely letter from Shirley. She's written a lot since my cable (which she says she's having 'blown up' and put on the walls, especially the bit about 'no more partings'). Today I finished rough drafts of my accounts and got over the difficulty of devaluation and everything worked out fine. Now I have to do fair copies. I have now recovered my spirits and appetite somewhat. My appetite went away almost completely for three or four days. It began returning the day before yesterday. I was very depressed. Recovery simply comes slowly after a struggle.

Today was the fifth day on the accounts and overall I have enjoyed doing them. The 40-minute walking sessions are now regular as clockwork, having begun last week. One of the things I have done in getting out of this depression is to almost convince myself there is a good chance of something turning up in 'Bountiful March'.

I am now in the eighth month and perhaps something will turn up. Something important, if not release. I tell myself repeatedly that 'Something good is coming!' I am not sure whether I believe myself or not.

Signs of spring are more strong now. Temperatures are in the mid-30s every day and the light lasts well beyond my dinner at six o'clock…. Sao Kao and Lao Chiao are both quite friendly these days, which I take as a good sign. Today's letter said there was a piece in *The Times* (London) about me on 19 February, which somehow I found faintly encouraging. In her letter on the 27 February Shirley said a very lovely thing: 'that no love, historical or fictional, could be better than ours'.

I have decided on a new creative and more vigorous approach for March and to try to solve the sleep problem and inject a new mood of endeavour into my life. Sleep has improved the last two nights, after the worst-ever spell. A trip upstairs two days ago to get the account forms revealed a terrible state of dustiness. Dust everywhere. I am at present enjoying very much Nicholas Monsarrat's World War Two compendium novel, *Three Corvettes*. Very thought provoking and entertaining, and its stories of courage by British men put new heart into me. What is my ordeal compared with those of my countrymen during that war?

REFLECTIONS · 6

Thursday 28 December 2006

The massive, despairing depression of 24 February 1968 and the strange pretended 'discovery' inside myself of a new 'super-ingredient' have always stood out vividly in my mind as possibly the starkest and most harrowingly unforgettable memory of all the turning points in my strange two-year incarceration in China's capital. The diary entries, however, most noticeably contain only the bare bones of the fierce and terrifying feelings I experienced at that time. And perhaps because of this I allowed myself in these sections to hint obliquely at deeper and darker things in those strange little remarks placed in brackets beginning rather formally and academically 'NB'.

Having just checked in the dictionary the precise meaning of this Latin abbreviation found most frequently in academic books, I rediscover that it means in full 'nota bene' or 'note well'. That now seems a curious little device, a kind of verbal manhole cover to protect me from the darker shafts in which lurked my most intense inner fears. They allowed me to hint mildly at something for the record without expressing it openly and unequivocally.

Among the things which I remember and did not dare mention at all, even in a 'note well' aside, was the fact that in my desperation I feared I might somehow commit suicide in my sleep. I felt I had enough self-control and will to live to resist such an act whilst awake. Yet so convoluted were these inner fearful contortions as February 1968 wore on, that I made sure before getting into bed each night that all my razor blades were wrapped in waxed paper and inserted or wedged into an old matchbox so that if I did sleepwalk to them in the scullery to slit some vital part of me whilst unconscious, the fumbling to extract the wrapped razor blades from the matchbox would cause me to wake up and halt the process.

I could scarcely eat or sleep at all during this time and remember still that I often lay awake all night with the muscles of my back fluttering with sheer fatigue.

My heart seemed to beat so loudly inside my chest that I remember fearing constantly that some terrible cataclysmic pain might strike through it at any moment to end my life, so high was my sense of tension. I could not stop swallowing or clearing my throat, and the whole gathering sense of fright and disorientation after seven months alone seemed to summarise itself in those two lines of that 'horror poem' that my mind had seemed earlier to compose spontaneously of its own accord.

Each day crouches huge and menacing at the window
And only at midnight steals reluctantly away.

Writing this entry a few days after Christmas 2006, I have truly became aware at this point of what a 'saviour' my diary had by then become. I suppose at one level, a diary is something like a sympathetic friend who will listen patiently to you as you pour out your troubles and merely nod sagely in silence or repeat occasionally, 'Yes, I understand,' thereby approving or legitimising your soliloquy. It gives you a feeling that you have communicated, unburdened yourself, got something off your chest, cleared out something that might have been injurious if it remained inside.

When you are an innocent, completely isolated prisoner thousands of miles from home, subject constantly to silent hostile stares and endless small attempts to ladle humiliation into your daily diet, the waiting pages of the diary are your only comfort-zone. Perhaps they are too a little like a metaphorical APC or Armoured Personnel Carrier into which you can clamber once a day and pull down the steel hatch with a clang to feel self-protected, in a small way at least, from the slings and arrows of outrageous fortune which have unjustifiably been flung at you.

Only recently did I become aware that journal writing had become an essential part of some contemporary Further Education teaching syllabuses, particularly in the social sciences and self-development, life-coaching and self-help studies. Earlier I had independently read with interest that research had proved that those people who kept diaries or journals definitely lived longer than those who did not.

All this eventually intrigued me so much that I began to research the subject a little further and only in the last week or two have I discovered that Japanese high-born females were believed to be the first recorded personal journal-writers in history. Ensconced idly in the court of the Emperor, they seemingly wrote in detail of their fantasy lives as well as everyday events. Britain's most famous diarist, Samuel Pepys, like fellow Protestants of his day, discharged into the pages of his journal descriptions of daily life and confessions framed as though to be presented to a vigilant disapproving Divinity.

Puritans on the Mayflower linked journal-keeping to their own personal disciplines and tendencies to self-analysis and later American writers like Emerson and Thoreau became known for their diaries of 'self reliance'. They and pioneering literary and psychology luminaries, like Carl Jung and Anaïs Nin, drew attention to how the writing of a journal or diary permitted its owner to tap valuable inner resources.

Anaïs Nin in a preface written in 1976 to one of the most comprehensive and authoritative books on the subject *The New Diary – How to Use a Journal for Self-Guidance and Expanded Creativity*, by Tristine Rainer, describes how she and the author taught a course in diary writing 'as an exercise in creative will'. It was also taught 'as a means to create a world according to our wishes, not those of others; as a means of creating the self, of giving birth to ourselves … of reintegrating ourselves when experience shatters us, to help us out of the desperate loneliness of silence and the anxieties of alienation.'

Those words, written seven years after my own hostage diary was completed, could hardly sum up more succinctly what keeping my diary had unconsciously meant to me. Tristine Rainer's work in fact opened my eyes to many other ways in which my diary had helped me without my knowing it. She described how it was found to be common experience among diarists that anxiety or depression disappears once they have found an image to express it in writing. She quoted an entry from a diary of Virginia Woolf, in which the famous Victorian novelist said:

Why is life so tragic, so like a strip of pavement over an abyss? I look down, I feel dizzy; I wonder how I am ever to walk to the end. But why do I feel this: Now that I say it, I don't feel it.'

This made me reflect that inventing those two lines about how each day 'crouched huge and menacing at the window' may actually have helped exorcise or diminish the mounting panic I felt at dealing with the terribly slow and ominous passage of time, rather than just being the tip of an iceberg which I did not dare to describe further.

Tristine Rainer also points out that when witches were burned at the stake in less enlightened times, their diaries were invariably burned with them. This caused me to reflect that if my diary had ever been discovered, and if China's Public Security Bureau and the Foreign Ministry could have found an English translator who also knew shorthand, some of my forthright and even vituperative remarks about my guards and the Cultural Revolution might have occasioned some very unpleasant form of retribution, a formal trial or at the very least a new mass struggle meeting.

I find myself wondering today at my temerity in keeping such a document going so painstakingly throughout the whole period of imprisonment. I did not really have a particular end-intent in mind in keeping it. Certainly I never then felt I would ever publish it in its entirety – yet the tenacity with which I kept it and kept it hidden proves that instinctively I realised it was a fundamental and vital part of my survival effort that was worth every bit of the risk and danger involved in compiling it.

So far the narrative has shown an overall picture of me reaching and grasping successively for devices and solutions to keep me afloat on the sea of uncertainty and fear that was to be, for the entire 26 months, a period of unknown duration. Up to this point it shows me hitting on a series of different ideas and strategies, doing my best to implement them, falling from grace, devising others, stumbling again, yet somehow, one way or another, keeping on keeping on. The diary was obviously a keystone in all this activity, giving me a chance to refer back and compare and analyse what had already gone before, what had worked and helped.

I have often said that not knowing how long I was to be held was the very worst aspect of the ordeal. There was no definite calendar of time from which to tear off the months as they passed to show that release was getting nearer. There was never any definite 'sentence'. There was no way of knowing whether a significant proportion of the time had yet been endured. In this vacuum, the pages of the diary, I can see now, became the most important piece of driftwood to cling to in that seemingly Pacific-sized sea of uncertainty. And as February 1968 became March l968 I went on clinging to it for dear life, not knowing that another event of major importance would soon be showing its mast tips faintly above the distant horizon.

7
THE MAGIC MOMENT

Friday 1 March 1968
31-day Plan for March

It is aimed at inducing a more creative approach and stepping up vigour.

1   Rise earlier than nine o'clock. Wear shorts and singlet and do exercises with energy and vigour.

2   Target of five complete 'saleable' crosswords at the end of the month (if possible eight). These are to be done basically before breakfast if possible.

3   Continue studying from *Atlas of World Affairs* for the whole month.

4   Write! After description of an 'Ideal Sunday', your short stories and other things.

5   Read! Fact in the late afternoon and fiction at night.

6   Generally attempt to be more self-disciplined than during February. Use 'Seven-Months-Plus Determination'! Remain optimistic. Things are surely better now.

Sunday 3 March 1968, 4.15 pm

Spring is definitely on the way. Today's afternoon walk temperature was 42 degrees (read from the thermometer on one pillar of courtyard gate). The weather itself has given me a lift in the last few days. Yesterday in the latest *Peking Review* there was an item of small encouragement. It told how three Hong Kong newspapers had started up again after being closed for six months. There was not tangible encouragement in it, but it suggested an improvement, which might lead to something for me in the long run. I hoped and prayed it would.

The main point of writing this note is to record that yesterday's guards began guarding me with new *Little Red Books*. During the walk they now hold new *Little Red Books* in their right hands across their bodies. There is a little gold head of Mao embossed on the fronts, which sometimes glints in the sun. Some of them hold it across their chests in the region of their hearts; others look a little embarrassed and let it dangle in one hand. It is not clear whether after my seven months of suffering this is supposed to frighten me further, impress something on me, or whether it's for the guards' protection – something to counteract the effect of their standing alone in the presence of a 'reactionary' – to ward off evil spirits in fact! I chuckled at the mentality of the person who gave this new order, without reaching any great conclusion on its merits. It could only be, I thought, a determination to show how rightly he is following instructions – a kind of self-preservation again.

The book is held almost like a weapon in the hands of a sentry. Also on the night before last there was another innovation. After the leader has sung the first line of 'The Helmsman', instead of 'One, two, three!' there is now a full-bodied chant of '*Mao Chu shi wan sui!*' which is slightly jazzier! Such are the major moments in my life at present!

Today I finished my first 'professional standard' crossword and it has given me lots of satisfaction. I intend to turn out as many of these as possible in the next few weeks if I am not released. Yesterday I had a third letter in three days from Shirley. Very loving, talking of dreaming about my present and how she had received a picture of me. I love her so much and really long to return home and marry her.

Wednesday 6 March 1968, 1.45 pm

Today sounds of a march, as though heading to a big rally in the Square. First rally for many months. Last night, late, there seemed to be sounds of celebrations. The last few days have held more noise of marching and chanting of Mao's name ('Great teacher, great supreme commander, great leader and great helmsman!'), than for many months. Yesterday I wrote a cable to Mum and it went to the Foreign Ministry.

Yesterday letters came in from Angel and Emerita, yet contained nothing tangible. Angel's had a cutting about Freddie Forsyth disappearing, probably to Nigeria. I am in the middle of crossword mania again – this time compilation! Today I am on my fourth and can hardly bear to stop doing them, even at meals. Rose at 8.30 today and was working at 9.30 on the design of the puzzle, which gives me considerable pleasure.

The day before yesterday I was asked if I wanted a haircut. This seemed unnecessary, since normally the barber just comes. I thought it might be a sign of improvement. Lao Chiao, bless him, yesterday afternoon said to me when Angel's letter came, in a quiet voice, 'Is that from Mummy?' He was so obviously trying to be nice to me after I had earlier asked to send a cable to my mother. Weather continues to be warm. Tomorrow it is one year since I left England. I hope soon I shall be returning.

Bestselling thriller writer, Freddie Forsyth and I worked for a similar four-year period on the Eastern Daily Press *at different offices in Norfolk where Freddie, then in his mid-twenties, was already a larger-than-life character. An ex-National Service RAF jet pilot, ex-student of a Spanish university, driver of a fast open sports car, he always did everything with an unusual flourish and brio which set him apart. We both later joined Reuters about a year apart. Freddie was posted to East Berlin, where I later eventually succeeded him, after he was brought back to London following some florid over-reporting too rich for the Reuters news agency daily brew. Successful fiction writing was obviously awaiting him even then. He joined BBC TV news briefly and later got personally involved in events in Biafra, after reportedly 'disappearing there' – all this before writing his first, career-making thriller novel* The Day of the Jackal. *Shirley enclosed the cutting about him because she knew of Freddie through these connections and we had several mutual friends.*

I eventually compiled nearly 300 crosswords, up to the end of 1968, and some 50 of them were published in a paperback book by Penguin in 1975, entitled Crosswords from Peking. *Glancing at the cover of this book of puzzles, for the first time in over 30 years, I find with a very real sense of pleasure that it says the author 'perfected the art of compiling crossword puzzles under the noses of his communist gaolers' and added, 'Professional compilers have paid tribute to his self-taught expertise in brevity, ambiguity, deception and all the verbal dove-tailing of the game … evidence of courage and resource, they are entertaining problems in themselves, notably less frustrating than the treatment that occasioned them.' If I had known those modest means of filling the void each day would eventually get such a 'rave review' back home and be enjoyed by legions of Penguin puzzlers, I would have been beside myself with delight!*

Monday 11 March 1968, 11.30 pm

Feeling slightly sleepy and just about to go to bed. Tonight at dinner I received a much-wanted letter from Angel. It contained a cutting of a Patrick Campbell article, which made me laugh a lot and made me feel better. Six days without a letter now seems a long time. I am being over-indulged by too much goodness. This morning I rose earlier than for many months, at about eight, to get ready for a haircut. Last Monday Sao Kao had asked me if I wanted one. Then yesterday (Sunday), Lao Chiao passed on a message from the police that the hairdresser would come today between nine and ten. Somehow I construed this as evidence of a change of attitude, although very, very slight. Before they have never asked me.

With last Sunday's 'straw in the wind' about the papers re-opening (in

Hong Kong), I have allowed myself to feel the smallest encouragement from this. Perhaps March, as I have told myself, will contain some bounty for me. I realised today that it is seven weeks to May Day. I expect it will go quickly enough.

Tonight I reached the end of *Les Liaisons Dangereuses* by Laclos, which I have enjoyed. Two days ago I began *The White Nile* by Alan Moorehead, which is a fascinating account of the exploration and opening up of that river, which was all unknown to me before. Find it very interesting. My Angel's letters continue to be very loving, but I sometimes think they annoy me a little because they reflect so little deep compassion about my predicament. But I always immediately conquer this feeling, which is unfair. Shirley in fact is being magnificent.

She sent me a crossword puzzle, today saying she thought 'it might amuse you'. That is quite good, after nearly eight months and about 60 puzzles! And today I compiled my own ninth puzzle! The temperature is up to 48 now in the afternoon and is splendid. No sign of buds on the trees yet. Gosh, I love and miss my mother and my Angel. Mum's cable has been at the Foreign Ministry six days today. I had a moment of fury at this incredible stupidity this afternoon. But it passed.

Patrick Campbell, who wrote a regular weekly column in the Sunday Observer, *was an Irish humorist, who in normal times often had Shirley and me in stitches when we read him. He had a famous stutter and was equally funny on television in 'Call My Bluff'.*

Wednesday 20 March 1968, 11.00 pm

A short note to record that yesterday I walked outside without a coat for the first time. Today the little buds on the trees are looking green and just ready to burst out. Spirits have been reasonably even for about ten days now. Squadrons of girls and boys and men can be heard every morning marching and shouting '*Wan shou wu chiang*' and the 4 greats – leader, teacher, supreme commander, helmsman. Before 8 am each morning there are loudspeakers with 'East is Red', 'The Helmsman' and lots of *Mao's Thought* talk.

Tonight I managed to sort out the problem of my accounts for the first time and am very pleased. I completed my eighteenth crossword today. My morale is good. Yesterday the house was inspected by a gang of workmen. Could this, and the information of a haircut and the little note in the *Peking Review*, be the start of something big? About three days ago there was a piece in the *Peoples Daily* about Hong Kong and the New China News Agency. Couldn't understand it, but prayed it was good. I hadn't asked for the paper for days and it was delivered on a Sunday night. There were no exclamation marks or signs of 'Imperialism' in the headlines, so I hoped it might be good.

Saturday 23 March 1968, 3.45 pm

Yesterday about this time Sao Kao came in with a book in his hands which had translations of words like 'phlegm', 'blood' and chest' and other parts of the body and illnesses. He made a gesture with his hand, saying he had noticed I looked ill. No, he said, the police hadn't asked him. Did I want a doctor? I said, 'No', but asked for tea, fruit juice and milk.

This morning I had my first drink of anything except water and black coffee for seven months. A glass of pineapple juice; it was super. Any moment I expect some tea. 'Tea at four o'clock?' said Sao Kao very endearingly. A little smart policeman had been talking to him down below before and followed him down afterwards. At dinner time I told him I couldn't sleep with the noise of the guards and he conveyed this also. There was telephoning. As he went to leave later, he was called back and questioned again.

I have put this down along with other tiny things – like the haircut information, the piece in the *Peking Review* about Hong Kong newspapers re-opening, a piece in the *Peoples Daily* about the New China News Agency and Hong Kong as 'intimations of returning normalcy'. I only hope there is something in it. The day before yesterday – 21 March – the first leaves broke out on the tree in the courtyard. This tiny evidence of the renewal of life was more important to me than it has ever been before, giving me hope of 'renewal of life for myself'.

Thursday 28 March 1968, 7.15 pm

Today it rained for the first time for about six months and I walked in it. Was slightly pleasant after long months of dryness. Today the problem of the accounts appears to be solved, after getting a sum of money from the bank, indicating how much the outstanding amount was. Completed my twenty-fifth crossword today. The past 28 days have been more or less devoted to that and the accounts. It has been quite a good month so far. I miss Angel immensely and still pray fervently for something to happen soon. But really it still seems 'somewhat early', I tell myself.

Sunday 31 March 1968, 8.45 pm

Today a lot of activity downstairs during the day – apparently cleaning. Then tonight guards clumping up and down, seemingly getting something to eat or drink. So the invasion gets deeper. There was some chanting of ' *Wan shou wu chiang*' after the meeting with my two staff, as apparently someone was inaugurated.

The leaves on the tree are now coming out, although small. Today's afternoon temperature was 62 degrees and it was warm, I threw off my winter sweater and put on a wool shirt. Yesterday a letter came from Emerita containing no encouragement and the day before a letter from Shirley rather infuriatingly said, 'You were mentioned in the House', but didn't say anything else. Felt a little fed up this afternoon, but not sufficient to call a depression. Last Sunday's *Peking Review* told of a three-year sentence on a British 'spy', and this didn't make me feel any better!

Review of March: today one thing is very clear. I am not going to be released until one or all of the Chinese correspondents in Hong Kong are freed. It is now eight months and ten days and I am calmly reconciled to nothing happening for some months. The situation seems quite flat. I don't think Hong Kong will release anyone before a year, and perhaps not until long after.

I thought tonight: 'It is simply a matter of time.' Silly phrase in the circumstances, but true! God knows – it may be 18 months or two years. I can remember writing in my little cell, 'Perhaps I will be here six months or even a year' and feeling very bold and daring! I write now about 18 months and two years and hope fervently it will never come to that. But it may well do.

March has been a good month. I completed my twenty-eighth crossword puzzle this afternoon. My plan has been very successful. The early rising, the exercises and the puzzles have been continued right through the month. I have never been depressed and have kept busy the whole time. Quite the best month I have had, I think. Yesterday I was pleased to find more novels upstairs. I have now 12 in hand. I still hope against hope that something in the way of improvement or release will turn up. Perhaps house repairs will produce something. But what else there can be, I don't know. I do so miss my lovely mother and Shirley, and have just prayed very fervently for some help. (March also saw the successful completion of the accounts, which pleased me a lot.)

Oh what a joy it would be if I could be released! It is almost unthinkable. I still tell myself something good is coming. And why not? Letters recently have revealed that David Oancia is leaving and perhaps Jean Vincent too. This impressed me anew with how long I have been here. It seems that the guards don't sit outside the door now at night, but remain in the room. This was possibly a result of Sao Kao's questions. Sleep has been better altogether this month. And now for April and I hope this, too, will be a 'good month'. (I also hope there will be no trouble in Hong Kong this summer.)

The British 'spy' was George Watt, an engineer from Northern Ireland working for Vickers-Zimmer somewhere in northern China not far from Lop Nor, where China had a nuclear facility. He came to seek me out in London after his release and we compared experiences. George told me with great good humour that he had given his guards the impression that he bowed gravely each morning before the portrait of Mao in his cell – whereas in fact he had fixed a British postage stamp, bearing a picture of the Queen, in a drawer beneath the portrait and was in reality bowing loyally to Her Majesty! George later wrote an ironic book of his experience, called China Spy, *because he was quite obviously nothing of the kind.*

Some ten or more other Britons in addition to George Watt, the Vickers-Zimmer engineer, were eventually held in different circumstances and in different places around China largely without any realistic charges being made. They included Norman Barrymaine, a 66 year-old journalist held incommunicado without reason in Shanghai; Peter Will, a 46 year old captain of a passenger cargo ship held without explanation in the port of Tangku; David Crouch, a 29 year old second officer of a Blue Funnel cargo liner accused of 'contravening harbour regulations' in Shanghai; and David Johnston, a Shanghai bank manager working for the Chartered Bank who was arrested as 'an enemy of the Chinese Peoples Republic'. Several other British individuals working for the Chinese government in Peking in different roles also disappeared and were held without explanation, in some cases with members of their families, until after my release. They included Mr Eric Gordon and his wife Marie and 12 year-old son Kim; Israel Epstein and his wife Elsie; Mrs Gladys Yang, British-born wife of a Chinese subject; and Michael Shapiro, a former Stepney councillor.

Monday 1 April 1968

30-day Plan for April

Aim: extend and consolidate the new creative and active approach begun in March.

1 Continue crosswords: aim - create total of 50 by May Day.

2 This month must see some further creative work. Writing: study of Cultural Revolution; some Situationer material.

3 Try to get typewriter to type accounts and crosswords.

4 If it seems possible, try to get radio.

5 If it seems possible, ask to write letter (this depends on Mum's cable to large extent).

Monday 1 April 1968, 4.30 pm

Downstairs at this moment one of the guards is reading to the two staff. This began yesterday with Lao Chiao alone, after a preliminary on Sunday with Sao Kao. They shout and sing just like at regular guards' meetings; then a long editorial is apparently read to them from the paper. It took an hour yesterday but today was shorter...

(It is now 7.50 pm. I was interrupted by a guard ordering me out for walk and now have just had a rotten meal of tough meat!)

There was a lot of clowning downstairs last week. I think a 'shrine' to

Mao has been set up down there in the basement kitchen. In the last three or four days there has been new ritual added to the guards' morning and night 'performance'. Some stand to attention and salute on entering the door before Mao's portrait. But at the end of the complicated ceremonial they now wave their books rhythmically from side to side, while shouting three times, 'Long live Mao!' Then there's another shout and they turn and dismiss. The impression is of increasing drill. When answering the telephone, everyone now uses one of three phrases: '*Wan shou wu chiang!*', '*Mao chu hsi wan sui!*' or '*Ta tao su hsui!*'.

It seems there is to be no end to the complications. I hope they don't start including me in those damn things. I am somewhat fed up today. I have paid new three months' rent and car bills today. I wrote a truculent note to go with rent, until I thought better of it. In the end I put it down the lavatory.

'Ten thousand years without limit!', 'Long Live Chairman Mao!' and 'Down with Soviet revisionism!'

Thursday 4 April 1968, 11 pm

Today was a strange day of dust storms, which left brown sand, presumably from the Gobi Desert to the north, covering the courtyard. They also produced a strange light. Was somewhat fed up, as for sixth day there were no letters. Began to wonder if they have been stopped again. Although quite fed up, managed to prevent it becoming too bad. Today I did 'weekly wash' of socks and handkerchiefs, which is a disgusting affair. Last night I began reading *Something of Value* and today started a Peking Foreign Languages Institute book called *Vietnam Studies*. I finished *Queen Victoria* by Lytton Strachey recently, having enjoyed it immensely. I have also been dipping into *Whitaker's Almanack*, which is also very interesting.

Something of Value *is a novel by Robert Ruark, set in Kenya during the Mau Mau uprisings. Both revealing about the strange and violent ritual killings and the white colonial reactions to them. Most of all a touching love story, which I found moving and uplifting.*

Tuesday 9 April 1968, 5.30 pm

Today it is becoming unmistakably clear that those fucking bastards have again stopped my mail! It is now ten days since I received a letter, and 11 since one came from Angel. During March they came on average every three days. One is completely lost in wonder at the spiteful petty-mindedness and arbitrary little ways of these people. As if I am not in enough trouble that, without any reason, they should decide to stop the tiniest crumb of comfort that I have from the outside world. They are despicable!

I received a cable from Shirley quite incongruously on 6 April saying,

'Usually we would start the Easter holidays today', and asking me to look after myself. Last night I had the tiniest and most nebulous feeling of intuition that perhaps there was something good on the horizon. I can't explain it more than that, but it heralded a break, I feel. Just now, while praying, I stopped speaking completely and felt that the 'Power of God' was expressing itself. I had just said how much of a helpless wretch I was, but that God was all-powerful, when the unusual feeling came. I believe these two things are connected.

Today Amah returned to work in the house for half a day (after her long illness). Is that also a good sign? These first eight days of April have been somewhat unpleasant. But the depression never really got out of hand. Perhaps this is because I have the measure of the situation more now. The daily 'indoctrination' of the staff continues and one day a whole song was taught to Sao Kao downstairs in the kitchen.

Wednesday 10 April 1968, 11.45 pm

Today the white and red blossom on the tree outside was coming out full and beautiful. Today, after 36 days, I was allowed to send my cable to Mum. Today I got two letters from Emerita. She said she was sure that her debt couldn't be allowed to get much higher. I finished writing a second piece about sun and rain. I read for the eighth day about Africa. I was not too depressed. I was not happy. Time passes without much meaning. Amah, here again today, has definitely returned to work. On Monday (8 April) I asked for a typewriter.

I believe Emerita, who had once visited the Reuters house socially before my arrest, had been doing her best in phone calls and letters at the start to be optimistic and encouraging about the likely length of my captivity. I think she had optimistically predicted that I would not be held for very long and had perhaps undertaken lightly to pay me something, say £1 for every extra week perhaps, beyond a certain predicted early release date if she was wrong.

Thursday 11 April 1968, 6.30 pm

(Writing seated at my dinner 'table'.)

Tonight for the first time since I moved into this room I have eaten dinner without the light on. This has just occurred to me. This evening there has been a very powerful sense of almost supernatural quality. Before my dinner was brought up, I stood looking out of the window – something I haven't done before at this time, my habits being very regular – and the pink and white blossoms on the tree, blowing in a strong breeze in the evening sunlight, were very beautiful. The setting sun shone through my open door from the lounge and fell brightly on the wall of this room. There was an almost tangible feeling of goodness and beauty.

I went into the bathroom to look at a tiny flower of blossom I had brought in from the courtyard this afternoon, all crushed in the warmth of my hand as I carried it on the walk. I had put it in a little water in the lid of my boot polish tin. And to my surprise it seemed to have closed up neatly with the refreshing water.

While becoming aware of these things, unusually strong shivers ran down my spine, which I have come to regard as almost a sign of God's presence. All these things together give me a new, strong feeling of hope. I am sure something good is coming. I don't know what, how or when. But the enchanting sense of goodness and the pleasure of God I am sure were much too real to mean anything else. Now at this minute the sun has set and the courtyard is in shadow. The magic moment has passed. I shall continue with new hope, awaiting my release into full life again.

Sunday 14 April 1968, 4.00 pm

Easter Sunday. I have just been in the lavatory praying beside the bath with all my might for help in this terrible isolation. Downstairs the staff are being taught a song and the sound has driven me almost to distraction. This is one of those times when it seems impossible for this terrible nightmare ever to end.

The singing and shouting goes on day and night and demonstrates the terrible 'mindlessness' of the period. Outside the trees are heavy with blossom. My tree is thick with white blossom in full spate and outside the back wall, one is in bloom in pink. It is now one week to 21 April, which will make it exactly nine months. Recently this has been the mark to which I have been aiming. I shan't expect anything to happen on it, but I suppose it makes me feel that then I can start getting my teeth into the three months that remain to make a year.

I suppose again that a period of a year feels manageable – and perhaps even longer. Will somebody somewhere ever do anything about my wretched plight? But realistically, at this time I don't expect anything even at the year. In my most optimistic moments I now feel the earliest time my release can be expected is in the autumn. But all the other factors involved – the pressmen in jail in Hong Kong, calm in the colony, the Chinese determination not to give in until they get everything they demand, and the whole terrible situation in general – leave me almost no hope of release for even longer. What a terrible position to be in!

I have done nothing to deserve this; I don't know how long it will last. I am so totally isolated in a most terrible alien-ness that it makes it almost impossible to take a reasonable view of things. Nothing ever seems to happen to encourage me. I suppose, at best, I write these words now so that one fine and beautiful day I can look back on them and be thankful for their passing.

But now my situation is miserably grim. I try to be optimistic, for that is the only way to survive and I do want to survive! I look frequently at the picture of my lovely Shirley and long to be home and married to her. There are times when I can believe that something good will come soon. Please let something happen to encourage me. For so long I have had to be my own encouragement and I desperately need help now.

About three days ago the guards stuck up a new permanent portrait (of Mao) over the front door with red-flanking strips. All these growing signs of permanence don't help. I curse myself for ever being foolish enough to come here! What a wretched man I am! God please bring me deliverance soon!

Wednesday 17 April 1968, 11.00 morning

Today the courtyard is covered with the white flecks of the blossom falling profusely from the tree. This morning there has been much marching and hoarse shouting of slogans outside, as some big rally builds up. Drums, too.

Lao Chiao, this Monday, told me it is to be a meeting at Tien An Men. Yesterday I asked for a needle and cotton to sew my trousers. After checking with the Foreign Ministry – would you believe it? – and half an hour wait, I was granted permission. My mood continues to be up and down, with some depression, but I am managing to hold it 'off the bottom'.

Two days of examinations in current affairs have occupied me this week. (NB My learning my *Atlas of World Affairs* by heart and then testing myself in very small writing!)

Thursday 18 April 1968, 5.30 pm

Today the temperature is 68 degrees. The blossom from the tree fell around me like a snowstorm as I walked in the yard. Have just finished again the messy business of washing socks. Today I had my hair cut very short.

As the nine-month mark looms in sight, things seem to be worse rather than better. Yesterday I was granted the use of the typewriter I asked for nine days ago. But, for the first time ever, a guard came and sat in the room beside me. After I had spent two hours and more typing up eight months' accounts, they were taken from me to go to the Ministry. Why, I am quite baffled. The guard snatched them away as if they were gold dust. There is something strange about it which disturbs me. Do they want to know how much it costs? Do they think I want to send them to London? Whatever it is, it is quite clear that the persecution is not easing up. On the contrary, they are determined to keep up this terrible game. This makes me more depressed.

Also today the barber arrived completely by surprise, before I was dressed. This destroyed my illusion of last month – when they asked me a week before if I wanted a haircut – that there was an attempt to be more correct by me. The doorbell rarely rings any more. That pretence has almost been dropped of it being answered by my staff here. Now papers are pushed through a hole in the gate. Sometimes the bell is rung, but rarely – and it doesn't always mean there is a letter for me when it rings.

Another week has passed letter-less. So all the good signs of March – better nourishment, mail every three days with morning deliveries, the haircut thing, the enquiry after my health – have been nullified now. And I am in the depths of despair again. I am disgusted with life and with the unthinking nature of the British Government and the intransigence here of this one. Today I have corrected all the things I have written, panicked into this by events yesterday and keenness to know what I was writing. My routine has been broken this past two days by these things and the haircut. My life is completely becalmed at the moment. And there seems no early prospect of anything good coming now. What am I to do? I need a miracle to save me from this terrible isolation!

Sunday 21 April 1968, 3.45 pm

Today it is nine bloody months! Nine incredible months of my life have passed as a prisoner. What do I think? I don't know what to think. There is still as little prospect of release as ever. It now seems it could go on 18 months and – heaven forbid – even longer.

How I have stood it, I don't know. How I will stand the rest, however long it is, I also don't know. I only know that I have stood it and that I will stand the rest, however long it is.

There is so little to give me hope at present. What a terrible Sunday afternoon. How I long for England! Yesterday a letter from Shirley cheered me up a lot. She said, 'How horrible it would be if we had never met.' Shirley is so wonderful in all this. How lucky I am about her. Two cadres visited yesterday, but although they had a conference behind closed doors, as they did on 14 February, I was not involved. The fat police cadre peered through the crack in the door at me. It is sometimes very hard to believe that it will ever end but I suppose it will one day.

Tuesday 23 April 1968, 7.15 pm

Today the nine-month spell of isolation was broken! Donald Hopson and John Weston visited! In the morning a lot of fuss was made about opening the side door into the lounge. In the afternoon the fat cadre appeared for the second time in three days. Then about 3.30 pm the interpreter enters with a colleague and says, 'I am instructed to tell you that today at four o'clock two officials of the office of the British Chargé d'Affaires will visit you. You must abide by the following conditions:

1   You must use standard English.
2   You must exchange no documents, letters or papers.
3   You must not record or take photographs.
4   We reserve the right to terminate the interview at any time.'

I asked for a repeat of them, and then sat down to wait for 35 minutes. A cadre had come into the room and I had been ordered to sit down, so as not to see somebody enter across the courtyard below the level of my view from the window. Who it was, I don't know. Just before 4.00 pm I was led into the other room, which had been set up with furniture from upstairs and cigarettes.

When the gate opened, I rose to peer out and saw Hopson and Weston – I was immediately struck by the fineness of their suits after nine months of seeing only drab coarse Chinese cottons. They came in and said, 'How are you?'

I replied, 'All right.' And all the time I was gripping Hopson's hand with one hand and John's with the other.

We sat down and Hopson read first a letter from my mother and then a message from (Gerald) Long. Mother said something about making the first attempt in the hotel trade in Scotland. Long ran on about 'constant striving' again, I think; I paid little attention. Then Hopson told me that Red Guards had burnt down the British Office last August. He said the visit was in return for a special visit to 15 communist newsmen in Hong Kong today.

He said the political situation here and in Hong Kong was better and 'although your release is not just around the corner, things are better now than nine months ago'. George Brown had twice offered to swap Hsueh Ping for me, he said. This made me feel better. There had been questions in Parliament and Western newspapers had taken up my case.

I asked if the Chinese had said anything about me and he said, not apart from discussing the visit. Reuters had tried to send a representative to discuss my case, it was said. I was somewhat nervous and almost felt tears come to my eyes when John asked if there was a message for Shirley and I said, 'Tell her I love her very much and that she means everything to me that I mean to her.'

I said that Mother must be told that I looked all right, no matter how nervy I was. I said I had sometimes felt on the verge of a nervous breakdown, but that was probably the isolation. Hopson said that I looked not much different.

He had sent Macmillan's memoirs, John had sent another parcel in December, Mother said she hoped I had got the parcel she had sent. There was a message from Reuters editorial in London saying they hoped that they would see the Anthony Grey by-line on the file again soon. (For some odd reason I felt tears start to my eyes at this.) Hopson said the Hong Kong people could send letters and I should ask. I got a tiny bit angry here, having said I was intending to ask, and he appeared to be trying to tell me what to do.

But it was wonderful to see them – their colourful neckties, their suits, their English faces (Hopson looked incredibly brown, John pale). I shook hands again very warmly as they left and both gave me messages from girls and wives, but I didn't really hear them. Outside on the porch I managed a small smile for John and he made a nonsensical remark, 'Keep it up.'

It was just wonderful to see them. Hell, it has been nine months since I saw anybody like that. How incredible!

I told them I had been living downstairs from mid-August.

John said, 'When the Red Guards came?'

Hopson said, 'Was there any violence?'

I replied, 'I don't think there is any point in going into that now.'

I also said I had been ill and had had the doctor once. I said I had 40 minutes' exercise a day. I was perhaps a little guarded about the 'average day', which John asked about. Hopson asked a stupid question about whether I was playing 'Patience' (the solo card game).

John asked about chess and I said I didn't get access to a board. And then he asked, did yoga help – yes, I said, I had learned a lot about self-control.

When did I know about the visit? they asked.

Twenty minutes before they arrived, I said.

And how many guards were there?

'Three,' I replied.

Always one who speaks English?

Never.

Hopson took a cigarette and held it up enquiringly.

I said, 'Help yourself – I don't know where they came from.'

Before, Lao Chiao had asked (at the prompting of the guard) if he should bring tea; I said I would tell him when they were there. He brought it anyway. But we left it untouched.

Lao Chiao had also asked if I wanted to change, pointing to the darned hole in my trousers. I said no. He had the temerity to say, 'I think you should change.'

I said I would remain as I always was – and did.

John also said at one point, 'We hope to repeat this.'

I asked for books and a Bible with big print, histories and economics that I could get my teeth into.

What does it mean? It means that I am irretrievably linked with the 15 'news workers' in Hong Kong and won't get out until they do. In psychological terms, it was a wonderful boost just to see friends, shake hands, talk and look at them. It has been an encouraging day. It has broken the long, terrible, empty nine months of not knowing, and thinking all kinds of strange things.

It is a reassuring sign although it doesn't mean the end is near. I shall re-dedicate myself to endurance as a result of it.

George Brown, the British Foreign Secretary of that time, had offered to swap me with Hsueh Ping, the first convicted press prisoner in Hong Kong. I appreciated Mr Brown's straightforward commonsense approach, although it seemed unlikely that it would succeed in the way that expedient spy swaps had worked with the Soviet Union. At least I felt he had done his best to do something quick and effective for me.

George Brown was perhaps most famous for becoming 'tired and emotional' on television (this explanation became a widely quoted satirical euphemism for 'drunk'), after being hauled out of some private function into a television studio to give his first reaction to the tragic news of the assassination of President Kennedy. He was also later the butt of many jokes about his personal idiosyncrasies regarding drinking and womanising - yet this one act endeared this controversial rumbustious man to me for a lifetime.

Wednesday 24 April 1968

One other thing: yesterday morning while repeating to myself my daily 'mantra' that begins, 'Nothing but good can befall you', I interjected at the end, quite why I don't know and quite differently to any other morning, 'Something good is coming – sooner than you expect.'

This feeling of premonition built up while I was exercising; it came to me, saying something good is going to happen today, there is a feel of it. When at breakfast the accounts were on my desk, returned from the Foreign Ministry, I deliberately refrained from writing this in my diary, telling myself, 'I will wait until the second thing happens.'

This is no idle reconstruction after the event; it was real premonition. Thinking about yesterday when I was made to sit on my chair and a guard came in, closed the door and kept me from the window, I now guess it was the recording equipment going in and out. No important persons were present, so it could only have been an object. The writing cadres were just a front.

Hopson also talked some nonsense about asking for a telephone. It seems the walls were almost stripped of posters and I sat under the 'Down with A. Grey!' slogan on the dining room wall. That must have been noticed by the other two.

(I have been meaning to note for some time now that about ten days ago the 'book-holding' by the guards stopped during walks and the sessions downstairs have eased off too.)

Monday 29 April 1968, 10.30 pm

Suddenly today summer came. For the first time I left my jacket off all day and went outside without it. The air was filled with flying flurries of blossom and seeds, small ants crawled everywhere on the ground (normally one is in too much hurry to notice this) and the temperature went over 70 for the first time, at 75. Tonight I sweated for the first time in my room here, where the temperature is 72 degrees.

Today, for the first time since last Tuesday's event, I managed to stop thinking about it. Every day since then has been taken up almost entirely with re-creating it, worrying about how wet I must have appeared, thinking what I should have told them and how bitterly I should have castigated the British Government and their non-interest in me.

It has occupied almost all my waking hours, but now it is slipping away. My attitude, of course, is different because of it. It has given a different perspective. It makes me even more certain that I shall be here for some long time yet; however certain that may have seemed before, it is concrete now.

So this has strengthened my resolve to 'buckle down to a three-month grind' through the hot weather. There is little that can happen now. I pray tremendously fervently that nothing will happen in Hong Kong and harbour the hope that autumn or early next year will be possible for release.

(I just broke off to watch one of the incredible little silver moths flying crazily about, then resting on the floor. They are very beautiful.)

A letter from Emerita on Saturday gave me the first outside reaction. She said: 'We all think you are wonderful – and are glad to hear you are bearing up so well.'

Tuesday 30 April 1968, 20.10 hours

Review of April 1968

April contained the biggest event of the house arrest so far – the visit by Hopson and Weston. It changed my perspective, helped me in a strange intangible way and kept me thinking about it for days. April also saw a cable go to my Mum, saw me type accounts watched by the police, and I put in a request on the twenty-fifth to write letters.

Today I completed my sixtieth crossword puzzle. I wrote several things in a small way, read for 18 days the Kenya-based novel *Something of Value* and, towards the end of the month, Alan Winnington's non-fiction book *Tibet* and several old *China Quarterly* magazines. I was depressed to a certain extent off and on in the early stages, but this, I think, was due to the comparison with March – a very good month.

Since 23 April I have been calm. Today, preparing for new month, I am praying for same. Tomorrow I change into summer trousers and shoes. My trousers and shoes of the winter are worn out and very tired and dirty looking.

(Today a picture in the paper looked like President Liu Shao-chi.)

I have decided to learn Chinese this month. I more or less make it a six-months' plan. I regard the next three months of the summer as a whole as my current 'struggle'. I vaguely hope nothing else goes wrong in Hong Kong, and that something might happen in the autumn or early New Year.

I had bought just before leaving London – in a Highgate bookshop – a Chinese language primer in the famous yellow-and-blue-covered 'Teach Yourself' *series. That series covered every conceivable subject from needlework to home plumbing, I think. I had already found and brought down to my room this* Teach Yourself Chinese *volume. It had been among the books in the upstairs sitting room of the house among the curious collection of books brought and left there by previous Reuters incumbents in the post. This part of the 'plan' for May 1968, however, was not carried out. I simply shirked it, I think, because of the enormity of the task.*

REFLECTIONS - 7
Sunday 31 December 2006

In retrospect it is clear that the 'magic moment' I describe as occurring just before sunset on Thursday 11 April 1968 was unique and of the highest importance. Although fleeting, it was perhaps the most profound, condensed experience of all. That lovely image of the pink and white blossoms swaying on the tree in the bright evening sunlight has returned to my mind spontaneously on many occasions since then.

I am surprised to find, all these years later, that I did not mention it even briefly in my unusual summary of the highlights of the month written on 30 April. Its power and the 'enchanting sense of goodness' were very tangible and strongly felt at the time. I was very deeply moved. Yet the experience was subtle and, although intense while it lasted, was difficult to define in words.

Obviously it was overshadowed at the time by the massive impact of seeing my first friendly familiar faces on 23 April, after nine months of traumatic isolation from the world. The entry of Sir Donald Hopson and John Weston in their 'glowing' suits and ties was a sort of small scale 'relief of Mafeking' for me. It was a halfway house of sorts, because while I remained physically a prisoner, their visit did at least temporarily lift my mental siege and relieve a lot of the tension that had gathered in me since that distant day in July 1967 when I had been confined to my house alone after John drove me to the Foreign Ministry. Seeing him and Donald Hopson again reassured me that I was still part of the real world, although tenuously.

Their visit also encouraged me to think that at least some modest improvements had occurred in the political situation surrounding me and all was not hopeless. Clearly it made me feel that there was more prospect of being released than there had been up to that point. This helped me find new inner strength to endure the hot summer months that followed.

Over the much longer term, however, the more subtle experience which preceded the visit by twelve days has possibly had a greater and deeper long-term influence. 'There has been a very powerful sense of almost supernatural quality' is how I struggled to describe something that was largely beyond words. Yet it was gentle too, sweetly inspiring and comforting at the same time.

Nowadays I would not personally use the term 'God' in attempting to define such matters, since that one simple word is open to so many different subjective interpretations across our troubled world and is cited imprecisely for so many diverse purposes by people of many faiths that it has become possibly one of the most easily misconstrued words in the entire human lexicon.

Now I think I see that 'magic moment' as a time when a veil of sorts was briefly drawn aside. I simultaneously glimpsed and felt something very rare, experienced briefly what I would now more comfortably describe as a state of 'pure consciousness' or a hint of a higher order of existence. My circumstances and my reactive thoughts, it is clear to me at this distance, had led me directly to those moments when I slipped off the ordinary plane of existence, the everyday level of 'conditioned consciousness' and onto a higher, more beautiful and more elevated level of awareness beyond thought.

The full importance of it was obviously not fully discernible at the time – and may not be fully realisable even now. Yet a seed of something additional was sown then, I have no doubt. Some new awareness became an essential part of me and it still flourishes and stimulates further undogmatic searching and seeking, even today.

In its essence what was perhaps taking place at that time in April 1968 was an unknowing, inadvertent surrender of my own egoistic mind to that greater wholeness and unity of which we and everything in our existence are seemingly an integral part. In my case, that all seemed to happen accidentally. Yet the hostage situation is obviously not the only circumstance that can produce such a feeling of profound realisation in an individual.

Being innocently imprisoned amidst great hostility does have the unique effect of forcing that individual into a profound process of inner and outer examination. He searches for new inner resources that he might not otherwise seek. Arthur Koestler, who experienced solitary confinement under sentence of death in a condemned cell as a News Chronicle journalist during the Spanish Civil War, later described that experience as 'a spiritual hothouse' and the modern hostage experience also potentially possesses that quality par excellence.

Re-reading and reviewing those journal entries for April 1968 have brought me a very strong confirmed conviction of what was earlier only a vague and undefined instinct – that there was something of so far unconsidered value to be re-excavated from the diary's pages, even after nearly four decades. In a very modest way it is, as my strange little recent dream suggested, like unearthing my own small-scale army of Terracotta Warriors, re-investigating my own personal 'distant' past in China.

Perhaps processing the diaries to prepare this book has in a way taken on the characteristics of an archaeological dig. First, in Jersey in the Channel Islands in 1970, I translated with the help of a portable typewriter the meticulously contrived shorthand symbols that had been written with stolen biros and pencil stubs into little exercise books in that sweltering eight-foot-square cell and later the adjoining room. These typewritten transcripts, gradually yellowing with age, were preserved over the intervening years with the original diaries themselves in bank deed boxes that were like personal time capsules.

When 'dug out' from those deep bank vaults, the transcripts were newly processed electronically onto more durable computer hard drives, floppy discs and CDs. In this form – onscreen – I have been able to examine them minutely and clinically, dust them off, clean them up and prepare them like historical artefacts for further display and consideration, perhaps in a small corner of some future and imaginary Museum of Humanity exhibition called 'The Inhuman Condition'. By then let us trust, nobody will be able to understand how human beings could have once wished to harm each other by, among other things, unjustly imprisoning innocent individuals for long periods without cause.

Setting irony aside, however, as I read through these diary entries now, stage by stage, writing each of these interleaved Reflections before I move onto the next phase, I do have a curious feeling of reliving the whole experience day by day and month by month. The intrinsic memories of the experience embedded deeply in my DNA feel as if they are also undergoing a similar positive process of progressive review, being brought into the light of day and understood better, cleansed and refreshed – and perhaps finally dispersed.

That relatively short entry for Thursday 11 April 1968, describing how I was transfixed briefly by the beauty of the late sun shining on the blossom of the tree remains deeply moving, even uplifting – particularly in its conclusion. 'Now at this minute the sun has set and the courtyard is in shadow. The magic moment has passed. I shall continue with new hope, awaiting my release into full life again.'

Something, I knew had been stored and added to the practical inspiration of the consular visit and the imagined life-saving new 'super-ingredient' I pretended to discover in myself in February during the most frightening period of depression that I ever encountered. All these things together, it seems, were working away together as I prepared to endure that long hot summer of 1968, fighting in different ways the recurrent waves of negativity that were still to roll up on my mental shores with variable strength and severity for many months to come.

8
DREAMS OF HOME

Wednesday 1 May 1968

31-day Plan for May

Make good use of time; don't waste time and energy being depressed!

1   Learn Chinese two hours a day.

2   Compile big crosswords for the month.

3   Write two short stories or articles.

4   Remain positive! This thing will end some time!

5   Innovate where possible (Good luck, Boy!)

Thursday 2 May 1968, 2.30 pm

Yesterday was May Day. I saw the fireworks spring up for the third time in the evening above Tien An Men Square and I was fairly disinterested. I had a feeling that by the next set, for National Day on 1 October, things might be slightly different. During the night of 30 April into May Day, I dreamed that I asked Lao Chiao if he knew when I should be released. He said he knew. After a long pause I asked when. He said clearly: 'October.' During the day there was much singing of Mao songs. Towards the end of the afternoon, crowds marched to the square for the evening celebration. The shouts and singing of the endless Mao songs and the inevitable 'Wan shou wu chiang' and 'Four Greats' drifted into the distance and renewed themselves. This surely is the most incredible mass indoctrination in the history of mankind. I put on my summer gear and felt very 'summery'. The trousers are tight and I wondered how long they could last. Today is hot. I have completed two new big crosswords on light paper. That's all for now.

This dream was eventually curiously prophetic and precise.

Sunday 5 May 1968, 7.30 pm

Yesterday afternoon a doctor came after I'd had severe stomach pain all day. But I told him I didn't ask for him. After examination there was a lot of chat, after I had repeated I didn't ask for him (having been told there was nothing much wrong and I could have some doses if I liked). A little man in light-blue cottons told me through the translator, 'This is a socialist country and we are responsible for the health of these other people (guards) as well – that is why we have come.'

The doctor was young and I thought prepared to talk this time; the translator was civilian, not Public Security Bureau. The tension was higher than last time. Today Lao Chiao brought a coffee tin asking for 'sample from lavatory', but only after Sao Kao had gone. I had the pain badly from the morning. So there was no sample. The whole thing is rather a farce. Despondent today that there have been no letters. The Ministry is clearly holding things up deliberately again. Bastards!

Tuesday 7 May 1968, 3.30 pm

Today another small 'needle in the side', which immediately infuriated me again. Asking for books, as I have at least on three other occasions, I had to wait while they telephoned for the first time. Then instead of going straight upstairs without checking, as before, Lao Chiao was told to tell me, 'Tomorrow.'

Furious! How absolutely without reason! After fuming about hate, etc. for a few minutes, I dropped to my knees to pray by the bath for strength. Now, half an hour or so later, I reflect how particularly damning to them such action is. How pathetic that they should go to such lengths to persecute and annoy one solitary Briton. How indicative of their lack of humanity and confidence. They have the lack of grace of uncivilised people.

Also I've had no letters since Emerita's on 27 April. It appears that I get letters only every two weeks from England now. Again, how pathetic that they should feel the need to introduce a rule like that, when they have me so completely down and out!

Wednesday 8 May 1968, 3.30 pm

Another infuriating delay in the books' question. Another call to headquarters and then – nothing. The boards in my room have now been here 44 days. They say, 'The force at the core leading our cause forward is the Chinese Communist Party, the theoretical basis guiding our thinking is Marxist Leninism.' (Later in the afternoon I got books, but when I asked about getting a book left in the car in the garage, they had to ring again.) The other board says, 'If anyone attacks us and if the conditions are favourable for battle, we will certainly act in self-defence to wipe him out resolutely, thoroughly, wholly and completely. (We shall not strike rashly, but when we do strike, we must win!)'

This last one seems to sum up their attitude to me and their contest with Britain. Today I completed what turned out to be a brilliant crossword. Just one of those days. The compilation was best, and most of the clues funny or clever or both.

There have otherwise been tiny alterations in routines. The recent 'Long Live Mao!' chant before the singing has been replaced by the former 'One, two, three!' chant. People are beginning to say the usual '*Wei* (Yes?) on the telephone again instead of the other political quotations. The singing has stopped downstairs this afternoon and yesterday there was nothing. Very small things, but nevertheless signs of a very slight lessening of extremist enthusiasm.

Friday 10 May 1968, 8 o'clock in the evening

This second the infuriating blasts of raucous shouting and sounds of 'Helmsman' and the other '*Wan Suî* s have just finished in my old dining room. How annoying and loud and pathetic it is. Today there was no mail, so bang goes the theory on two-week intervals. It is a long time indeed! Tomorrow it is two weeks since a letter of any kind (from Emerita) and I'm missing these letters very much.

I have just been reading adverts in the London *Times* Personal Column, which take me back to London flat life again. Hell, this is a terrible existence. Today I had to pay 8 yuan for the doctor I never asked for. I was a little mad at the time.

Monday 13 May 1968, 8 o'clock

Yesterday a long gap in postal deliveries was broken. Three letters from Shirley, posted on 23 and 25 April, were delivered. I don't know how they came, since Lao Chiao brought them in just before lunch. No bell was rung. They had been held since 29 April, according to the Peking postmark.

I thought how pathetic that they should feel the need to resort to such twisting of the knife in the wound. The letters told how two Daily Mail men had brought the news of my diplomatic visit to Shirley and that Erdmute had rung. Also Shirley was furious at being left out of the messages arrangements for the visit and felt hurt. She was also upset at Idiot (David) Oancia's report that I had received letters from a friend.

Yesterday the courtyard was filled to a greater extent than ever before with Gobi Desert sand and dust, and a most unhealthy light existed all day. The sky was brown and light came through in strange blue shades. Unreal.

I was surprised at the amount of detail about my visit that had been given out – also in the strong interest of the press at home. The London *Times* said I had been fed a 'basic' diet which was a good phrase dreamed up by someone.

My attitude at present is to endure the summer; it's as simple as that. I hope only for letters and expect nothing else. I aim at clearing May, June, July and August before thinking of hoping for release. I pray that there will be no trouble in Hong Kong. I am calm and even quite cheerful today. Today the 'heat was turned on'. It was 84 degrees in the courtyard and I believe the summer has begun. Roll on the end of August.

Erdmute Behrendt, Reuters outstanding office secretary in East Berlin for many years, including my two years of tenure there, became a life-long friend of Shirley and myself.

Tuesday 14 May 1968, 1.15 pm

Last night I dreamed again that I was home. And in the dream I said, 'This time I know I am not dreaming, because all the shops are recognisable in the right order.' And as I looked from the platform of a bus, there were the shops slipping by seemingly correct and in order. Then all of a sudden the reality dawned again that, while dreaming, I knew I was dreaming and nothing had changed.

Many times I have dreamed of being home. Sometimes it has been with the proviso that I must return again. Several times I have dreamed about buying Sunday papers in a dream, and then in another dream going to the same shop thinking, 'Now I am really home and here is the shop I once dreamed about.' But always, before the dream ends, I know I am dreaming and not really free.

An hour ago I got three letters and a card. This included one from Mum – only the third in nearly ten months. Dear Mum. How I love her. Shirley said (David) Oancia had written that I had 'shown only a glimpse of his struggle against loneliness'. I expect that was when I mentioned nervous breakdowns. It is 80 degrees again today.

Thursday 16 May 1968, 17.00 hours

After 12 days at the Foreign Ministry, my letter to Shirley was posted – 82 cents. I also received a letter from Shirley and a card from Germany of August last year telling me she had just heard of the house invasion. Strange detail. Yesterday a glazier came to mend the windows. The window in the bathroom was un-nailed, but nailed up again.

He knocked the glass about on the floor of the bedroom and afterwards I found splinters everywhere. Today's mail brought incredible total of 12 pieces in five days – the most dense mail period so far. Shirley is an absolute love. Having had an operation for removing a mole, she is now buying things for the house and having it painted and saying she is doing everything to keep up to scratch, so that I shan't be disappointed in her when I get home. What an angel!

Last night I finally got started on my ten-year-old short story idea about a criminal scientist. It goes without saying that these 'mail days' have been much better for me than many others. (Two days ago the temperature reached 90 degrees for the first time – it has cooled a bit since, but nights are hotter.)

Saturday 18 May 1968, 6 o'clock in the evening

So today reveals one of the most infuriating situations to date. Yesterday two letters – one from East Berlin – dropped through the letterbox with the papers. I heard them and saw them as I walked. During my walk, the original 'Ferret Face' guard who has returned in the last few days, walked out, picked up the letters and after trying to slip them into his pocket, screwed them up in his hands and walked indoors with them, leaving the papers lying there.

Yesterday they weren't given to me and today they weren't given to me. So now letters, after arriving at the house, are not given to me. I am having to employ all my powers of self-control not to get really furious about this. Last night I was also infuriated by the singing of the little fat spitting guy. I leapt up and shouted for the paper to try to introduce a diversion. (I had closed the windows inside first.)

He, without jacket or hat, was a bit nonplussed, but refused to give me the paper. He came in and said something I didn't understand. Today there was a long meeting in the morning and I thought there would be some reprisal. I expected my outside walk to be cut. But nothing happened. So still the tremendous humiliation continues!

Sunday 19 May 1968, 22.00 hours

It seems these days are taken up almost entirely with holding my nerves steady against singing and spitting. This morning the 'Grinning Lunatic' was awake at seven o'clock, singing over and over in the next room '*Dong Fang Hung*' (The East is Red). Just these words over and over again. On his own last evening, he did the same with 'The Helmsman' over and over again, like the idiot he clearly is!

All this afternoon the little guard, 'Slack Jaw', has been singing over and over downstairs for the staff, and later upstairs all three were yelling out. In between they are spitting! It is a crazy hell-like existence!

Today a letter from Mum and a card from Shirley, but no sign of the East Berlin letter delivered on Friday 17 May. What a crazy game they play. Today I finished off my first short story and am at present reading *Roxana* or *The Fortunate Mistress*, having recently finished John Steinbeck's *Tortilla Flat* and before that the Africa book. I prayed extra fervently tonight for the coming week and that perhaps there was the chance of something unusual happening in the next seven days.

Roxana *is by* **Daniel Defoe,** *author of* **Robinson Crusoe.**

Monday 20 May 1968, 12 noon

Have just been counting my mail. After 15 days without any letters at all, one on 27 April and one on 12 May and five deliveries in seven days I have now received 14 items. Truly the richest mail week of the whole ten-month period. I have hesitated to do such a valuation, since such things are reserved for bad times. Still no sign of the letters which were delivered on 17 May. I am resolved to wait a little longer. In the past two days since the 'incident' with 'Fat Boy', the paper has now been brought to me at dinner.

Wednesday 22 May 1968, 12 noon

Today, I write a diary of misery. I have just tried to say a special prayer for help. Last night at about ten, a carpenter rushed in and nailed up the window in my room. This I had opened about three days ago because of the heat. There is nothing but a sheer wall outside and last November when I was moved in here, I was told I could have it open when I liked. This act of the guards (incredibly vindictive and swinish) threw me into the deepest misery I have known for some time.

Sat drooping with horrified misery. They had made as if to nail up the tiny window in the bathroom, too. I had gone in to try to stop them. But they did nothing. I was unable to not show my anger and the 'Wizened Chief' who has returned in the last week, stood staring at me, as is their wont, to indicate displeasure.

So with yesterday's refusal to give me the *Peoples Daily* newspaper and with the letters of last Friday not appearing for the sixth successive day, things are indeed deteriorating again. I am so desperately miserable and desolated. Yesterday it was ten months; how many multiples of this will it be before I am released?

This morning for the second day a crowd of slogan-chanting marchers streamed by in the street. Through the gate, as it opened briefly as a guard went out, I saw they carried slogans on sticks. They shouted, 'Down with American imperialism!', 'Down with Soviet revisionism!' and there was the sound of shouting the usual '*Wan Sui's.*'

They sound like hordes and hordes of demented, tormented, crazy souls being driven from hell. These are the cries of my world on this day of misery. But I have noted before, it is often darkest before dawn, and hope something will come soon to lift my spirits.

Thursday 23 May 1968, 4.00 pm

A moment ago I was in the toilet praying. Outside the screams and yells of the demonstrations going by ripped and tore at my nerves. I feel very desperate again. Now at this moment they are running by. There was no magic today on the twenty-third day as there has been in the last five months. I feel very low again. I must brace up. I gasp out prayers many times a day. The demonstrations, I find from the *Peoples Daily*, are in connection with some riots in France, presumably against Vietnam and America.

In Paris the famous May 1968 left-wing student street riots went on for weeks and became an historic landmark protest. The way it was reported in the Chinese press made me fear a communist revolution was breaking out in Western Europe and all would be changed if I ever got home.

Friday 25 May 1968, 5.00 pm

This afternoon I watched the guard come from the gate carrying the papers and at least two letters. I saw them partly covered on the table as I came in from my walk, but they haven't been delivered to me. There is clearly a new game being played with my mail! This afternoon I wrote some more of the story about psychoanalysis which I began last night. This new writing form of diversion is giving me considerable pleasure.

The weather has been cooler for the past two or three days and the effect of the closed windows at night has not really been too bad. The demonstrations, which went on for three days, were dying out today. The papers show lots of pictures of France. It is difficult to understand what is going on, but it is clearly anti-American. There is a map that almost seems to suggest there has been a revolution in France. I am very keen to see the *Peking Review* this week. (During this week I have had strawberries twice a day and they are delicious!)

Monday 27 May 1968, 10 am

Yesterday was quite a good day. I received a letter from Shirley at breakfast in which was a hand-made chess set. I was quite overwhelmed with the loveliness of this act. She really is an absolute angel. Also, Sao Kao was allowed at last to get the book from the car, which pleased me immensely (NB Edgar Snow's *The Other Side of the River: Red China*

Today). I had forgotten about it and given it up. Somehow, I don't know why, I see this heavy, thick, hard-covered, red-jacketed volume as a symbol of good. I feel things are improving now, very definitely.

The day before, there were two letters from Shirley, one giving details of the letters from the Westons about my visit. I was surprised after all the fuss she had made about it, that she said nothing about my actual message. I am now hoping and looking forward to a reply to my letter, which Shirley must have received now.

Yesterday afternoon I again saw letters carried in by the 'Looney Guard', but they weren't delivered to me. May has been 'a month of nails and strawberries and a book from the garage and a letter home'. I am now looking forward to getting on with June. Last night I finished my short story about little Sigmund and so completed the two ten-year-old stories in my mind. I saw this as quite an achievement. Another little premonition yesterday; as I shaved I was talking to myself, saying: 'There is something coming today!' 'Oh,' I answered, 'You think so?' Then I replied to myself again: 'Yes, I know so!' Very strange!

Reflections - 8

Wednesday 3 January 2007

A Man Alone

A man.
Sitting.
Alone.
Sitting alone for a long time.
Sitting alone for a long time in a room.
A room which he may not leave.
A room which has four walls, a floor and a ceiling.
Six sides of a cube.
A cube like a dice.
Like a six-sided dice.
And the man is sitting on a chair on the floor inside the cube.
If it were a dice it would be a loaded dice, he feels.
Loaded against him.
Loaded by himself sitting on the floor of the dice he feels.
If it were picked up and rolled it would always land up the same way.
Because the weight of the man is on the floor.
And the side showing to the world outside would be bland.
Featureless, bare, the upper side of the dice, the ceiling.
Telling nothing.
A kind of blank dice.
Loaded against himself by himself.
Loaded to, for, with, from and by himself, he feels.

The man is sitting alone for a very long time.
A very, very long time.

And because he is alone for a very long time with an empty mind, he dreams.
With his eyes open.
He dreams with his eyes open but always returns to reality
Within the six-sided cube.
After a very long time alone it is difficult for the man.
It is difficult for him to know whether or not he is losing his mind, going insane.
He dreams with his eyes open, he dreams deliberately.
But he always returns to the sickening reality of the six-sided cube.
And for this he is grateful eventually.
Because he comes to believe that insanity is the inability to wake up.
To wake up from dreaming with eyes open.
To remain sane inside the six-sided cube he dreams desperately
With open eyes.
But sometimes he fears he may not be able to stop his open-eyed dreams.
Perhaps the reality is that the insane dream all day with open eyes.
And never wake again.

Perhaps they try to wake but don't succeed.
But the need is compulsive.
Man must dream.
He must walk the thin line between dream and finite reality.
Perhaps fantasy is a way of assuring himself of his reality – by contrast.
A distorting mirror which he holds up to himself.
And somehow illogically sees in it his reassuringly ordinary earthbound image.
And so draws perverse comfort from his own physical inability to escape
Into the intangible world of unreality.

And sitting alone.
Sitting alone in a room.
Sitting alone in a room for a long time
A man.
Sitting.
Alone.
Dreams.

This is an 'invisible' entry that was deliberately withheld from my secret shorthand diaries. Entitled simply *A Man Alone*, it is the first of four such entries and they all remained otherwise 'invisible' because I never wrote any of them down – even in shorthand. And now in early January 2007 I cannot find even a passing reference to them in the transcripts of those diaries – or even any mention of the fact that I decided to retain something invisibly by 'writing' it only inside my head and learning and repeating the words constantly until I remembered them as if by second nature. My 'security', it seems, was total.

I anticipated that before my release I would be minutely searched and everything in my possession removed from me – particularly my shorthand diaries and the thirteen short stories I wrote secretly throughout the burning hot summer of 1968 to help me survive the emptiness and desolation. I was ready to lose them all, yet resolved to preserve at least some crafted fragments of my reflective thoughts, some typical mementoes of that often unreal-seeming experience and what it had induced in me. And this was the first and chief one of those four mementoes.

So this account, I feel, would not be complete without them and the other three pieces are entitled respectively *What Is The Universe In?, No Story and The Play*. They will follow as further *Reflections* interleaved after the following diary entries along with a yearning, sentimental poem I wrote in that same period entitled *Snow in England*. The four 'invisible' pieces appeared first in print as introductory passages to some of my short stories when seven of them were published in a slim volume in 1971 under the title *A Man Alone*.

9
THE OLD MAN AND THE LEAVES

Saturday 1 June 1968, 9.45 am

30-day Plan for June

1   Write to Mum.
2   Ask for radio.
3   Write at least two short stories.
4   Compile 30 small crosswords.
5   Immense iron self-control to keep up morale.
6   There is a feeling of importance in the air, I think.

So June begins. I have just finished my exercises, in which I now work up quite a sweat. Summer is really on now after a fairly cool May. Yesterday I received two letters from Shirley and one from Mum. Shirley said she had a 'faith delivery date' of before the beginning of next term. This added to my optimistic impression of improving prospects of release. If only there will be no trouble in Hong Kong and things go well, perhaps in the autumn there will be some chance.

John and Sally have said they hope to get leave in November – another pointer. The getting of the Edgar Snow book I saw as an omen. I am reading it every night now, having just finished Dorothy Sayers' book of short stories. Yesterday I broke the record for compiling large crosswords, with a time of 1 hour 48 minutes.

The Snow book has helped me to think of the Chinese in a more rational light and encouraged me to think they won't really want this to go on longer than it has to. I can't think that June in itself will bring anything concrete, but once it is past I shall have 11 months under my belt.

The letters delivered to me yesterday could have been held a week. If tomorrow there are more, I will be almost certain that they are being held for a week in the other room. The one from East Berlin I have written off. I think they have decided to cut out all my mail from other than Mum and Shirley.

My mood is fairly calm today. It falls with the arrival of letters, I find. The day before yesterday I had dropped to my knees by the bath and prayed with great emotion, but on getting the letters my attention is taken up and I feel happier. Then as the time wears on and no more come, I become more 'unstable' as it were until the next arrival. But overall I am supporting myself with the hope of something in the autumn again, or even before.

Tuesday 4 June 1968, 7.30 pm

I am sitting sweating like a pig in a temperature of 84 degrees with all the windows closed. Today I asked very politely if I could have the window left open in the afternoon. (It is very difficult not to smash something at the moment, since the mind-crushing whine of the 'Deep Brown Vest' team leader is going on and on next-door, reading items from today's paper.)

With absolutely undiluted vindictiveness, this request has been ignored. With nothing to be gained by it, with nobody knowing about it, with no possible reason, the request is refused and I am subjected to extreme discomfort purely for the sake of it – absolutely clear vicious vindictiveness!

If ever I get out of this, I shall make absolutely sure to have this completely incredible viciousness made known. The sweat ran off my face at dinner tonight. During the day the temperature outside was 86 and my shirt under the arms and at the back became covered in sweat. The backs of the trousers are streaked with two big black marks where my arms sweated during the walks. The heat has suddenly come with the beginning of June.

There is to be now three months of this before cooler weather. But I am determined to last it out. These bastards shall not have the last laugh!

Thursday 6 June 1968, 14.00 hours

Today it is very hot again and I couldn't eat all my lunch. The hot weather seems to have started earlier this year. Yesterday the temperature rocketed to 98 degrees in the yard in the afternoon and an incredibly hot wind blew as if from a blast furnace. Yesterday was a good day. No less than four letters from Shirley and one replying to my letter of 16 May, which arrived on the 20 May.

Shirley is such an angel really. She is so loving and faithful. I spent almost the whole day reading the letters and the enclosures from newspapers, etc. It really made a wonderful day. Four whole letters! Just before dinner Sao Kao came up to announce that the window (which Lao Chiao had closed at 4 pm for the second day running, after my request to have it opened) would be opened, but the screen would be nailed up. I said this wasn't good because I wanted to breathe. He talked to the police, but said they would have to ask the Foreign Ministry. So it was left at that with just one nail in to keep the screens closed.

It helps a lot, of course, but I miss the breeze. The exercises in the morning are now tremendously sweaty affairs. The guards wander about stripped to their vests all the time and some play dominoes, I think. Yesterday's window incident followed what I thought was a deterioration in the situation, since I waited for 45 minutes before being allowed out in the afternoon. I thought I was being penalised for asking to have the window open.

Shirley seems convinced that the autumn will see my release and this makes me believe that my guess for the same time must have something in it. (Shirley's enclosing of a Psalm of David echoed many of the things I had also said in my prayers.)

Saturday 8 June 1968, 13.45 hours

Two days ago I asked for the 12-inch square window above the nailed up one to be opened by Lao Chiao. It is sealed only with paper and I could have opened it myself. He said, 'After lunch.'

When by late afternoon he hadn't done it and I asked him again, he said the guards were telephoning the Foreign Ministry. Since then nothing!

The days seem cooler now after the terrible 98 degrees a few days ago. Every morning now since the hot spell began I can sleep no longer than seven o'clock. The open window also brings in the noise outside, and the filthy hawking and spitting of the guards in the morning make it impossible to carry on.

This morning a piercing bloody bird woke me tweeting in the tree outside! Last night I had lychees for the first time. Today and during the night I have had more tummy pains and took two tablets this morning after breakfast to try to clear it up.

I have eaten almost no lunch for three days. Each night I intently read Edgar Snow's book. I am also writing another short story called 'Indecent Exposé'. I would very much like some encouragement, as I am now within 27 days of my thirtieth birthday. The two quotation boards are still unchanged since 25 March or so.

At the moment the sun is shining outside (it is now 5.30 pm) and the whole vista in the courtyard looks unusually white. Black night, last night. A tremendous storm with wind blew up and it thundered and lightning flashed, but it couldn't seem to rain. Finally it rained and began to grow a little brighter. When I had my walk just now, I found the air was at last cool.

The sky is now in fact incredibly blue with fleecy white clouds. This seems somehow symbolic to me of delivery from the darkness of fear into the light. During my walk I saw into the kitchen in the basement beneath my room, for the first time ever, because the lights were on down there, and I could see pictures of Mao on the walls with red posters. I could see no signs of daubed slogans. On the roof two basket chairs were leaning against the parapet.

These two things helped my train of thought, since earlier today I fancied I perceived a change in the rhythm of my life, possibly a span of weeks away. I believe that, in these tremendously isolated circumstances, such perceptions may be possible. They come in peculiar little fleeting, almost unrecognisable flashes of feeling that perhaps soon there will be things possible other than the narrow compass of each day's activities. Anyway, I prayed just that my 'fancied perception' would be true.

Sao Kao just wandered in with cigarette in cigarette holder to ask for money for medicine, and to give me the paper. He never says thank you.

Tuesday 11 June 1968, 5.45 pm

As I came in from my walk just now I saw on the dining table in the guards' room a pile of at least three letters topped by a green postcard. Looked like today's delivery. Yesterday a plain envelope came with a reminder about rent. Then this morning there was a rather touching thing.

I had left the photograph of Shirley, Mum and Grandma on the desk. As Lao Chiao cleaned the bathroom he suddenly stopped and came through and pointed to it and said something about, 'Is that your wife?' or 'Who is that?'

I said it was my 'wife' and her mother.

He looked again very hard and said, 'Good, eh?'

I said, 'Very lovely.'

At breakfast he came in with the tray and took it up again. 'Your wife house London?'

'Yes.' Then I showed the photograph again and said, 'That woman was mother's mother.'

'Oh. How old wife – 30?'

'Yes.'

'Then this one 70?'

'Yes, more perhaps, maybe 75.'

'Oh,' concluded Lao Chiao, nodding.

All this set me grinning, for it was the first such conversational exchange of any kind here for perhaps almost a year. Bless Lao Chiao!

Friday 14 June 1968, 5.30 pm

This afternoon the shambling guard carried in the papers while I was outside, strangely, and it looked as if there was more than one letter inside. It is now nine days since I was 'granted' a letter. There is little else to report, except I have been taking increasing notice of the dates in the past few days – working out how long to the eleventh month, how long to my birthday, how long to the one year mark etc. each day.

I keep telling myself that now it will be possible to hope for something after the year is up – and I hope and pray the autumn will bring something for me. Today I conceived the idea for a new 'spoof' story that would end up with the characters talking about the writing of the story.

Yesterday and the day before, I conceived the story of 'The Old Man and the Leaves', but haven't written it yet. As I write the sun shines peacefully on the wall outside. The streets have been quiet for days since the pro-French demonstrations.

Sunday 16 June 1968, 3.30 pm

Yesterday two letters and a big card from Shirley. Posted end of May. Therefore 16-day time lag. Ten days since the last delivery from the room next door on the 5 June. The bastards! Bathed today in a hurry after oversleeping a little. Not as much as three days ago, when I managed to doze until about 10 am. But normally I am awake very early these days.

The window is open, therefore I get all the noise of the guards spitting, hawking and throwing out water and the street noises. Wakes me about 6.30 am or 7 am. I am praying fervently for the time to pass. At lunch time today there was a lot of running back and forth to the gate and telephoning by the guards. I began to think someone had tried to hand something in.

Two nights ago I began reading the thriller novel *Midnight Plus One* by Gavin Lyall. I am now also in the middle of writing the story called 'The Old Man and the Leaves'. I love my Shirley very much and long to be with her, loving her.

Thursday 20 June 1968, 7.30 pm

Today was sock-washing day – another week gone. Now on the verge of eleventh-month anniversary. I desperately want some encouragement and sign of hope for release. Two letters and a card from Shirley came on the 18 June and one began, 'I hope now it will be very soon that we are together.' It was probably just wishful, but it helps, that kind of thing. I am furious this afternoon about the ridiculous way my mum's letter is being held up. Tomorrow it will be 18 days since I handed it over to these swines to look at. How bloody-minded that they should hold up my dear mum's desperately awaited letter!

Outside in the courtyard the tree, strangely enough, has been shedding its leaves for the past few days. It doesn't look healthy, or it is having an early autumn ahead of the other trees. The temperature is still reasonable, although I sweat fairly continuously. The room temperature is constant day and night around 80 degrees. The outside temperatures generally speaking haven't been much above 82 or 86 degrees.

The letter, which I saw brought in with a bill for the papers on Monday last week, 10 June, hasn't been given to me. It seems the guards are still playing a very funny game with my mail. On the 18 June there was a 'recorded' delivery, I think the bank statement, but that also hasn't been handed to me. Given the fact that since the visit by Hopson and John, I've had no mail except those early ones from Emerita, so it is a bloody retrograde kind of activity!

It is now 18 days without my mum's letter going off; the windows in my room are nailed up; other people are cut off from writing, delays of my mail continue to be in the next room. Bastards!

Last night I finished the very good Gavin Lyall thriller *Midnight plus One* and enjoyed it very much. I'm not writing any short stories at the moment, having just finished 'The Old Man and the Leaves'. I am still reading Snow's excellent book.

My trousers have come back, looking excellent, from the cleaners. I am wearing my grey ones at present and getting used to them for a week or so. I am still trying to beat this stomach trouble. Yesterday and today I complained to Lao Chiao about the cloudy water I have to drink. I have not eaten any fresh vegetables for two days. But still my stomach is bad. My throat and chest are a little better, but these worry me too. I long for a sign of something happening.

June has been a pointless month so far. During the past few days, I have been watching the dates very closely. Anxious to get to 21 June to start climbing to the one-year anniversary. I do hope and pray something good will come soon. Will it be in September or October, like I have long thought? With the parallel with Wilbraham? Oh how I hope something will come! It is so desolate and never-endingly boring at present. I do so much need some help.

Arthur Wilbraham was a young Englishman, like me, in his late twenties, who had been arrested and imprisoned in East Berlin on charges of helping some East Germans escape to the West. I had covered his trial alone in East Germany because other Western correspondents were not accredited in East Berlin and were therefore not allowed to attend. I had interviewed Wilbraham exclusively in the courtroom after his sentence – so remembered the plight of this evidently decent young Englishmen very vividly. Exactly what 'parallel' I was thinking of during my own captivity now escapes me. Perhaps he was eventually released in these same autumn months and perhaps there were undertones of some behind-the-scenes negotiated deal, linking his freedom with the freedom of other prisoners with communist connections in West German prisons.

Friday 21 June 1968, 5.45 pm

Today it is 11 months. As I walked in the courtyard this morning I was very angry about my letter to Mum still not having come back from the Foreign Ministry. I was desperate for some encouragement and prayed very ferociously. After the walk, Mum's letter was handed back to me with a letter and card from Shirley. Lao Chiao sent it off.

This afternoon when Lao Chiao came for food money, I asked him if he had been to the hospital and he said, 'Yes.'

When I asked whether it was a holiday, he said, 'No.'

So I said, 'I suggest you have holiday', and after bit he said, 'No holiday, too much work.'

I had asked him if 'they' had said 'no holiday' and he just grinned. This afternoon Lao Chiao brought me 60 cents' rebate on the bill, which had come with the papers.

I draw no conclusion from these two events since every time I have done this in the past, nothing has happened The return of my letter made me feel a little better today. I love my Shirley very much. After today I can start on the twelfth month to the year anniversary.

Saturday 22 June 1968, 5.30 pm

It seems quite incredible perhaps, but while walking just now in the yard it occurred to me for the first time that the events of 18 August were a trial. I don't know why I have never thought of it before. When Hopson asked me if I had been accused of anything, I said, 'No', without hesitation. But I suppose then I was accused of being a reactionary. As I walked in the yard, the bell rang and the electricity man came in to read the meter. I felt some embarrassment at being watched by a stranger. The guards, etc. are all familiar. It was an uncomfortable experience and made me freshly aware of my humiliation and complete lack of dignity. So now we are inside the twelfth month. I hope I am near the end of this ordeal.

Monday 24 June 1968, 5.30 pm

Today temperature in the room is 86 degrees and outside 89 degrees (Fahrenheit). I think the big hot summer began yesterday. During the night I received two bites – one on the ankle and one on the thigh. It is bloody hot. I sit and sweat while completely still. I drank four bottles of water yesterday. My stomach became bad again today. It seems to have gone on now for about five weeks. I keep putting off having a doctor, but perhaps I should.

Wednesday 26 June 1968, 15.00 hours

Today it is 87 degrees inside, but yesterday it was 89 inside and 91 outside.

Yesterday I sweated right through my shirt and was very uncomfortable. Today only two degrees less and I am quite comfortable, I think because there is a breeze. Yesterday I broke all the rules and read an entire book, *The Deadly Affair* by John le Carré, starting about 3.30 pm and finishing about 9.30 pm. Fascinating and brilliantly written book. A thoroughly enjoyable day, otherwise there is nothing to say. Two days ago I asked for the gauze door to be closed and it has been closed ever since. It is just the hot middle of the summer without the hope of early release time. My feelings are under control and I live for release.

My thoughts are more sexual than usual and I had a very sexy dream last night – very strange. In it 'A' offered me his wife and she came willingly but I, having accepted, finally refused. I suppose I am fairly tortured in this respect and the dream reflected it I expect. I have just caught sight of another damned letter (at 5.30 pm)! As I walked I saw a letter with Chinese stamps on stuck in the letterbox with the papers. The 'Pervert Jaw' guard was very sneaky in hiding it and bringing it in. All other letters I have seen in this manner (two!) have disappeared without trace. It will be a change if it doesn't do so this time. The temperature was at 89 outside (inside is 87).

Friday 28 June 1968, 17.30 hours

Today is a nothing day. I have started a temperature graph. Today is 83 outside and inside and rising again after a spectacular fall yesterday with the rain. Last night a great cricket came into the room. I called the attention of the guards to it, picked it up in a towel and motioned for them or for me to put it outside the door, two steps away. But the imbecile answer was, 'No.' I let it fly out, but it didn't go near the guard. I then covered it up and put it out of the bathroom window. The two guards came in and I again got the horrible feeling I get when they come near me.

A letter yesterday from Shirley said a small voice told her it wouldn't be too long now. I got a new supply of razor blades today, Sally's Christmas present having completely run out. Yesterday's letter also said Bible and other books had been sent. I notice that most days the bell is rung now with the papers. Yesterday with the mail came the bank statement delivered on 18 June. This was clear proof of a nine-day holding by the guards. Shirley's letter had been held six days. I am praying very hard not to hit these people! My stomach is half and half at the moment. Still getting no fresh vegetables from the cook.

Sunday 30 June 1968, 1 pm

Bath this morning and sweated for about two hours afterwards, right through the back of my shirt. Today the humidity is increasing. The air is heavy and smelly and hot. And one feels as if one could bite it. A few days ago I asked for a fly spray because of gnats (mosquitoes) at night in the room. But I wasn't allowed to have it in the room. Today it is one month since I had a letter from my lovely mum! The funny bastards have again stopped her letters!

Yesterday I noticed, as I came in from my walk, a Peking letter on my table that looked like it was from Emerita, perhaps a birthday card. Doubt that I shall get it. As June ends, I am happy to be getting into the twelfth month and hope that after August things will happen. Who knows what I will do if nothing happens this autumn. Ray Witney (a First Secretary at the British Mission) got an exit visa the other day, according to Shirley. I construe this as slightly good. Yesterday Chou En-Lai's speech for the Tanzanian President made no mention of Britain, which I find encouraging. Today's temperature: 85 degrees inside and outside at mid-day. It will be hotter later.

REFLECTIONS - 9
Thursday 4 January 2007

Snow in England

It is Sunday morning in winter,
Snow has fallen freshly during the night
And now, in the early dawn
The English countryside lies quiet and beautiful
Beneath a coverlet of white.

The birds are hushed in awe;
Black branches bear their bright burden with pride;
No foot's left its print,
No eye roused from sleep yet beheld the joy
Of the cold winter outside.

There is enchantment in snow;
Its very presence thrills the soul, although unseen
And coming on first sight of it
By chance, the heart delights, exalts and cries out
At its beauty pure and keen.

The magic quilt settles soundlessly
Comes, like love, with quiet mystery about the door
And in its silent embrace
The earth, a willing mistress, an enraptured woman
Is more lovely than before.

But now the summer sun burns down
On me, and perhaps on her, for we're far apart,
But when the snows return to England
To embrace her, I too, will return to settle
Once more, quietly in her heart.

June 1968

The rather sentimental poem opposite grew out of a piece of prose I started to write in early April 1968. I was trying with great concentration to set down in simple words an idyllic beginning to a perfect day at home, which I had first created in my mind in the earliest days in the eight-foot-square cell. When reading over the first paragraph I was struck by what I imagined was its lyrical quality, so I wrote out the first paragraph again, line by line, into the opening five lines of a poem. I put it away in my pocket and only took it out again in June to add the shamelessly nostalgic sentiments about my own country where I wished so fervently to be. I also wrote into it the closing prediction to bolster my optimism that by the winter I would be home – and perhaps in an attempt to mentally cool myself as the heat of summer approached and increased!

10
Himself

Monday 1 July 1968, 8 pm

31-day Plan for July

1 Intensively ignore guards and confine yourself to absolutely neutral relations.

2 Re-introduce absolute self-control on yoga lines (calm for July and August).

3 Write three short stories.

3a 31 big crosswords.

4 Write to Shirley.

5 Remain tremendously determined to succeed.

6 This will be a hot, tough month but it will be crushed by your will!

Today three small happenings: first, after my morning walk, a bottle of cold water stood by the thermos flask, put there quite voluntarily by Sao Kao. I had drunk most of it before lunch with pleasure. When he came to collect the tea things he brought – again without asking – a small bowl of ice with a spoon. This afternoon I asked him about the house insurance. He finally said he couldn't understand and I wrote it out and it was taken to headquarters.

Temperature outside 88 degrees, inside 86 degrees, a not unpleasantly hot day. I completed a good crossword, first of the big ones, and re-read a bit of *The Flying Fox*, a novel set in Malaysia.

Wednesday 3 July 1968, 08.30 hours

Today the temperature inside was 89 degrees and outside perhaps over 93 degrees, but the guards messed about with the wall thermometer. I went upstairs to get some summer shirts, found only one and had to cut the sleeves out of a white one and sew it up (badly). Yesterday I had a haircut, very short, and washed it.

Also, in the afternoon a cable arrived from Mum; a birthday cable; delivered the same day only 8 hours or so late. I saw new things put with other mail. Today I brought the vacuum flask into the battle, using it for cold water instead of useless hot water. Last night I started DH Lawrence's book *The White Peacock*, having finished Edgar Snow's *The Other Side of the River* the night before. An excellent book. Strangely the temperatures of the past two days haven't left me so hot and bothered as the same ones three days ago, when I sweated right through my shirt. I suppose it is less humid at present.

Today the bill for the rent came and it made me realise that for the next three months there is little hope again. How long time is! But I am managing not to be depressed. The rent thing isn't final, I told myself. There is possibility of change, perhaps in September.

Thursday 4 July 1968, 7.45 pm

Today the temperature dropped back to 88 inside and out. Lao Chiao announced to me that he and Amah would begin two weeks' holiday tomorrow. On Monday I checked up with Sao Kao about the house insurance. This afternoon I washed socks and handkerchiefs – the weeks seem to fly between these little jobs! This morning a letter and card from Shirley told me she was going on holiday. No letter from Mum again. But I did get a cable from her yesterday. I realise that I have just about finished being 29. On the eve of my 30th birthday I don't want to be 30 and I have also felt a little depressed today and yesterday – but only a little. The bloody rent bill did it. It still seems a hell of a long time before September and even then nothing may happen. I told Lao Chiao it was my birthday at lunch time, but it made no impact on him.

Friday 5 July 1968 – my birthday

(This is in fact being written on 6 July at 5.15 pm.)

My thirtieth birthday was uneventful. I completed the creation of a record big crossword in 57 minutes and spent the entire day writing a letter to Shirley and Mum. I handed it over this afternoon, after much worry about a passage in it about how bitter I was about no help from London.

On my birthday I put on my tennis shirt and clean white trousers, and this made me feel good in the morning. I woke later than intended, since I was kept awake long into the night by the bad little guard spitting outside my window (NB guards walk up and down in darkness outside window in summer during night, their feet making soft regular noises directly outside the open window), a treacherous noise which almost brought me to the verge of losing control, but I just managed to control it. (I lifted my foot as I lay in bed to bang it down and make a noise, but resisted it eventually.)

Nevertheless I exercised and bathed, standing up in cold water. Breakfast was routine with lemon juice, three pieces of toast, scrambled egg, coffee and a peach. Afterwards I walked for 40 minutes. My companions staring at me at each end of the courtyard were 'Pervert Jaw', 'Little Chou En-lai' and 'Shambler'.

Before lunch I completed the design of a puzzle in an incredible 32 minutes. With lunch – minced pork, cabbage and rice with a misshapen peach that was too hard to eat, ice and water – I read some of *The White Peacock*, which I am enjoying very much.

After lunch I completed the clues to the puzzle in 25 minutes to make an incredible new record, beating the small record too. After this I pulled the table out and began a letter to Shirley. I got out all the letters I have received, after writing a couple of pages, and began looking through them. Sao Kao brought tea and made great point of arranging the cups and things on the tray after setting them down. He gave me no sign of knowing that it was my birthday.

After dinner of very tender beef and potatoes and a peach and soup (during dinner I did *The Observer* crossword, not quite completing it), I continued writing the letter. I walked only for a half hour, because I was so busy at it. The storm broke as I wrote and purple white lightning flashed and it slashed down with rain for one of the first times this year.

For the last half hour or so before bed I read Lawrence again. I said several special prayers during the day for better things now I am 30. Today (6 July) I pored over the letter morning and afternoon, and eventually decided it was more or less OK, after changing 'anxious and black despair' to 'things like that'. Now I must start my crossword puzzle for the day, very late.

I think it is possible some letters came today. Clearly the Peking ones I saw nine days or so ago haven't been given. Yesterday I also cleared out my desk. What pathetic reading this makes!

As I look round the room now I see a line of books on the window sill, a peach on a plate served up for the evening, two sleeves cut from a white shirt; several cards from Shirley provide some colour; Edgar Snow's book

The Other Side of the River on the bedside table; two blankets piled on the bed, because there is nowhere else for them (NB at night I put them on the table before getting into bed), clothes in a heap beside them, a fly swat, a pair of shorts used for exercises; on the table before me a dictionary, *Whitakers' Almanack*, *The White Peacock*, a pen box, a notebook for new words, a bottle of cold water just brought in by Sao Kao, a glass, a small serviette and two copies of *Peking Review* (a week old) which I am leaning on; in the corner a pile of *Peking Review* on a box containing letters and magazines and papers.

The walls are still covered with the same slogans 'Down with British imperialism' and also 'down with me'. Three feet from my elbow on the wall is a colour picture of Mao. The quotation in Chinese that was put up some time ago is again from the wall above my head. The temperature is just 83 degrees. A small square mat lies beside the bed. Otherwise the red wooden floor is bare.

Five feet away on two chairs at eye level are two quotations from Mao which have been there now for over three months (25 March, I think they were last changed). One begins, 'If anyone attacks us and if the conditions are favourable for battle, we will certainly act in self-defence to wipe him out resolutely, thoroughly, whole and completely ...'. The other is the first in the *Little Red Book* about 'The force at the core ...'. Marxism is spelled wrongly. The thermos flask of hot water is on the windowsill; a dead telephone is at the other end, beside a pile of dead papers. The chair in the corner has a cloth over the back.

The sun shines very beautifully outside, the temperature is low, at 75 degrees, and the leaves of the tree look very tired and droopy, as if it was already autumn. On the back of the door hang my maroon dressing gown and my leather jacket. This is my world on or about my thirtieth birthday. I wonder for how much longer.

I shudder a little at the start of 2007, as I read the insulting names I gave my guards. Perhaps there is some slight mitigation in the fact that I chose names that at least might amuse me each time I identified them silently to myself. 'Pervert Jaw' a particularly unkind nickname that raises an inward chuckle from me even now, was in fact given to a decent enough Public Security Bureau man who did not, as far as I remember, ever go out of his way to be especially unpleasant to me. He was quite small and quick moving, yet did have a very pronounced, long, square jaw-line, which made him instantly identifiable at a distance. I think I did also consider calling him 'Peking Man' – after the famous big-jawed Stone-Age skeleton discovered near Peking – but it was not as insultingly funny as 'Pervert Jaw'. 'Little Caesar' was highly officious and made fast hand gestures on giving me orders. 'Shambler' was so named, obviously, because of his ungraceful gait and 'Little Chou En-lai' kept his uniform neat and tidy and had a hint of the quiet spruce charm of China's urbane prime minister.

Wednesday 10 July 1968, 5.20 pm

There is nothing tangible to say. I noticed about five days ago that the guards had stopped taking meals here in the house. (NB They had previously brought in mess tins from headquarters.) I draw no conclusion. Today the temperature is 92 degrees outside and 88 inside – the same as yesterday roughly. I have two tremendous cold sores on my bottom lip, which at present itch like fury. The days are hot as hell, but I can still stand them well enough at these temperatures. The worst is still to come, I suspect in the next month.

Tonight I shall finish *The White Peacock* by D.H. Lawrence. I am finding it difficult to start on a short story this month, but thought of an idea yesterday – my old one about the body as a factory or business concern and the characters are all individual brain and other living cells.

Days are long and without incident. Tomorrow it will be a week since I had a letter. The six-days' interval thing (between giving me my letters) has obviously been changed, since the item that was signed for by Lao Chiao on the 4 July – I think it might have been the car licence – hasn't reached me. I have been really somewhat depressed this morning. The end still seems impossible. Please make it soon.

When completed and entitled 'Himself', this short story, set inside one human body, would several years later appear in Playboy Magazine and also become a BBC Saturday Afternoon Theatre radio play.

Saturday 13 July 1968, 13.00 hours

Today I received six pieces of mail: two letters from Shirley, two birthday cards – one from Shirley, one from Mum – plus a card from Shirley and the car licence bill. This was a relief after nine days without a letter. It told me Mum was going back to Norwich from Scotland for a holiday with her new friend Geoffrey (a 'permanent' relationship it seems, says Shirley). There were pictures of Shirley and another, slightly fat and well-looking one of Mum.

During the night there was heavy rain, which brought the temperature down a bit. Then this morning the first flower had bloomed in the yard. It blazed red and caught my eye through the window as I came out of the bathroom. The leaf that has been shading the bud for several days, now seems to be very frantic to get out of the way of its beauty, so proud is it of its charge.

Also after the night's rain, the most amazing thing seems to have happened to the tree. Small new green leaves have sprung out on the branches among the old brown ones. The tree has found a new lease of life. I try to see that as rekindled hope for myself.

Otherwise my mood is low key. It has been for some days now. Perhaps it is the weather, which is really quite humid today after the long rain. How I need some sign of hope. I wonder if this is to go on for a long time yet. This is the most terrible ordeal and the most awful life.

Addendum: I have just eaten a small roasted chicken brought up for supper by surprise by Sao Kao from the kitchen (at 7.10 pm) and almost the first thing I came across was the wishbone. I thought this was a good omen and worth recording. I have preserved the bone and wish for release soon.

Wednesday 17 July 1968, 11.20 am

Last night about 9.45 pm, as I walked my regular evening inside walk back and forth towards the door facing the 'guardroom', the team of guard 'Number 28' (the number on his red basketball vest) were playing chequers. They were lying across my dining room table looking disgusting in their vests, belching and laughing like bloody oafs!

Yesterday it was raining heavily in the morning and I almost didn't get my walk outside. But about 12.30 pm 'The Idiot' suddenly motioned me out, to my surprise, holding open the door and smiling. He was almost alone in the house and was unsure of himself about the rain not having quite stopped, I think.

The temperature is now 81 degrees and has been lower these past few days. Humidity has risen. There is little to say. Yesterday I was misled into thinking something was happening. The 'Pervert Jaw' leader came back with the day shift, after being on all night, and I thought this was significant. Lunch was served 30 minutes later – quite unprecedented.

But after much excitement and a small 'emergency' prayer as I sat here, it turned out he was only deputising for the little 'Fat Guy' who went off at lunch time, probably ill. I try not to lose hope and I try to endure this bloody awful ordeal. I am reading *A History of the Canadian People*.

Friday 19 July 1968, 7.15 pm

Today I received three letters from Shirley. In one of them she told of a visit to a fortune-teller. The woman had told Shirley she knew I was in difficulties and they would begin to resolve themselves in September and be completely cleared up in October.

I believe this could be the sign of hope for which I have been asking so fervently in my prayers these last few weeks. And Shirley said another woman had said exactly the same thing. This also fits in with my dream of last year, with the 'Wilbraham Theory' and with the logical reasoning of the situation.

So perhaps there really will be some good action in the September/

October period. The letters also tell me that Shirley went off on holiday on 3 July. I expect she is finished by now, or nearly so. Temperatures were 80 degrees outside and 83 inside. There has been no rain for two days. It seems a strange period, with less than maximum heat. I expect the real burn later this month or in August. Last night I finished my story about living cells. Tonight I am going to correct it.

Tuesday 23 July 1968, 3.00 pm

The one-year anniversary has come and gone without incident. It has become very warm now. Today I think is the worst so far. Lumps of distemper and plaster fall from the ceiling and walls, the cracks in the door (through which I could watch what was happening in the next room when I wanted) have closed up with the swelling of the door. The temperatures are well below those of the early part of the month, but today I sweated right through my shirt while drawing up a crossword table at breakfast. The walk outside was hardly any cooler.

Yesterday it rained during the night and since then it has been really humid. In the bathroom the pipes are dripping with water and great yellow marks have appeared in the sink and bath. Something in the water, I know not what. Meetings have begun again by the guards, about one big one a week. Today there was one. Also they have begun eating here again, although only one at lunch time seems to eat here.

Lao Chiao came back from his holiday yesterday. I was glad to see him, because even though largely silent, he is non-hostile. On 21 July I conceived a new idea for a story about an actor, planned it that day, wrote most of it yesterday and will finish today, I hope. I believe it is a good story. I thought up a new ending for it last night. It has prompted me to finish the crosswords early, both yesterday and today, to write it during the afternoon instead of only in the evening.

Today's temperature in here is 84 degrees and about the same outside. I wonder if it is going to be as bad as last year in a few days' time. I still think of the letter from Shirley as containing a good prediction about September and October.

This week's *Peking Review* on Sunday had a colour picture of Mao as a young man striding over the hills. I have eaten so many peaches recently; I have become almost tired of them. I am still reading *A History of the Canadian People*. I noticed yesterday and today that a curtain in the guard's room is daubed with a huge black slogan saying 'Down with A. Grey!' I believe the curtain is one that was moved from the end window, nearly out of sight to me. The material is good and heavy and has been clearly laundered. That is all for now!

Wednesday 24 July 1968, 12.30 pm

It can now safely be said that the long-awaited Big Heat is on! Yesterday was a day of clammy sweating all the time. At present I am sitting with my shirt soaked right through, having just come in from my morning walk. The temperature has shot up (86 in here already) after a week of steady level in the lower 80s. As I write this, my wrist and hand are making wet marks further down the page and sweat is standing out on my fingers and face.

This morning a letter and card arrived from Shirley on holiday. Interesting thing was that it was postmarked as arriving yesterday at the house. So that is the first time such an early delivery has been made for a long time.

This is a period I have been dreading and waiting to get to grips with. Perhaps three or four weeks will see it over. It is bloody hot and unpleasant.

(Same day, 5 o'clock.)

This is a repeat of those days last year with sweat dripping from me on to the desk. It is running off my face. The sweat soaked the papers as I tried to write today (checking on the story I have been writing called 'Fog and Orange Gloves'). My shirt was soaked through from early on. This is truly the beginning – earlier than last year – of the big heat.

Saturday 27 July 1968, 12.30 pm

What a life! The temperature in here at present is 85 degrees; outside the skies are grey and heavy; the humidity is average today. My 'barometer' is the cistern in the toilet. If the water drips a lot from it in condensation, then I know it is humid. Both 24 and 25 July were terribly humid – up to the standard of last year's 'dripping at the desk' days. I am faintly depressed. Today I am 'provisionally' writing off my letter no. 3, written on 6 July to Shirley. It is now 21 days since I sent it to the Foreign Ministry. Last night I didn't sleep too well.

Recently the new problem of the guard sitting outside on the doorstep has arisen. This means that it is in fact worse than when they sat outside the door inside the house, since the open window affords no sound barrier at all. I hear every creak of the chair, every grunt and spit. And last night the little fat bastard played very funny with the courtyard light. Turned it off a little after I turned my light off, but turned it on again to look in at me in very offensive manner – little shit! He had it on and off four times after that. Perhaps this was the reason for the bad night.

The heat alone is bearable. It is the extra noise that is difficult. Last night I began reading a new book, *God has a Long Face*. Yesterday I began rewriting my first month's diary into shorthand in another book. I shall feel happier when this is done. I have completed 16 pages out of 50 so far. The past four days there have been crowds going by, shouting and banging drums and cymbals. I have found that, even now, I am still anxious in case they are coming here.

I thought I heard 'Down with Reuters once, but there has been nothing in the papers to confirm. Sao Kao refused to say anything when I asked him. Small rash appeared on my stomach and on the crack of my right arm, but so far hasn't developed. I am praying very hard for strength to beat this terrible weather.

Monday 29 July 1968

Yesterday I had two splendid letters from Mum. One had been going more than a month, since no stamp was put on it and it came by surface mail; she told me she had left Scotland and was going home with Geoffrey. I was very pleased to hear she was happy with him.

I also had a letter from Shirley on holiday and a card and some crosswords from her Mum. Suddenly yesterday it became strangely cooler with the temperature dropping down to 79 in the afternoon – the lowest for over a month. The humidity has fallen off, too, almost completely. This is a tremendous respite for me. I am very glad. But I think perhaps it is only a respite before a bigger heat wave of the summer in early August. But at least it gives me a chance to prepare for the final effort. The letters and the cooler weather have given me new heart. I feel sure things are going well and there will be something before too much longer.

REFLECTIONS - 10

Saturday 6 January 2007

What is the Universe in?

Left alone for an eternal long time, the mind of the man begins to conceive
the very strangeness of reality.
Wage packets and mortgages, tube trains and buses, jobs and homes,
families and wives and friends and enemies … all are as nothing.

Left alone for a long time, the most overpowering question for the man is:
What is the Universe IN?
When looking at the blank wall of the six-sided cube for a long time,
And after a lot of thought,
The man is often on the brink of the answer.
He feels that suddenly he is about to become aware of total reality.
It's on the tip of his tongue.
Total understanding is at his elbow.
Sometimes it moves even closer.
But close as the final explanation comes
Closer than it ever came before
Or was ever after to come,
It eludes the firmness of his grasp.
Nevertheless the hint remains.
The Universe is in something.
All life must be relative.
The bacilli in a gathering wound,
The ant hill,
The teeming capital city

Are all of a relation,
Are of a progression.

One day far ahead when man is woman too in one body,
He will walk to the top of a hill in the dawn, thoroughly complete.
And everything a million years old will explode in a shower of light.
Perhaps some unimaginably gargantuan figure inside which our Universe
resides unseen
Will say to his equally gargantuan wife:
'Ouch! That pain in my toe of the past few days got much worse just then.
But now it seems to have disappeared completely!'
Oppressed by such thoughts the man of terrifying smallness and insignificance
Dreams his wide-awake dreams
It seems in total isolation that his dreams are the one thing that give him
stature.

This obscure metaphysical musing declared itself in almost precisely these
words some time in the Spring of 1968. If such things are possible, it insisted on
forumulating itself in my mind and being remembered in this form, for reasons
perhaps best known to itself.

11

THE 'SCALES' WILL TILT IN MY DIRECTION

Thursday 1 August 1968, 8.30 pm

The 31-day Plan for August

1 Let this be a creative month!

2 Continue to intensively ignore the guards. (Last month: well done!)

3 Be sure of your eventual success; this month will see the defeat of the weather by your will.

4 Write short letter to Shirley.

5 Write three, if possible, short stories.

6 Remain absolutely calm.

7 Compile 31 more crosswords.

As I begin this month my mood is fairly constant. The weather for the past five days or so has been kind. It is getting hotter, but the humidity has disappeared. Perhaps it will return now. My sleeping has become a little ragged. Today I was awoken at about 6.30 am by the radio noise in the next room and the guards making a racket; plus the noise of the Red Guards in the streets. Then I dozed until after ten.

The past three days or so I have been up writing this diary – copying and scraping out the original handwritten stuff. An extreme bore. For the past six days I have been reading *God has a Long Face* by Robert Wilder. Not bad, but not good. I have 'written off' my letter to Shirley. It has clearly not met the approval of the Chinese authorities. I shall write only a short one this month to save wasted effort. August seems a long grind to go, but it is the encouragement that it will see the end of the really hot weather and take me close to what I believe is hope for me.

The last two nights I have eaten grapes as I read late at night. Grapes and peaches are in season at present. My appetite is surprisingly good and has been all through this hot weather. Letters from Mum on 28 July were a very welcome surprise. July otherwise was not eventful apart from my birthday and my one year anniversary on the twenty-first. I don't expect anything from August. I must, I suppose, learn to expect nothing from the days ahead unless I make myself too hopeful. Life really is terribly empty!

Sunday 4 August 1968, 21.00 hours

It is nine o'clock and 85 degrees hot. I am sitting. Outside the guard chief has just this minute finished watering the yard. The red and yellow flowers stand visible in the moonlight. It is Sunday night. Today I handed over my fourth letter to the guards. It was three-and-a-half pages long. Short, compared with the ten-page efforts of the first three. The July one didn't come back from the Ministry.

Yesterday I began to worry about it a bit. Why has it been stopped, and what are they likely to do about it? Today I finished my 'security check' by going through all my books and papers to see if the guards might object to anything if they searched me thoroughly. This check started with the scraping out of the longhand of last July and August in this diary and copying it into shorthand. This has taken about a week I suppose. Now that it is done I feel that I can get on with writing something this month. But what?

I am not sleeping well again now. Last night I was awakened for a very long time through a din. The funny thing is that for the past week or so I have discovered for the first time that I have a cockerel for a neighbour – one with a wretched little strangled voice. I hear it now, whereas I never did before. Before I seemed to wake in the early part of the night. The main reason at present, I believe, is the noise made by the guards who sit on the porch and I hear every movement and sniff they make. I need help soon. I am so down at heart.

This morning I bathed after doing exercises. This week I have barely had time to do exercises, since I have often finally fallen asleep late in the morning after being awake in the night and not woken properly until after ten. This has meant cutting down on some of the exercises. I try to tell myself the hot days must be near to an end.

The 'Dog Days' should end on 15 August and I remember clearly that last year it wasn't so hot, after one month down here away from the air conditioning in the bedroom. Please speed the end of this hot weather! Strangely enough, I have had a ravenous appetite through all this hot weather and tonight I asked for extra bread. But the humidity hasn't come back really since that bad spell at the end of last month.

Last night I finished reading *God has a Long Face* and finally decided I liked it a lot, after earlier reservations. I also washed my hair. I look not bad really. I am pale but don't feel too bad. The unhealthy spots and rash that appeared during the humid spell have all gone. I have been reading the copies of *The Times* I have recently, and last night I did something which I thought was very good; I finished *The Times* crossword, got it right, and in 64 minutes! This was the first time ever with *The Times* and I regard it as the peak of my crossword-solving career.

It was strange to do something of which one was even a little proud again. It is a week since I had any letters and this makes me wonder whether they have decided to cut these off as a punishment for my transgressions in the last one I wrote. I hope against hope that there will be something in the autumn, in September or October.

The 'Dog Days' associated with the 'dog' star Sirius, are the annual period from roughly mid-July to mid-August, which are regarded as the most 'unwholesome' in the Northern Hemisphere. Then, during a time of heat and humidity, bugs and insects proliferate. This was more noticeable in Peking than anywhere else I had lived until then.

Tuesday 6 August 1968, 5.30 pm

At present the temperature is a splendid 77 degrees in here and 69 outside. It fell further today with more rain, after an initial fall yesterday with wind and rain in the morning. Today I got my raincoat from upstairs, under escort as usual, to walk in quite heavy rain in the morning. There have been no *Peking Reviews* this week and it seems a little unusual. But one must wait and see.

Yesterday I conceived and wrote what I regard as quite a good short story: 'The Crooked Mile', a sports story. Today I am checking it. It was the first story thought out and written in one day. Yesterday I noticed, on going out for my afternoon walk, a small pile of letters on the table. And the top one was an airmail envelope. The day I handed my own in (4 August), I saw it placed with another one with a single stamp on it which could have been a local letter going back to the Foreign Ministry.

Yesterday there was drumming in the street almost all day. This followed more than a week of drumming and demonstrating over I don't know what. There have been no letters for nine days, it has been a long time; I miss them very much.

Things really are unbearable, but my mood is controlled. I am taken up with my writing perhaps. During the night for the first time in many weeks I found myself pulling my sheet over my body. This was because of a temperature of 77 degrees. For many weeks it has been too hot to have a sheet or any clothes on the bare part of the bed. This was quite an event.

Thursday 8 August 1968, 12.30 pm

Yesterday saw the fantastic arrival of ten letters and two cards. It also saw the surprising posting of my letter to Shirley, which I had long ago written off. I couldn't remember afterwards whether it had the part for Mum in it. But it was truly an incredible day. Made more so by the fact that if 11 pieces of mail in the morning weren't enough, another one was handed over, oddly enough, at teatime.

Lao Chiao had just brought in the tea tray when the other, which arrived here apparently on 2 August, was given to me. (The arrival dates on the letters range over 15, 29, 30 July and 2 August.) The contents were very interesting. Mum's told me of her arrival home, a local reporter calling, and more details of a row with June, which had led to her and Geoffrey leaving Scotland.

Shirley's letters were interesting, mainly from the point of view that there were articles on me in the papers for the anniversary of my arrest. She quoted one which said, 'Friends of the sandy-haired reporter described him as very determined – a real bull-dog.' Shirley thought this was making me sound like 'a moronic thug', which made me laugh.

There were lots of lovely ones from her on holiday, lots of enclosures from the leader pages and other places, which I read all day and night. I didn't touch my *History of Poland*, which I started three nights ago. Shirley gave more details about the fortune-tellers: one had said September, with the possibility of the end of August or beginning of October, the other starting September completing in October. I do so hope they will be true.

I had a terrible sleepless night last night, with guards outside in the courtyard with both lights on. I have only just decided not to complain. I never went to sleep once during the night of the first three shifts; I must have dropped off at about five, to be woken up by the sound of the watering of my yard and singing by the bloody moron of the first line over and over again of '*Dong Fang Hung*' (The East is Red). Feel headachy and could do no more than warm-up exercises today. It is still only 78 in here, but I fancy it is becoming humid again. Yesterday's arrival of mail was the most fantastic of the whole time.

Tuesday 13 August 1968, 8.30 pm

This morning I woke so late, I had no time to do my exercises and had to do them at lunch time. It isn't so pleasant then. But it shows how slack I have become. I today completed a small crossword in 43 minutes – 6 minutes outside the record of 37 minutes established a few days ago. Last night I finished writing something entitled 'Hips and Haws', a biographical piece about my very first memory of life – but I am slightly displeased with it. Today I am trying to put it into some shape. While I was finishing it last night, the bloody guards made so much noise cackling and fooling around in the other room that it put me very much on edge.

I wore no pyjama jacket last night, after wearing one for three nights after the drop in temperature. But today it is quite humid again. Lao Chiao made a kind of pancake in which he put meat for lunch and there were some half sour grapes too. It is still a time of no action.

Shirley, in letters received on 10 August said eight exit visas had been granted to British diplomats here. I wasn't sure how to receive this news. It could be that it means that the diplomatic problem has been solved without me, which is bad; also it could mean that the problem is beginning to 'break up' and something good for me might follow. I do fervently hope for some sign in September. I am prepared for nothing this month.

Thursday 15 August 1968, 7.30 pm

Right in the middle of the night I was awakened by a cacophony of drums and cymbals. They came slowly down the street, and got louder and louder in the dead still night until I thought they were in the courtyard itself. I had fallen asleep with the distant sound of them in my ears. Today there have been more, but not a tremendous amount. I have no idea what it is but the sheer incredible situation of it happening in the dead of night infuriated me. I thought to myself that, by the day China gets a 'Noise-Abatement Society' and a Noise Abatement Act, the world will not have many problems left.

Today and yesterday I have been re-reading the last pages of Edgar Snow's book *The Other Side of the River*. It is very good and instructive. I've not written anything for two days. I have also not had mail for five days and I am missing it. The most unpleasant thing of all happened two nights ago. I had torn up my ragged, worn out pyjamas after dinner. Two guards ('Angela' and 'Shambler') came in and looked round as I read. I thought this was strange. Later five of them came in, led by the 'Sneaky One'. He picked up the tiny remains of my pyjama trousers and kept poking them around and asking something.

I got really furious and, after trying to ignore them, I leapt up and said that they were 'finished'. I showed them the torn off bits. My fury towards them didn't please them and as I sat down again all five stood together and stared at me like a Kafkaesque dream: five heads all looking down, one against the other. It upset me for the rest of the night and next day. I wondered whether there would be reprisals, but so far there have been none.

Today Lao Chiao said no shops had shaving soap. This made me depressed unreasonably for a while as I have run out.

Monday 19 August 1968, 9.15 pm

I have nothing to write about really. Yesterday the anniversary of my 'invasion' and solitary confinement passed without incident. I had feared some marking of the anniversary. I keep my shoes on at night as I read, just in case. A short while ago I dropped to my knees beside the bed and let my head fall on the bed in a kind of despair. It takes one like that sometimes. I have said a couple of special prayers today in the bathroom.

Yesterday it rained all day – the longest I have known it rain in China. The temperature dropped to 65 outside and 76 inside – the coolest of the summer. Today it is now 78 degrees in here, which is pleasant. I hope the worst of the hot weather has passed now, but I am not certain of this. I expected the cook back from his holidays today, but he didn't appear.

I haven't written anything for about a week, having felt lazy. I have read *Whitaker's Almanack* instead. I have read the paper and continued creating crosswords. I am enjoying *The Tree of Man* by Patrick White. It is good and has an original, ungrammatical style, which I found irritating at first. There have been no letters for nine days. I was very angry this morning because of this. But what difference does it really make?

I am so hoping that the September–October prediction made known to me through Shirley's fortune-tellers will come true. I don't know how I shall continue to bear this through the autumn and winter if they don't, but I am sure something will happen soon. It must. I have taken my final deadline as 9 November, the day I was moved into this room. But I think October should see some action. I think perhaps after 21 September there will be something; this is because with reading the *Almanack* the other day I came to a piece that said, 'On 21 September the sun moves into Libra.' Although this doesn't mean 'freedom' but 'scales,' the sense of the word is 'freedom' for me. Then the 'scales' will tip in my direction.

Thursday 21 August 1968

This morning, with some relief, I received four letters (one from Mum) after a gap of 12 days. Towards the end of that time, I became very much in need of those letters. One said the *Far Eastern Economic Review* had said Reuters and British press were playing down my plight. A small cheer for the *Review!* A tiny champion entering the lists on my behalf at last?

Mum's letter told me she and Geoffrey had started work together at a hotel in Great Yarmouth. I love my dear Mum. Shirley still seems certain I shall be released soon. I have become quite convinced by her that the autumn will bring something. She said also that Theo Peters arrived home and mentioned my name in his statement.

Yesterday I finished writing another story – 'To Cut a Long Story Short' – and I was quite pleased with it. It might sell. I think it is almost literature!

Two nights ago the Sneaking Chief and his men spent the whole evening until almost midnight putting up no less than 15 portraits of the Chairman. They cover one wall and obliterate that slogan saying 'Down with A. Grey!' on the far side of the dining room. The 'Basket Ball-Playing' chief looked in a couple of nights ago, too. Perhaps they have decided to step up surveillance.

Mother said in her letter that Colin Chapman had been in touch with her. I thought that was nice of him. I had a bath at lunch time. There is really not much to say. I am reading *The Tree of Man*. It is very good and perhaps has already won me over and influenced me with its style. I was becoming very fed up until I got those letters today. Now I expect there will be another big gap.

I learned after my release that the British Foreign Office had advised Reuters and other newspaper editors at the outset that it was felt that there was a greater chance of my being freed if my plight was played low key. Incredibly this advice was largely accepted for some 18 months and no great emphasis was given in Britain to the story and no newspapers, as far as I am aware, campaigned before then for action. This did not change until towards the end of 1968. Even all these years later, it is a pleasure for me to re-discover that a publication a long way from Whitehall in Hong Kong had the courage to break ranks on that advice.

Theo Peters, a commercial counsellor at the British Mission in Peking, was evidently one of the first British diplomats to reach home after the year-long restrictions on their movements and the withholding of entry and exit visas which followed the Red Guard burning of the Mission and the 'Battle of Portland Place' in London outside China's Embassy.

Colin Chapman has been and remains a lifelong friend. He was a fellow junior reporter with me on the Eastern Daily Press *and by this time had become foreign editor of* The Sunday Times. *Colin did his best, to my certain knowledge, to drum up helpful publicity during a visit to Hong Kong and Australia and it was almost certainly through him that the* Far Eastern Economic Review *learned of the Foreign Office 'advice' about playing down my story in the British press. Leading Australian newspapers took up my cause during his further visit there about this time.*

Saturday 24 August 1968, 9.20 pm

I haven't got much to say. This seems to be a time of great emptiness. But I want to record the small sign of yesterday – a sign that things have almost come full circle. As I walked near the bottom end of the yard, I looked down and saw a fine wing of a moth moving and turning on its tip. Of course at its base was an ant, turning it this way and that and shoving it mightily.

It could have been exactly a year ago that I saw a moth's wing in the tiny eight-foot-square cell, moving across the floor propelled by an ant. It is a sign of full circle, which I experienced in East Germany just before I was assigned here. It means quite definitely that soon this will end and I shall be free. I am almost counting on it now – but not quite.

If nothing happens by November, I shall get my chess from upstairs, I shall ask for a medical examination, and try to get a Bible. I had strong desire to read the Gospels today. I was reading the dictionary on the meaning of 'evangelical'.

Tuesday 27 August 1968, 12.45 pm

The important thing to record is that, not last night but the night before, there was much noise. During the evening, as I read, there was noise of drums and fireworks from the square and I thought this was a rally. But although I read later than usual, waiting for it to finish, when I put the light out I could see bright lights there and drums coming down the street. I tried to sleep and did drop off, but was awakened repeatedly by the deafening clash of drums and cymbals and gongs right outside the gate, again and again. They stopped there.

There was even one shout of 'Down with *Lu-To-She*' (NB Reuters). This kept me awake until three or four I should think. It was incredibly infuriating. It continued during the morning and I actually shut the windows during breakfast despite the heat. I have no idea what it was. I thought perhaps it was a celebration of a new Central Committee meeting and some significant decision. But it could be just another 'reception' by Mao I suppose. The fireworks were a new element. It was strange how many drums stopped and started right outside the door here. Otherwise there is nothing.

It is a particularly empty time. It is now five days again without letters. I miss them so much. Last night I thought of a new idea for a funny story about a sub-editor who speaks only in journalese. There just is nothing to say. I am hoping frantically for something in September, but mainly in October. Last night I began *Asia's Bright Balconies*, having finished *The Tree of Man* the night before. The Tree was very good indeed. I think it taught me something about writing.

Asia's Bright Balconies is a good travel book about Singapore, Hong Kong and Macao, geographical 'balconies' on the southern facade of Asia.

Thursday 29 August 1968, 12.45 pm

I am delighted to write that the summer is ending and that there are signs of impending autumn. The night before last, the strong breeze rocked the door of the bathroom as I was having my late-night wash. This morning there is a fresh cool breeze blowing in through the bathroom window and in here. It is still hot and I fear that, if I say my battle against the weather is won, it will become very hot again!

Last night I slept again bare-chested and often without a single sheet over me. The day is very bright, without sun, but perhaps it is slightly brittle and autumnal. I think the heat must end completely soon. Time is punctuated by the plop of big berries falling from the tree and hitting the courtyard. This sometimes happens very quietly in the night while I am still awake.

There is another 'one year circle' sign. While I walk in the afternoons, these tiny little flying insects with brown and white wings alight on me. I remember them last year on the windowsill of the little eight-foot-square room. Yesterday there was the incredible news that Soviet troops had 'invaded' Czechoslovakia! This came in a very late *Peking Review* special supplement. I couldn't get over it for a long time. This is the biggest event in the communist world since I have been really conscious of it!

I wondered today whether the improvements of last year would not be paralleled this year in accordance with the 'prophecy' from London. The slight improvements that came in my conditions last year might well be repeated, although I am freed later this year.

I said a desperate prayer on coming in from walking just now. There are times when I feel suddenly very miserable. It is now seven days without letters again. I feel this very keenly. Yesterday also I went upstairs to get more receipt forms for the wages. And I saw a new novel I didn't know about. The 'Perverted Shit' guard made me wait until after lunch before going up.

Saturday 31 August 1968, 6 pm

(With dinner on the table.)

Today the temperature outside didn't get above 76. Yesterday this invisible dip began; I think the weather is beaten. I have just looked at the beginning of this month for the 'plan' and see that it said, 'This month will see the beating of the weather by your will.' It is true. I believe the weather is beaten, although there will be an odd hot day. I am feeling a little lyrical for no good reason tonight.

Shirley, the absolute darling, sent me a cable yesterday. I love her very much. Tomorrow September begins. Today, sitting on the toilet, I thought that this month could well be called 'Flat August' and that September might become 'Smiling September'. I have high hopes of something happening in September and October. I have hope to be released. I am telling myself repeatedly that it must come now.

September contains the twenty-first, when the sun enters the sign of Libra and perhaps as I have noted before, perhaps there will be some effect from this. I long and hope and pray for release. I am tonight finishing my eleventh short story, so I believe the plan for it to be a creative month was fulfilled.

August was difficult because of the letters. There were only three deliveries on the seventh, the tenth and twenty-second plus a cable on the thirtieth. I believe this is part of the final pangs. The berries on the tree are beginning to glow red and the birds are pecking at them as I write. I shall be full of hope for September.

REFLECTIONS - 11
Monday 8 January 2007

No Story

When the man alone was younger, he had trained to be a newspaper reporter. The first thing the older men in the newspaper office had told him was that five questions had to be answered in every story he wrote:

What? Where? When? Why? Who?

Check before you write your story, son, they said.

See that you have all those facts.

What? Where? When? Why? Who?

And when you've written your story, check again.

To see if the questions have all been answered.

What? Where? When? Why? Who?

Now as the man sat in the six-sided cube alone for a very long time, he knew.

He knew that none of the questions could be answered.

What was he?

Of flesh and blood. Yet so were dogs.

Dissected, the body betrayed no sign of the soul, no sign of the 'I'.

Where had he come from? Where did he go when dead?

Nobody knew. So to 'What?' there was no answer.

Where was he? What was the universe in? Nobody knew.

So to 'Where?' there was no answer.

When was he? Now. But when was now? So, no answer to 'When?' either.

Why was he? The most clearly unanswerable question of all.

Who was he?

Take away the name that had been his since birth and he was a nameless package of tingling blood vessels with ultimately no sign of his 'I'.

Who was he indeed?

Five questions.

No answers.

So if there were no answers, there was no story!

Because, frighteningly, there seemed to be no story, the man alone dreamed one.

12
'SMILING' SEPTEMBER

30-day Plan for 'Smiling September'

Hope for improvement!

1 Write 2 complete stories.

2 Compile 30 crosswords.

3 Rise early and improve yoga exercises.

4 Hope for improvement, but be prepared for nothing.

5 Continue to intensively ignore the guards.

7 Remain absolutely calm.

Thursday 5 September 1968, 11.30 pm

Just received a letter from Shirley after a 14-day gap. What a relief it is. I have been desperate for letters. The rather naughty angel hadn't written for a week, so it appears to explain things. It contained a little encouragement in that Hopson (Sir Donald), was back home and had said something about me. Also an article in the German press on me. Yesterday I conveyed a letter to Mum to the guards. I spent a pleasant day writing it. I am beginning to have a strong feeling that something good will come before long.

Sunday 8 September 1968, 11.00 pm

A few days ago I remember complaining to myself, 'Nothing ever happens!' Well, several things have happened, although I find them disturbing. And it is difficult to know whether they bode well.

Two mornings ago I finished my exercises earlier than usual and after Lao Chiao had finished cleaning, I decided to clean off the shelf in my bathroom. As I stood on the chair – which I have never done before – I saw at least two civilians come out of the police room with some of the police. There had apparently been a visit. I absolutely don't know what to make of this. Consular access? Period check? Is some change foreshadowed? I honestly don't know and think probably it will be like every other day and have no outcome.

Then last night, just before the shift ended, the 'Playboy-Reading' guard switched on the light outside. And then a drumming of feet upstairs and then three broad-shouldered thick-looking police tramped through my room to the bathroom – a complete change of guard. The last time was November 18 last year.

This morning there was more activity and a new face at the table. This could be connected with the cadre visit. But it can hardly herald a quick release. It is slightly depressing, I am forced to admit. But it doesn't entirely rule out release this autumn. Perhaps it could be the beginning of something happening.

Yesterday I also had a haircut. On the evening of the 6 September, the firecrackers started going in the distance and were followed by passing drum units. These went on quite late. Then yesterday morning the noise became deafening again for long periods and I find myself once more cursing the strange stupidity of these people who just kick up fantastic amounts of noise all the time, which is quite incomprehensible. (I thought: this is the only country where demonstrations take placed organised by the authorities instead of against them.) Even a short time after it, like now, it is difficult to remember how infuriating the noise of these drums is. But it is past.

One particular guard I noticed invariably crept very very stealthily upstairs at some point during the night, whenever he was alone as the solo overnight shift man. My hearing seemed to have become more acute with my lengthening isolation and, even with my bedroom door closed, I could hear him clearly head into the upstairs lounge above the dining room. I deduced that he had discovered a pile of magazines there which included one or two copies of Playboy *as well as* Time *and* Newsweek. *Either he was unusually sophisticated for a Public Security Bureau foot-soldier and was very interested in current events worldwide and therefore catching up on the never-before-seen editions of* Time *and* Newsweek. *Or his eyes were being knocked out by explicit glowing naked photographs of bronzed American college co-eds and Playboy bunnies. Hence his nickname the 'Playboy-Reading' guard. I trust I haven't done him an injustice. Maybe we will meet in Beijing one day and he will tell me the truth!*

Tuesday 10 September 1968, 12.15 pm

After almost three days of the 'new guard', things haven't so far deteriorated, but the new style is very strict. The most noticeable thing is the quiet. It is almost uncanny sometimes. They are still in the stage where they keep their voices lowered when speaking. I have seen them all now and they are not particularly hostile. Some are quite 'presentable'.

One wears white gym shoes with no laces with his uniform. Another has apparently hammered metal studs into the rubber soles of his soft everyday shoes, which make a curious clicking noise when he walks. The different styles of these new guards are very interesting in other ways too. So far there have been no morning meetings. So far there has been no indoctrination of the Reuters staff. So far in fact things are perhaps pleasanter than they were under the old regime. Except the walking, which is more uncomfortable because some of the idiots feel they must stare at me. They leave the house to take lunch breaks and don't eat (yet) on the premises. The only intrusion so far was two nights ago, when one walked into the room about 11.30 pm. But even as I pause in my writing, there is belching and farting from the next room.

I don't know that any of these slightly promising signs will last. I expect as they settle in they will be noisier. During the night one demonstrated a very loud and persistent cough. It is too early to draw conclusions really, but it seems likely that a new order has been deliberately introduced.

I am trying hard to think of it in no other way except that it means release is not far off. I half expect to receive no letters in this new regime. I hope I receive them. But if not, I shall take it as a sign of release coming. During the day I finished reading a *Maigret* novel and during the days now I am reading *Khrushchevism*, a very interesting book by an Indian communist writer.

Thursday 12 September 1968, 10.45 pm

This morning a fantastic clang and beat of drums outside again. And last night my heart sank as I heard the sound of fireworks starting up about 10 pm in the Square of Heavenly Peace. Then came the drums outside making their usual evil din, like a banging of big tin trays. It went on until about 2 am. They had begun early this morning. As the noise outside becomes unbearable, my face contorts as I curse and swear at them. Mindless morons!

This is the fourth demonstration in about a month. I expect it will go on all day again. The last one was less than a week ago. Seven days without letters again, and my mood is affected. I suspect this time, however, that they may be stopped altogether because of the new guards. It makes me feel very cut off. I manage to tell myself that release is coming and it doesn't matter. I hope so. Yesterday there was a small change. Amah came in to clean and got my breakfast; she was quite sweet. Lao Chiao is ill. What a terribly empty life. Last night I began reading Len Deighton's *London Dossier* guide book and don't feel too sentimental. Perhaps it is a sign of release.

Tuesday 17 September 1968, 11.30 pm

I have just spent 40 minutes standing outside watching the rain. It is pouring as it has never poured before since I have been here. I have just changed into my white trousers to let the others dry. They became wet even though I stood under the porch.

I tried a faint smile at the guard when I came in at a run; he tried a faint smile back. On 14 September I had two cards from Shirley, which relieved the idea that the mail was stopped, but it is still a possibility. I am still hoping something will turn up soon.

After ten days the guards have developed some of the bad habits of their predecessors, but not all of them – yet. They spit and cough and sit outside at night. Two of them have taken to using the bathroom upstairs. I have heard Sao Kao reading an editorial one afternoon, but who to I don't know. Otherwise they haven't done propaganda on my premises. Lao Chiao has been ill for a week now. So far there have been no morning meetings. No doubt since I write this, there will be.

Last night I began *South Wind* by Norman Douglas. I had read Deighton's *London Dossier* and also *Khrushchevism* by an Indian woman; both were worthwhile. I became very fond of Inspector Maigret in the short space of one novel. I am still hoping against hope for something this month or at least next month.

Friday 20 September 1968, 13.30 hours

There has been a remarkable change in the weather these last few days. The heavy rain of 17 September was followed by another rainy day on the eighteenth. Then after a dull day yesterday there was a most tremendous wind last night. It caused a strange incident. About 9.30 pm as I walked inside, the lights, which had been flickering from time to time, as they always do in the wind, went right out. There was a strange noise outside and then more flashes and then a strange greenish-white flash and sparks from the direction of the porch.

I thought it was a thunder-bolt. I was very startled and was about to throw myself on the floor in the darkness. It was a moment of fright. One wondered whether it was an atom bomb or earthquake or what it was. It only lasted a few moments, but in these moments it was terrifying. I don't know what it was, except perhaps there was a short of some kind, but no damage seems to have been done.

The guards were startled, too, and looked all over the house and peered up in the dining room at the top of the wall behind the door. I really thought a fireball had landed in the street. But I think it was only the electricity in the house. Perhaps it is a freeing force at work?

These last few days I have tried, not very hard, to think of a story, without success. I have been very lethargic. I have read The Economist during the day and I am now reading South Wind at night. I had a day off from crosswords the day before yesterday, to celebrate reaching a grand total of 200!

I have that half-imagined feeling that perhaps release can be near. And yet I also feel depressed since it is six days again without letters. It is practically a month now since 22 August, which was the last time I had decent letters. Only on 5 September and the fourteenth, when two cards came, has the silence been broken. It is very depressing and I long for letters and some sign of encouragement.

The guards are still fairly quiet. I suppose they are not a bad bunch. They haven't had meetings yet and they haven't done propaganda downstairs.

Last night I put an extra blanket on the bed. The temperature during the night fell to 67 degrees – a ten-degree drop in three days! Until a few days ago one could hardly bear a sheet on. I am wearing my wool cardigan during the day. I must try to be more constructive at this stage, believing something is coming, but knowing that it might still be a month or so away.

Saturday 21 September 1968, 11.15 am

Every few minutes this morning a most unearthly din breaks out in the street outside – music and singing and quotations in a great cacophony of sound. Last night there was a practice (I think) in Tien An Men Square for the National Day. This begins late in the afternoon and really gets going after midnight. There is incredibly loud noise crashing out over the whole of Peking, well into the small hours. It is quite outrageous. People are marching up and down the street with whistles and shouting. It is almost unbelievable in the middle of the night. The guard kept the ceiling light outside my door on all last night and I wondered if something was planned, so I went to bed in my clothes, just taking off my trousers.

(At this moment Sao Kao entered without knocking at the door, he placed a bill for electricity on my table and went out – without closing the door properly. How I detest that man!) In the night I took off my socks when I saw the light in the guard's room was out. I am very fed up this morning. It seems I truly am a victim of all sides. I hope something will happen soon, for I am very low.

Monday 23 September 1968, 12.15 pm

Last night the guards put up a curtain across the room where they sleep. This produced a slight depression, since it wouldn't be there if release was due soon. As I write, whistles blow and girls are shouting as they march by in the street. They are praising Mao, as usual.

Last night as I read, the awful sound of roars from many throats and the tramp of feet came from outside. Also the thud of running feet in unison. All very terrible. They were on the way to the Square to practise for 1 October, National Day. I have this morning looked up last year's diary and the same thing occurred.

They shout, praise Mao, blow whistles and make a very intensive noise. Then they come back, all through the night it seems, making just as much noise! I prayed very hard yesterday for some enjoyment in the seven days of this week. But I begin to fear nothing will happen during September – and my faith in October swings back and forth.

I try to have faith in it and still think it is possible something will happen. All the indications point to October. (Reading last year's diary for this day, it spoke of terrible depression, very difficult to shake off. I suppose I have learned not to get into such depressions: what a lesson!) This morning, as in the last few days, there were roaring loudspeakers outside.

Wednesday 25 September 1968, 16.00 hours

Today a letter from Shirley. It was postmarked 29 August. So it had been held in the guards' room four days short of a month! These fucking bastards, bloody filthy shits! The letter covered a period of nine days while Shirley was in Germany. It said the Daily Express had asked its readers to send cards to me; what do they think this is – a fucking game? Bloody wretched bastards! The letter did nothing to cheer me up. Quite the contrary! I am extremely fed up. I am now beginning to think of this going on until Christmas and long after. This is the first time I have expressed such a thought, I believe.

I now begin to see the 14 months I have been here as being quite pathetically small. What about 18 or 24 months? I have been so hard done by! I have been wretchedly deserted by everybody. But I will fucking well survive! Damn it!

Monday 30 September 1968, 12 noon

I have been very lazy with regard to this diary recently and there are a number of things to record. Yesterday there were 13 pieces of mail. Last night a dirty filthy bloody spittoon and a lavatory brush appeared in the guards' room.

On Saturday 28 September, there was a total of about six or seven guards here, in and out all day, going upstairs frequently and at lunch time the staff had a big meeting with them in the room. I saw this through the keyhole. This led me to believe I was to be moved upstairs, but nothing happened.

On Friday 27 September the weather suddenly broke again. It had been building up slowly again to the mid-70s, after the big drop a week earlier. On Thursday I took a bath and was back to short sleeves again and cursing the weather for not getting cooler. But during the night of Thursday–Friday it rained and went downward. Not only was I quickly back into my woollen cardigan, but I soon had my leather jacket back on. Whereas I had begun taking off the heavy blankets from the bed, they were now back on with a vengeance again. For the past four days it has remained cool, with temperatures in the 50s and 60s inside and outside. I put on my thick tweed trousers on the day it rained to save my light summer ones from the wet. I have got them on.

I had only intended to change from my grey suit trousers to the white ones on 1 October. The weather change has been very sudden. The grey suit has been cleaned. The reason for the meeting of the staff with the guards and the activity upstairs is not clear and I expect it will remain so.

Yesterday's letters from Shirley: I saw Lao Chiao come in to clean with a thick wedge of airmail in his hand and rushed through. There were odd ones, but most had come to the house on 21 and 23 September. They spoke of Shirley getting things done in London, stories about me in the papers regarding possibility of a swap and another cable to the premier by Hong Kong journalists. They were very encouraging after such a long spell of nothing. They included many touching things (cleaning pads!) and crosswords, etc! I love my Shirley very much and went about all day calling her a treasure.

There has been another addition to the bloody noise from the Square at night (which has itself subsided a lot). There has been, every morning, loudspeaker music blaring into the house. And yesterday afternoon there was a full-length performance of *The Red Lantern* opera. It was tremendously loud and stopped all mental activity. The other daily blasts keep up an incredibly monotonous repetition of Mao's thoughts, mentioning him over and over again.

The spittoon: I find the presence of the spittoon absolutely disgusting. It stands clear within view next to the lavatory brush, and the guards spit into it at nights. It is a most revolting sight. It is obscene.

I am praying fervently for release in October. But I have begun to think this last week or so of the possibility of it going on until Christmas; I can't think beyond that. It will be disgusting if I am left here by the British Government.

REFLECTIONS - 12

The Play

Characters: *Three highly prominent Orient-men; three highly prominent Occident-men. The face each other in two lines centre stage, both uncompromisingly haughty in manner*

Three highly prominent Orient-men: Now the thing is this you see. You highly prominent Occident-men were once very arrogant colonisers and threw your weight about in our Orient. Times have changed. But you have arrested and put in prison some of our Orient men. We don't give a damn about them really, but we wish to demonstrate that times have changed and that you can't do it to us any more because we have appallingly large numbers of people in our Orient country and you are small and now it is our turn to be arrogant. So we have put a poor, fairly insignificant representative Occident-man in a six-sided cube on his own and we'll keep him there until you submit to our will. So there!

Three highly prominent Occident-men: Look, I say, this is a jolly rotten thing to do. Well, I mean to say, it isn't even fair. (With a tone of staunchness creeping into their voices.) But we won't be intimidated you know. We are not entirely unarrogant yet.

Three highly prominent Orient-men: All right, all right. But we are going to hurt him. Nothing absolutely physical, you understand. But we are going to hurt him mentally and psychologically though – pretty hard.

Three highly prominent Occident-men: (Even more staunchly.) Huh! Think we can't take it? We can take it all right. We'll show you. It's not us in the six-sided cube, you know. We can take it. You won't find us buckling under quickly. It's not us in there.

Three highly prominent Orient-men: Heh-heh-heh, heh-heh-heh!

Three highly prominent Occident-men: (Craftily, with a gleam of self-righteousness coming into their eyes as if they have suddenly seen the way to utilise the right on their side.) Do you know what we shall do if you do not release our Occident-man from the six-sided cube? We shall cause questions to be asked in our House about you. And then the whole world shall know how wicked and unfair you are.

Three highly prominent Orient-men: Heh-heh-heh! In fact, ho-ho-ho! And ho-ho-ho-ho-ho! Do not make us laugh with such pathetic nonsense. Heh-heh, ho-ho-ho. How splendidly 'democratic'. Questions in your House. Ho-ho-ho! Heh-heh! Pardon us if we do not quake in our shoes in the face of such 'democratic' power.

Three highly prominent Occident-men: (From the saddles of their high horses.) It is only too patently clear to the whole world that your actions are not in keeping with the basic principles of humanitarian behaviour. You shall stand condemned in the eyes of the decent people of the world.

Three highly prominent Orient-men: (In a sing-song chorus, reminiscent of the fashion in which naughty children defy their weak parents.) We're hurting him, look, we're hurting him. We're hurting him and you can't do anything about it! We've been hurting him for a long time and you've not done anything about it!

Three highly prominent Occident-men: (Showing some signs of huffy exasperation but refusing to be drawn.) Pshaw! Pshaw! Be warned, if this continues we shall cause further questions to be put in our House about you.

Three highly prominent Orient-men: (Suddenly becoming serious.) You know, you people really are disgusting. Really disgusting. You profess to such beautiful ideals of humanitarian sympathy, such sincere regard for every single individual of your kind. And yet for a very very long time, you have let one of your kind suffer in that six-sided cube. You are truly disgusting.

Now we state quite clearly and categorically that everything within the compass of our rule is subordinate to the revolution. It comes first, the individual after. We are true to our principles. Ruthless they are, but we are true to them. But you do not follow your principles. Frankly we are greatly surprised. We had expected, knowing your principles, that you would have helped this unfortunate in the six-sided cube before now. But you have not. For reasons of arrogance and pride, ill befitting such smallness of stature, you have ignored him. You are truly disgusting. You surprise us, but you are disgusting!

In late 1999 under the 30-year rule, the previously secret British Foreign Office papers dealing with my period as a hostage in China were released for general public scrutiny at the Public Record Office at Kew in London. Before they were released, I was invited by the Foreign Office to look at them on the condition I took no notes. I scrutinised them briefly and quickly during a visit to London for other reasons, and to date I have never done more than skim through them on that one occasion. Yet in re-running the 'unwritten script' of the above play, I feel it is appropriate to set down here one brief extract from a mid-1969 internal Foreign Office memorandum which I glimpsed on that one occasion. This defined my 'burden' in a manner almost worthy of those three 'highly prominent Occident men' of my bitterly satirical mental playlet.' The memo said in part:

'Mr Grey in a sense has to bear a large part of the burden of safeguarding the wellbeing of millions of people in Hong Kong for whom we are responsible. We have the difficult task of asking him to sacrifice his liberty for a very long period without being able to consult him or explain the significance of his privations. However, this does not mean we should let the Chinese force us to give in to their demands to obtain his release.'

I think it is true to say the very last thing I expected to do on being assigned to China by Reuters was to spend a couple of years 'safeguarding the wellbeing of millions of people in Hong Kong'!

13
ANOTHER VISITATION

Tuesday 1 October 1968, 12.30 pm
(National Day, People's Republic of China)

I have just looked back a year at the diary for 3 October last year. I wondered then whether I should still be here 'for next year'. How ironic! I hardly dare put words to the idea that I may still be here next 1 October – but anything is possible in this terrible predicament!

I got very little sleep during the night. The National Day crowds started going past towards the Square of Heavenly Peace about three in the morning! They made the most terrible racket outside. Chanting, ridiculous noise and screaming and answering chants, and shouting – all making the most incredible din!

I looked at my watch at 4.50 am and it had been going on ages then. I eventually got about two hours' sleep between 7 am and 9 am. Then I had to get up, because the noise was so great. At 10.15 am or so the noise of organs playing loudly started to come from the Square, shouts and swelling music and 'Sailing the Seas Depends on the Helmsman' and so on and so on and one knew 'He' was there!

Then came the strange voice of the 'Second Man'. It is somewhere between a quavering Larry-the-Lamb bleat and the metallic voice of the villain in a science-fiction story. It keeps rising to senile shouts at the bits where the vast crowd of probably a million have to shout back. Then the music and the marching followed, and as I walked outside there was an explosion of red balloons and parachutes streaming away in the bright sun. Now there is a pause until tonight's fireworks. I have just set out the cold meat and eggs and cheese and fruit for my lunch, which have been with me on a tray all night. I had the same at breakfast. History repeats itself, as last year.

'He' was Mao Tse-tung and the 'Second Man' was his first deputy and already 'anointed' successor at this time, Defence Minister and Long March hero, Lin Piao. (Lin would later disappear mysteriously, allegedly in an airliner that crashed in Inner Mongolia in 1971. All its nine occupants are said to have been burned to death and charred beyond recognition. The plane was supposedly heading to Moscow and Lin and his family are said to have been on board, fleeing to the Soviet Union, having failed in a plot to assassinate Mao.

Lin Piao was not alone among China's gerontocracy of that time in having a curious voice. Mao did not make a public speech for many years, it is believed, because his Hunanese provincial dialect and general high-pitched mode of delivery in public were not considered to befit his enormous Cult of Personality stature.

Wednesday 2 October 1968, 11.00 pm

To my surprise the cook didn't come yesterday. I have just asked him about this and he told me there were 'too many people at 3 o'clock'. Yesterday really was unhappy. I had a rotten headache, which originated in the noise during the night. It was quite bad in the evening.

The dirty crocks and fag ends of food remained in a disgusting pile on the tray and I finally covered them with a cloth. I feel somewhat depressed about the prospect of release this month. I have to hope, of course, but there is so little sign of anything happening.

I continued to read *Commandant of Auschwitz*, the horrible story of the Nazis' attempted extermination of the Jews. (NB For many months I could not bring myself to read this horror prison story.) It isn't exactly designed to lighten the heart!

I keep re-reading the letters from Shirley. I love her so much. I really find it difficult to understand why there is talk of 'exchanges', as she mentions. There will never be an exchange for me. Surely the British Government knows that. They must know what is required very well, but simply refuse to do it. They want to teach the Chinese a lesson, I suppose.

I pray quite definitely for release in October. I hope something will come, but my mind is now getting used to the idea of Christmas here again. This really does seem likely; I suppose I must deep down believe in my release some time, but in a practical fashion it is almost impossible to envisage it.

The food situation is worth describing: on 30 September the cook brought up a great number of things for me to be able to eat in his absence. A big bowl of purple liquid and a small bottle marked 'poison'! I was to dip the salad in this, he said. There was a bowl of about seven eggs, a dish of pork, mutton and beef, he said (although I found no beef), slices of cheese and a small piece of butter, salt wrapped up in a small square of paper, and two bottles of water. Thinking he was coming in the afternoon, I ate almost everything at lunch. I decided not to touch the salad and the 'poison' bottle. I don't know why, just I suppose I doubt anything connected with poison.

I ran out of water in the evening. For dinner I had a small plate with one egg and some remains of meat and some cheese. It was very depressing, but I tried not to notice and got on with compiling a crossword. It was a drab day. It made me appreciate, perhaps, warm food and the small difference of having people bring me in food, which does break the otherwise terrible silence.

If my memory serves me correctly, all uncooked salad food was treated with potassium permanganate in Western households in China at this time, not least because of the widespread use then of human sewage as fertiliser. This was an interesting reminder of the process for preparing my food that was going on each day in the kitchen beneath my feet - and how it was not surprising I occasionally became ill with gastro-enteritis.

Saturday 5 October 1968, 3.00 pm

Today I think is special. Today a letter from Shirley (one of four) said did I know that those for whom I was a reprisal were due to be released in November? Just like that. Did I know! It is the most FANTASTIC piece of news since this whole thing began!

She added John (Weston) has told her he thought 'something lovely' might happen before Christmas. This is very interesting news. I don't want to go off the deep end about it, but it does seem to put rather a new complexion on things. I pray it means my release is now within thinking distance. It is the most hopeful sign of my whole time here!

Yesterday I spent most of the day checking a letter I wrote the previous day. After lunch there was a trample of feet and in came the 'Wet Guy' and Lao Chiao to give me a letter that I had earlier written to Mum, that had obviously been returned from its Foreign Ministry inspection. It was taken off immediately afterwards to the Post Office by Lao Chiao.

I handed in the next letter at dinnertime. Last night a new round of drum banging and cymbal clashing began. It is still going on. While it is outside, this noise is almost unbearable. I have no idea what it is. Last night, on bringing in dinner, Lao Chiao was so intent on pointing out to me a picture of a new river bridge at Nanking in the *Peoples Daily*, that he forgot to help me move the table and took the tray away.

Yesterday the rent demand for three months up to December came. After a tiny fit of anger, it didn't really affect me at all. I wrote a cheque immediately and put it on the breakfast tray. I refused to be depressed, since I had the feeling that these three months should hold something decisive. Today's four letters from Shirley also included the interesting information that the Chinese authorities had assured the Foreign Office that my health was all right.

In view of the fact that I have never been asked or examined, it is a very interesting statement. I don't want to go on and on about this piece of news today in case it turns out not to be correct. But it is the best news in 14 months. Let it be the first sign of good things to come. I was so bound up with writing the monthly letter to Shirley the day before yesterday that I forgot to compile a crossword and also to wash my socks. The discipline has gone to pieces recently. It is not unpleasing that it does sometimes!

Tuesday 8 October 1968, 1.45 pm

Today I find myself trying not to let time appear to go slowly. The news from Shirley on the fifth of this month has ever been in my mind. But it seems up to today I have been too busy to write a plan for this month – a month that started well in 'a blaze of pleasure' from the 13 delayed letters that arrived on the 29 September.

Then there was the unusual National Day without any cooking; then the accounts I was able to complete on the 2 October, then a letter to be written on the third and a cheque on the fourth. Then on the fifth and sixth there was a clue revision to be done for recent crosswords and the Peking Review to be read (yesterday). So here today I am ready to write the plan.

Again today it is raining. It began early this morning and I walked for ten minutes instead of 40 minutes today. Some seven or eight guards were here this morning. Some went upstairs for a while but I have no idea why they met. It wasn't a regular indoctrination as of old; there was no singing at the end. I don't think it has much significance. I hope that thing of Shirley's about release is right.

Plan for October

1 Write one short story.
2 Remain patient.
3 Compile small crosswords.
4 Try to learn some Chinese.
5 Hope for the best.
6 Observe strict neutrality with the guards.

Saturday 12 October 1968, 2.15 pm

Today one letter from Mum, to keep up the rate of one delivery of letters a week – also a bank statement almost a month old. Geoffrey has got a job but Mum hasn't. Kim (Davenport) visited her again, I was glad to see. Otherwise little news.

Yesterday I conceived a new short story plan to break a run of six weeks in which I couldn't or wouldn't think of one. The day before yesterday (10 October) the bloody stupid guards all came and stood around their room and the house all day – how annoying of them, making me think that something was to happen. They annoy me intensely since nothing they do is rational. Now they do 24-hour shifts. Sometimes they have four of them at night. The personnel of the shifts changes constantly.

Time, as I thought it might, seems to have slowed up since Shirley's letter of 5 October. The day before yesterday I read a quotation from Samuel Johnson which said, 'If you be idle, be not solitary; if you be solitary, be not idle.' I think it was this which spurred me to make an effort to think of a story. Although I haven't started writing it yet, I am pleased with it. (It is to be called 'The Proice of Fame'.) The day before yesterday I finished the two-day read of *A Kind of Anger* by Eric Ambler, which is very good! There is nothing to report, but I do hope for release in November.

Wednesday 16 October 1968, 16.05 hours

If ever I wanted to look back in later times on a completely empty moment, this would be it! I picked up this diary because of the fact there was nothing else to do.

The time hangs heavy.

The guards annoy me intensely now by holding stupid meetings. Yesterday they all wandered in during the afternoon and went upstairs to talk in my lounge! During the night I was woken by one of them using my upstairs toilet. This afternoon about eight of them wandered in and are holding a completely formless meeting in the upstairs lounge. These guards annoy me extremely by their meaningless action!

Sao Kao this moment has brought tea, muttered 'cabbage' and gone out to buy some off the streets, I suppose. (NB great piles of cabbages can be bought at street corners at this season.) I hope to be free soon. The days go very slowly now that I am waiting for November. But I am by no means sure of release. On 13 October four letters came from Shirley and one told me of a whole page in *The Economist* about me. Heavens above, my release must come soon. I really feel it must. Yesterday I completed the short story called 'The Proice of Fame'. I think it isn't bad. But my days remain highly meaningless.

Friday 18 October 1968, 12.25 pm

Who was the idiot who said about the new guards, 'They don't hold meetings, don't eat in the house – good sign'? Cunt! At this moment the bloody guards are streaming back from their meals. They were all here from the break of dawn. They made an unholy noise around nine am, so I had to get up and go into the toilet to get away from it. Now they have come back again, presumably to spend the rest of the day idling, loafing around as they have done twice before this week. They really are the most sickening cunts!

Yesterday it was cold enough for the first time for the guards to close the outside door of the house during the day, on their own account. But it is still open at night, despite my request of at least a week ago that it be closed. The fatness I have suddenly felt these last five days or so has receded a little. I have done exercises more thoroughly the past two or three days and have got up earlier and have eaten less. The roll of fat appearing suddenly was very unpleasant.

(14.15 hours, the same day)

The idiots have just trooped off upstairs. They make me fucking furious! In fact I am guarded by up to nine guards a day. I believe they just go upstairs to be comfortable. Fucking bastards!

Wednesday 23 October 1968, 20.00 hours

Tonight it is bloody cold in this room, 59 degrees to be precise. It is by far the coldest day so far and I have a scarf in my neck and my trousers tucked into my socks. The door to the outside is half open at present, by courtesy of the guards! It has been shut all day. The new 'awkward' shift has just come on. What is there to say? Today I have completed a rather clever crossword with seven different anagrams in it on the word 'trapped'. That is my sole achievement. The last two nights I have read Ernest Hemingway's *Death in the Afternoon*, about bullfighting – that is very good.

The time is definitely hanging heavily on my hands now. I find myself wondering what to do, to wait until my self-appointed inside walk time arrives at 8.45 pm. I have decided to ask to be allowed to go upstairs for books on 30 October. I am now praying for release in the first half of November, although I am ready to go through November with nothing. Am still managing to keep a fairly even temper, but depression has threatened once or twice in the last few days.

Saturday 26 October 1968, 13.00 hours

A change in the weather: it is warmer today. Yesterday I had the central heating switched on. The two days before I had been very cold, and I was almost shivering most of the day and evening. At nights I read with a coat over my knees. Yesterday I asked Lao Chiao to ask the guards to keep the door shut, and for the frame door to be put up outside for the winter. This morning things are back to how they were before, although it is warm outside, at 54 degrees. It was 48 on the two days before I asked for the heating to be put on. The guards have been very difficult about the door. Last night it was left ajar until I went to bed and then closed. It was open all day on the day it was 49 degrees. The guards have put on their padded underwear and all look like Michelin Men.

Today I paid the wages. My chest has been troubling me a little and I have almost made up my mind to ask for a doctor on 2 November. As I have already noted, I have decided to ask to be allowed to get more books on 30 October.

October seems to be dragging its bloody feet! I try to feel confident of release next month, but already I am beginning to think of it not happening. A big pile of leeks is heaped up in the courtyard – enough to last the winter. There are absolutely no signs of anything happening, it is very depressing.

Last night I dreamed that Lao Chiao said, 'In 30 days' time we shall move.'

'To where?' I asked. 'To the Wai Cha Ta Lo?'

'Yes' he said.

I don't put any credence on this dream. I try to tell myself that the changeover between the months of October/November has always been a lucky time for me. (I have met Janet and Mary and Shirley who have all been important in my life during this period of the year.) It is very difficult to imagine being released at all, but I know this is due to my isolation.

There was a ten-man meeting in the house this morning, after which the guards all sang 'The Helmsman'. This was the first 'old-style' meeting the 'new' guards have had. Yesterday there was also a ten-man meeting with singing afterwards. There have been a number of meetings, including some upstairs in my lounge. But this was the first of the old-style – another pointer to a long spell to go, ahead?

The cartoon advertising motif of the Michelin Tyre company showed a man composed entirely of rubber tubes.

Wai Cha Ta Lo was the diplomatic residential compound in an eastern suburb of Peking, close to the embassy quarter where, by this time, all foreign diplomats and foreign correspondents and their families resided. Public Security Bureau Guards manned all entry and exit gates

Wednesday 30 October 1968, 7.15 pm

Today new letters! Yet although I got four letters – three from Shirley, one from Mum – they contained almost no real new encouragement. Then I asked for permission to get more books from upstairs, as I had long planned through this month. The reaction was as incredible as any other!

After a lot of telephoning and waiting throughout lunch, I was told afterwards I had to write down the titles! I asked Lao Chiao to explain that I had four times before got books with the old policemen. (He said in a whisper, 'They are new policemen.') After about two hours in which they apparently did nothing, the guards then telephoned headquarters again about four o'clock and since then I have heard nothing.

I feel more than somewhat depressed. In Mum's letter she said Reuters had told her that I was 'one of their most brilliant correspondents'. My reaction to that is, Huh! Since they show it by doing nothing to help!

Shirley's letters also were a little annoying. One said John and Sally would be home in December and she hoped I would beat them to it. This seems like another of those empty expressions of encouragement that those safely outside feel obliged to make. I feel I must ask for a doctor soon. This is a very low time again. But I shall manage to bear it somehow, no doubt.

Friday 1 November 1968, 17.25 hours

November has dawned! The month in which I so hope I will be released! The month still seems enormous, of course, and I must be prepared for a disappointing 'nothing'.

Waterworks men came today. They mended the toilet and left water all over the floor, which Lao Chiao cleaned up afterwards. My state of mind is average. I am considerably worried about my chest, but above all hoping for release. There are many problems of administration of money and my passport, etc. I have suffered over 15 months here!

Plan for November

1. Take firm grip on yourself.
2. Write two stories.
3. Keep open question of doctor.
4. Compile 30 little crosswords.
5. Plan to be released, but plan also to be strong.

Monday 4 November 1968, 11.15 pm

Last evening as I said a special prayer before tea, I was almost overwhelmed with an exalted feeling. I felt very strongly that something outstanding would happen in the coming seven days. I felt this so strongly that after coming back into the room, I went back and prayed again for such a definite feeling. It was as strong as any of the correct feelings in the past. I feel very optimistic about this week. I didn't write the letter I normally would have done on the third day. Also today is the fourth day of drum banging, etc. in support of a statement of some kind. I feel sure release is near now. Please hasten it and deliver me safely to England to begin life again.

(13.00 hours the same day)

New arrivals have just come in for the day's meeting. There are meetings practically every day now. The day before yesterday 11 goons were present!

Tuesday 12 November 1968, 11.30 pm

Yesterday I was tremendously depressed. Sao Kao in the afternoon told me the guards said I must write down the names of books I wanted to fetch from upstairs. After talking to the guards, he repeatedly said I must write. This was the long-delayed reply to my request of 30 October..

I slumped to the floor in the bathroom, absolutely miserable, and prayed. At tea I asked if I could go up and look to see the names of the books. All this seemed to indicate a continuing harder line on me. And with no hope of release. Another guard change, bringing back the old guards, has also caused this feeling. I now feel again as I did long ago, with many months possibly lying before me.

I so expected all through last week for something to happen on Saturday. I decided more than once to ask for a doctor on this coming Wednesday, if nothing happened, but I am reluctant to do so now for all sorts of reasons. I am miserable and apprehensive and trying not to get depressed. It is only the twelfth, after all, but I begin to think that my release will depend on the release of the three other men in Hong Kong. How horrible and wretched this life is.

Saturday 16 November 1968, 15.00 hours

Two days ago I had a visit from a sweet woman doctor, who said perhaps I had bronchitis. She came on the second day after I asked. I asked to have the door closed, because of the cold, but this was refused. Last night the light in this room broke down. Today I was allowed a standard light from upstairs. I have been very, very depressed in the past two or three days. I have fallen to the floor in the bathroom in misery. I feel that this will just go on and on.

The guards seem more harsh than ever; 24 cabbages lie in a pile in the courtyard outside the window, enough almost until Christmas. I am trying to reconcile myself to having to endure for the next year, thinking of 18 months or two years as a term. It seems impossible that I will be released. I am very lethargic. I am very low in spirits — but I am still fighting.

Wednesday 20 November 1968, 15.30 hours

Today after stumbling through a week of pure misery, four letters from Shirley. One, by allusion to her birthday, seemed to suggest that I would be released by her birthday. She gave John (Weston) and perhaps (Len) Appleyard as evidence. Please don't let this be a disappointment.

Thursday 21 November 1968, 13.15 hours

Yesterday afternoon in the paper, I clearly saw news from Hong Kong about journalists. Probably their release. But how many? Thirteen? And does this mean I am to be released? Now I must be very busy. I am very, very hopeful but am trying not to discount the possibility of having to stay on. Shirley's letters seem more and more certain every time I think of it.

Friday 29 November 1968, 4.30 pm

The eight days since the last entry have seen a complete change in my fortune. Three days ago, on the twenty-sixth, all my hopes of release were shattered by a sudden and unexpected consular access visit by Percy Cradock. It was a bitter disappointment.

The effort of trying to change my thinking back to long-term misery has left me almost completely inactive for three days. I asked for a doctor immediately after the interview and three days later nothing has happened. I have been most deeply miserable and hardly know how to carry on. All through the summer and autumn I hoped and was almost sure something would happen. Now what? Several months at least I must face, if even the best happens. If the worst happens, it may go on for a time that is too horrible to write. So ends this book! (NB the exercise book.)

I shall try to begin again in another book – but this one finishes on a note of deepest misery.

(The same day, but writing this entry in a new blank maroon hardcover exercise book.)

I must begin again! At a quarter to three on the afternoon of 26 November, the shock and disappointment of another consular access visit came to me. The Number Two translator came in and read from his book, in the clipped prose of his race, the fact that, 'The Information Department of the Chinese Ministry of Foreign Affairs has informed us that ...'

I sat down disappointed and stunned. All my hopes, which had been very high after Shirley's letters about her birthday, sank. I couldn't think. I went to wash my hands and was called back by the guard in the room. I washed them with the door open. Shortly afterwards Percy Cradock arrived, with a wet-looking replacement of John Weston.

'Tony!'

He called my name and came in. He said he would read messages to me. I broke in and said, before he did that, could he tell me if there was any chance of my getting out of here soon? I had been in solitary confinement for 16 months and wasn't really interested in platitudinous messages.

I suppose it was rude and offensive. I can't remember his exact words, but he began by saying, 'Things are improving.'

I believe I blurted out that I had been told that seven months before, and he said, 'Don't think you'll have to wait another seven months.'

Later on he said he hoped that the publicity of this visit and the fact that Hsueh Ping (Xue Ping), and other journalists mentioned in the statement of 21 August, had been released would mean some improvement. Already there had been some evidence, he said. I listened without enthusiasm to the messages. (Gerald) Long (general manager of Reuters) came again with the rubbish that they were 'doing everything for your release' and 'thinking of me every day', etc. Crap!

Mother said letters were cause for great excitement. (David) Chipp said he would tell Mother and Shirley of the visit. Mother also said she hoped to see me home soon.

Then Percy began his brief. Hsueh Ping had been released on completing his term of imprisonment. All eight correspondents mentioned in the statement had been released. How many were left, I asked. Several, he said.

When I asked how long their sentences were he said something about how he believed one finished in 1971.

I fell back in my chair saying, 'Oh, my God!'

He said relations were improving and said publicity would show how badly China treated foreigners. I was amazed to hear him say this, with the two interpreters writing furiously. I believe I was so offensive that when I said, 'Have you finished your brief?' he left out some messages from people. He then said there had been articles in the world's press, questions in parliament and he had answered questions at a press conference.

He told me that the diplomats question (involving British diplomats in Peking and Chinese personnel in London) had been cleared up 'just because they decided to'. Apparently no concessions were involved. Chinese journalists in London, he said in reply to my enquiry, were not under restriction. Percy declined to be pressed on anything.

At one point, I believe as he was about to leave, I asked if I would still be here at Christmas and he dodged it the first time, saying he couldn't make any estimate. I believe I repeated the question and he said everything would be done to see that I wasn't.

I asked him for a personal assurance that he would try to do everything possible to get me out. He gave it, but I believe he said it was unnecessary because everybody was concerned, blah, blah, blah. I said I felt disowned and that everybody was cynical, etc.

I also said I hoped I had not been too hysterical and he said that no, I was obviously very sane and everybody admired the way I was bearing up, etc. I feel perhaps I had been rude to him. I said my reaction when I heard they were coming was to fight down my bitterness and anger. I didn't mean it personally. But, having seen the Hong Kong thing a few days before, I had begun to hope for release and now these hopes were dashed.

After his brief, Percy got around to asking, 'How are you?'

I began by saying that to be precise and exact I was not physically well. I explained I had a head cold and that also I was suffering from bronchitis. I said I had felt pains in my chest for three or four months and on 13 November had asked for a doctor. When one came the next day, I had asked the interpreter as they left what was wrong. He said, 'Maybe you have bronchitis.'

I said I told the doctor I was worried it might be tuberculosis and asked would it be possible to have an X-ray? The doctor said not at the moment. I had heard nothing since then. They had given me pills and liquid medicine. This had lasted five days.

'Ask for a doctor again,' Percy said.

I said something like, I would have expected some course of treatment. I said the whole attitude towards me was indifferent to say the least. And Percy said, 'Yes, nobody dare show you a generous spirit.'

He asked about my food and I said I had no complaints. Clothes? I said nothing.

Had my conditions improved? I said the windows had been nailed up on one side of the room and I had sat through the summer, without a fan, drenched in sweat.

He asked if this had been to keep out the light. 'No,' I replied, 'the effect was to keep out the air. I don't know the reason why it was done.'

I said that now sometimes I was cold in the room, since I couldn't close the door. I had asked to close the door when I was found to have bronchitis, but had heard nothing. Also I was not allowed to get books; I had several books, but had read them all. I read only one hour a day to ration things out, because I didn't know how long this would go on.

He said he was worried about my health. 'Do you think it is tuberculosis?' he asked.

I said I didn't know, but it was difficult enough trying to bear solitary confinement without an illness, but even more difficult with an illness preying on one's mind.

He said to ask for a doctor again and I said, 'Yes, I will ask for one today.'

He said the visit was in return for one to the remaining journalists in Hong Kong, which had been on offer a long time. When I apologised for appearing hysterical, the dimwit, named Roger, said he admired my command of words. I suppose it was a stupid thing to say on my part.

Percy asked if I had been accused of anything and if Foreign Ministry men had been to see me. I said I had seen nobody. I indicated that when the Red Guards came a lot of things had been shouted which I couldn't hear properly, but I had been told nothing else since. I told him also the four points that had been made to me:

1   I must respect posters and slogans;
2   obey guards;
3   remain in area defined by the masses;
4   await further notice.

I said my room was 12-feet square and I had a bed and a chair and a wooden table. It was adjoined by a scullery where the amah used to wash the clothes.

Could I go into any other room?

'No.'

'This room, for instance?'

'No. This is only the second time I have been in here; the first was when (Donald) Hopson was there. The guards occupy this room day and night,' I said.

'It seems to me,' he said, 'that your conditions have deteriorated.' I said I hoped he would be discreet over the publicity. 'That is just it,' he said, 'I want to help.'

'Well,' I said, 'I don't want my mother, who is the kind of person to worry herself into an illness, to think I am on the point of madness and death.'

'Oh no, you are not,' they both chorused. 'She is very well,' he said twice.

He asked if I wanted to give messages and I sent love to Mother and Shirley. To Reuters? What could I say to Reuters?

At one point I said I could only sit with clenched fists and try to control myself. He said I should keep trying to get upstairs, etc. I said, I wasn't stupid; I tried everything, but I couldn't win, I couldn't do anything.

I asked at one point if they could do anything else to try to get some books in to me.

They had tried that, he said. I told him that the guards looked from the room they occupied into my room and could also do so at night, since there was no curtain at the window and the light outside the door shone in through the fanlight. I said I hadn't said things before because I hoped for improvement. I was still understating things.

'Yes, I have some conception,' he said.

I told him my walks continued – under surveillance.

He asked about letters and I said I wrote one a month, it went to the Foreign Ministry and was returned a month later for dispatch. I believe he wrote this down. I said letters were kept in the guards' room, sometimes up to a month, before being given to me.

Did I see them arrive, asked the dim one. I believe I just stared at him. I didn't like to answer. I also didn't answer him when he asked if I could do exercises in my room.

I said at the end that the windows of the scullery were painted black. I told him I had asked to be allowed back upstairs, but I had had no reply.

How often did I receive letters?

I said most of them written by Mother and Shirley seemed to arrive.

I think that is all of importance that happened. Today is the first time I have felt like writing about it. And I am beginning to stop thinking about it a little.

After being knighted, the Rt Hon. Sir Percy Cradock later became Britain's Ambassador to China, from 1978-84. He opened and supervised negotiations on the Hong Kong Joint Declaration, regarding Britain's return of the colony to China, which eventually took place in 1997. After his six years as Ambassador in

Beijing, Sir Percy became Prime Minister Margaret Thatcher's foreign policy adviser in London from 1984 to 1992. He was also chairman of the authoritative and influential Joint Intelligence Committee from 1985 to 1992. When he came to visit me at the end of November 1968, he was already the Chargé d'Affaires in China, having taken over the British Office following the departure of Sir Donald Hopson. In 1993 Percy was made a Privy Councillor to Queen Elizabeth II.

My unkind references to Roger Garside are now hugely embarassing to read since I later came to know and like Roger in London where we met with our wives.

REFLECTIONS · 13
Thursday 11 January 2007

That second consular visit to me, of some 20 minutes on 26 November 1968, which sparked an immediately regretted outburst of anger and undeserved rudeness towards my two diplomatic visitors, proved to be a watershed moment in my enforced stay in China. I, however, would not learn any real details about its repercussions until I eventually returned to England.

Personal letters written to me about it from Shirley and others would be withheld permanently during the days and weeks that followed and only gradually was I able to piece together some ideas about the impact of the visit in the outside world. Percy Cradock, I was to learn much later, took the courageous step of calling a press conference in Peking after the meeting on that same afternoon and his words, I was very moved to find much later, made headlines around the world. In particular the British and international media quoted him as saying vividly: 'Grey lives in a void.'

Percy, a former law don at Cambridge, had joined the Foreign Office in 1954 and was serving as Head of Chancery at the British Office on my arrival. Although he had taken a long home leave in Britain after that and so missed some of the early build up to the eventual midsummer madness, he had returned in time to become trapped with Donald Hopson and the rest of the British diplomatic staff in the cataclysmic burning of the British Office. So I already knew and personally liked the quietly spoken thoughtful senior diplomat, who was widely respected for his formidable intellect and his insightful understanding of China, past and present. He could have been forgiven, I eventually thought, for thinking otherwise on that particular day.

One poignant line of a report on the Peking press conference by the new correspondent for the French national news agency AFP, who had replaced my dear friend, Jean Vincent, touched me deeply when I eventually read it a long time later. 'Both British diplomats,' the French journalist wrote, 'seemed to be having difficulty in controlling their emotions.'

At the Peking press conference, Percy's forthright and outspoken statement about my conditions was highly critical of how I was being treated by my Chinese hosts. I am not sure if these statements were made with or without the prior approval of the British Foreign Office in London. His telegram to his superiors in Whitehall was later very unusually issued verbatim to the British and foreign press in London, so it appears that if Percy Cradock took the initiative locally in Peking first, he immediately carried the day in changing the mind of the Foreign Office in London too – or forced their hand in making a significant modification of the previous and not altogether unfamiliar 'Play it down, old boy!' policy stance.

In any event his words broke the dam of officially inspired reticence at Reuters, and among the British press generally, about 'over-publicising' my plight. From this point onwards, vigorous press campaigns were launched in Britain and other countries, with Reuters full backing, and they were sustained and pursued until my eventual release.

Gerald Long, for Reuters, put out a statement that night in London saying, 'My reaction is one of horror at the conditions in which Mr Grey is held. I appeal once more to the Chinese authorities to release him immediately and I count upon the press, radio and television of the world to renew this appeal daily until he is released.' He and the Reuters board of directors thereafter repeatedly appealed by personal cable to Mao Tse-tung and Chou En-lai for my release.

The British National Union of Journalists, which had also accepted the previous Foreign Office advice, followed suit and mobilised its members to join journalists from many countries in protesting directly to China's leaders. Some 2,800 British journalists signed a petition arranged by a Fleet Street Action Committee and took it to the Office of the Chinese Chargé d'Affaires in Portland Place; the International Federation of Journalists, representing 60,000 journalists in 23 countries, cabled a protest from Brussels to Chinese Premier Chou En-lai with a copy to U Thant, Secretary General of the United Nations. The International Press Institute, Danish journalists, Australian journalists and the Berlin Foreign Press Association, of which I had earlier been a member, also cabled the Chinese leaders. Reuters colleagues and the Fleet Street Action Committee petitioned the Prime Minister, Harold Wilson, and he received representatives at 10 Downing Street.

The Action Committee, I was very touched to learn on arrival home, also collected money from journalists and arranged to have a leading psychiatrist standing by to fly to Peking to see me at a moment's notice. A request was made to the office of the Chinese Chargé d'Affaires in London for this doctor to visit me – but no response was ever received.

This move was obviously triggered by the line in Percy Cradock's widely published telegram report which said, 'He was obviously agitated at seeing the British officials and, as might be expected, under considerable general nervous strain as a result of his long solitary confinement.'

By a curious chance I have only today, early in the new year of 2007, become fully aware in detail of Sir Percy's feelings and thoughts about that distant disturbing consular meeting. Some 12 years ago, in 1994, after retiring at the climax of a highly distinguished career, after eight years as Margaret Thatcher's foreign policy adviser and a similar period as chairman of the Joint Intelligence Committee, Percy published a book entitled *Experiences of China*, focussing on the large part of his life that had involved him with the world's most populous nation.

A copy of the book has remained inexplicably unscrutinised amongst my large collection of books on China, which have most often been in store during a number of home moves over the past dozen or so years. Quite recently, with more space available in my current home, I was able to retrieve from storage a larger number of books and, aware that I had never found the time to read it, I included *Experiences of China* among many others still unread. However I placed this volume on shelves in my sitting room, still without then immediately investigating or reading it.

Only upon reaching this section of the transcription of the shorthand diaries, dealing with the second consular visit of November 1968, did I fully realise that it would make sense to look into the book by such an authority on China, to check what helpful references it might contain about the period of the Cultural Revolution which I am now reviewing.

To my surprise I found today that it included some illuminating and detailed references to my case and the former ambassador's repeated involvement in dealing with it. It also outlined the plight of some of the several other Britons who were additionally detained or imprisoned in China after me on various trumped-up charges and spurious pretexts.

In his first reference to my assignment in China, Percy wrote that I had been effectively 'pitch-forked into a revolution' with barely time to find my feet before realising that the Hong Kong crisis could have personal implications. After Xue Ping had been sentenced to two years' imprisonment in Hong Kong, he added, 'Grey was called to the Foreign Ministry and not seen again for two years.' When my telephone was cut off, he went on, 'another personal ordeal was added to the millions already imposed by the Cultural Revolution and another intractable problem presented to those who were trying to retain some sense in the relations between the British and Chinese governments.'

Experiences of China also revealed to me something I had not known at the time of that consular meeting – that Percy himself had been in the hands of the ten thousand-strong mob of Red Guards who had sacked and set fire to the British Mission, with the diplomats inside, only four nights after my own invasion, on 22 August 1967. Along with Donald Hopson – who received a bloody head wound that night – Percy had been forced to surrender himself into the crowd. He had been dragged around amidst the hysteria, 'jet-planed' on a soap box, photographed with his head forced down, to shouts of 'Lower your head!' until he finally found himself dragged into the gate-house of the Albanian Embassy on the opposite side of the street. There other British diplomatic personnel were eventually shepherded together by Peoples Liberation Army men for protection against further violence.

If, in my deeply distracted sub-conscious mind during that 26 November consular meeting, I was seeing Percy Cradock and Roger Garside as two of the obnoxious 'three highly prominent Occident-men' from my already mentally composed satirical piece, 'The Play' (presented unchanged at the end of Chapter 12), I could not have been more wrong. Along with all the other British diplomatic staff, Percy had virtually become a hostage in Peking himself for more than a year, restricted for the first three months following the Mission's burning, to home and office and the four-hundred-yard roadway between. 'In effect we were held under house arrest.' he said in his book.

Two days before the British Mission was set afire with all its staff inside, the Chinese Foreign Ministry – which had fallen into disarray under an extremist take-over – presented Donald Hopson with an impossible ultimatum over Hong Kong. Britain must cancel its ban on three 'patriotic' (pro-Communist) newspapers in the colony, declare innocent and release 19 'patriotic' Chinese journalists who had been arrested or imprisoned, and call off lawsuits against two newspapers and printing firms. This demand for total surrender and compliance or partial compliance was impossible to meet, said Percy Cradock in his book, given the legal processes in Hong Kong, and all that could be done was prepare for the siege.

Immediately after the trauma of the British Office being torched because of the failure to meet the demands of the ultimatum, on the recommendation of Donald Hopson and Percy Cradock, the Foreign Office in London placed restrictions on Chinese diplomats there, confining their movements to a radius of five miles from Marble Arch, compelling them to seek Foreign Office permission (exit visas) before leaving the country and keeping them under police surveillance wherever they went. These restrictions triggered the extremely bizarre 'Battle of Portland Place', which occurred on 29 August in London. That day Chinese diplomatic staff emerged abruptly from their offices onto the street swinging various implements, including baseball bats, axes and broom-handles, and started to mix it violently with the unarmed London policemen who were carrying out their routine embassy guard duties. There were injuries on both sides.

The very next day, Percy describes being summoned to the Chinese Foreign Ministry with Donald Hopson at two o'clock in the morning. There had been no contact with the Ministry during the seven days since their Mission had been burned down. The very timing of the meeting indicated the serious nature of the occasion. To emphasise this, the meeting was put back at the last moment from 2am to 3am.

So Britain's two senior government representatives in China made the journey to the Ministry by car in the small hours of 30 August, 'wondering whether we would be received as diplomats or held as prisoners'. John Weston, who had been with me on my fateful 'arrest' visit to the Ministry, was also accompanying them – and I was in all their minds then, because they anticipated they might possibly suffer a similar fate. 'We recalled how Grey had not been seen again after his call at the Ministry on 21 July,' wrote Percy.

In the event they were not held as prisoners and diplomatic propriety was partially preserved. In response to the restrictions imposed by the Foreign Office on Chinese personnel in London, the effective 'house arrest' restrictions already mentioned were at this point clamped on all British representatives in Peking; all exit visas were cancelled and all British personnel were confined to activities at their residences, or in their Office – which following the fire had been temporarily set up in one of their flats in Wai Chiao Ta Lou, the residential diplomatic compound. For any attempt to move outside that area, special applications would have to be submitted 48 hours in advance, they were told.

That next morning Donald Hopson and Percy, at the head of a British group, were forced to 'face the masses' again in a final confrontation, despite an appeal for protection to the Protocol Department of the Foreign Ministry. This time a big angry crowd gathered inside the residential compound, watched from their windows by diplomats of other countries and British wives and families who had been moved to the homes of diplomats of other nations. The crowd came as a result of the alleged 'fascist atrocities' and 'brutalities' committed by British police in the 'Battle of Portland Place' in London. 'This curious piece of theatre was undoubtedly engineered by the Chinese,' said Percy in his book, 'so that they could claim to match us in terms of outrage and work themselves into the position of moral superiority from which they loved to operate.'

He admitted that he found that final confrontation with the masses 'the most trying moment of the saga', because of the bleak realisation that the flats were not immune and that British diplomatic families too could face repeated incursions by violent men. He says he left his wife Birthe sitting on a laundry basket containing the Mission's remaining stock of money, to go with others and meet demonstrators because otherwise 'the violence could have become general'. More ugly scenes ensued, unsuccessful attempts were made to make Percy and others bow their heads and at one point 'one of the dervishes rushed forward and seized Donald Hopson's hair, forcing his head down'. To everyone's enormous relief, the demonstrators eventually marched away, having triumphed according to their lights.

From that point onwards the situation gradually eased, the epileptic spasms of China's body politic began to quieten. Before long it became clear that the torching of the British Office had been the climactic moment of the Cultural Revolution, as far as China's destabilised and erratic international policies were concerned. Decisions to restrain further actions against foreigners were seemingly taken by Mao in September 1967 and he also took his foot off the accelerator of the domestic Cultural Revolution too. The full restrictions on the movements of Britain's diplomats lasted three months, to November 1967, before being eased in response to a restoration by the British Foreign Office of the normal 35-mile radius travel zone for China's representatives in London.

Deadlock on the question of diplomatic entry and exit visas in both countries, however, continued until April 1968 and was broken only after the resignation of George Brown from his post as Foreign Secretary during that month and his replacement by Michael Stewart. Donald Hopson and Percy Cradock had been urging a unilateral British lead on this to encourage a Chinese response, but George Brown and his advisers had resisted, apparently wishing to show they could be as tough and uncompromising as China. (So perhaps if anybody remotely resembled my 'Three highly prominent Occident-men', it was surprisingly in the end, George Brown and his closest London-based officials – with possibly the addition of the Governor of Hong Kong, Sir David Trench, whom I discovered soon after my release had been firmly opposed to any early concessions on the prison sentences of the Communist 'news workers' in the colony against whom I was held.)

Mr Stewart, according to Percy Cradock's version of events, was more amenable to this unilateral advice from Peking and quickly removed the exit permit restrictions and granted outstanding entry visa applications. China encouragingly responded, at first, by granting exit permits for junior staff and entry visas for new incoming staff at the British Office in Peking – but still refused all applications in and out for senior diplomatic staff. This lowered temperature in the diplomatic confrontation accounted for the fact that my first consular visit from Donald Hopson and John Weston was allowed on 24 April 1968.

Tension later rose over Hong Kong again, however, in mid-year when American warships involved in the Vietnam conflict docked there, among them a nuclear-powered aircraft carrier. China immediately protested and the granting of new visas quickly ceased. Only when it was indicated by the British Mission in Peking that an internationally publicised diplomatic campaign was planned, to emphasise the continued 'imprisonment' of British diplomats in China, while Chinese diplomats could come and go freely in Britain, were normal travel conditions restored in late July 1968. Sir Donald Hopson finally left for home in mid-August – and Percy Cradock, self-confessedly shrugging off his own 'detainee' or 'hostage' status for a short while, left China for the first time in over a year to relax a little in Hong Kong in late October.

Except he seemed, according to his own account, determined to do much more in the colony than relax – perhaps influenced by the success with the Chinese Foreign Ministry of the threat to publicise the unequal situation regarding British diplomats in China and Chinese diplomats in Britain. By this time he had become Chargé d'Affaires, following the departure of Donald Hopson, and perhaps this allowed him to feel he had a freer rein in his decision-making from then on. The whole tone of *Experiences in China* shows the former law don to be a man of strongly independent and assertive mind, and although there was still some tension in the colony involving communist schools and home-made bombs, he had, even before his visit, initiated an exchange of correspondence with the Governor 'with the (British) detainees in mind, particularly Grey'.

Without giving precise details of the content of the correspondence, the author says the exchange became 'rather sharp' and that the Foreign Office in London did not fault his reasoning, but were upset by the tone of the telegrams exchanged with the Governor and gently said so. 'This,' he added, 'was not the last of such admonitions I was to receive.' The Governor, he added, who was not accustomed to having his policies dissected, 'was even more upset'.

He does reveal, however, that the issue uppermost in his mind at the time was whether the British Government was right to shun publicity over myself and the other British prisoners in China. He admitted that there were some good supporting arguments – it is usually easier to make concessions quietly and there was a particular danger with the Chinese that having taken up a public position, their national prestige would seem to be involved and they would dig in.

Although Reuters and the British press generally until then had accepted this advice, he said 'in Grey's case, the Chinese were now already on record. There were also vast resources of publicity worldwide that had not been tapped. Nor were the Chinese impervious to pressure. Their foreign policy was no longer one of total isolation and defiance; they were cultivating friends again and even considering establishing relations with new countries.'

As a result of all this reflection, he decided to use the occasion of his visit to Hong Kong to speak to the press – on the record – to express concern for the ten British subjects then detained in China and to condemn the Chinese refusal to grant consular access. 'This was thought rather daring,' he wrote, 'coming from one who had only just ceased to be a detainee himself. But it was a deliberate move, using an instrument that was available to us. I also pointed out that Grey, who was in solitary confinement, had not been treated in accordance with normal standards, had not been charged with any crime or sentenced in any court. He had been held without explanation. The Chinese incantation, "You are well aware why Mr Grey has been treated in the way he has," was not good enough. Again a risky line: the Chinese could have cooked up a charge and a trial if need be without difficulty. But the calculation was that the time for such antics had passed.'

Without my knowledge at the time, this press conference statement brought the plight of myself and nine other Britons unexpectedly back into the national and international limelight. Even now, all these years later, I feel like standing up and cheering that firmly taken initiative.

Of course being put on trial on faked charges had been a constant concern of mine during the whole of that time. After my release, I would discover that at a rally of 15,000 screaming Red Guards before whom my driver Lao Wang was 'struggled to the point of a long term mental breakdown', I was described as 'the big spy Grey'. This had been reported in a Red Guard newspaper. Looking back now, perhaps I lived some kind of charmed life, because had they found my shorthand diaries with their endless pages of hieroglyphics, they could easily in the hysterical circumstances have cited these 'coded' writings as evidence of my 'spying on China's internal affairs' and rapidly consigned me to an even worse experience in a worse prison.

On absorbing all this (to me) new information about the detailed thoughts and actions of Sir Percy Cradock during that critical period of Sino–British relations, I am newly aware and grateful that I indeed had an unsuspected personal champion of my cause in high places, along with those other contemporary British detainees. Of his visit to me in November following his return to China, Percy ultimately wrote in his book, 'Again publicity was very much an issue in late November when we were allowed a second visit to Grey and I went to see him accompanied by Roger Garside. It was not an easy interview. His mind was naturally on the Hong Kong prisoners. When would the last be released? I could give him little comfort … But later in a press conference and in a telegram home I was able to describe the conditions in which he was held. The telegram was published in full and the final sentence, "He lives in a void," got home. A storm of publicity followed. I think it helped.'

Percy Cradock eventually left China in early 1969, after a three-year spell of duty in China. He and his wife Birthe were tired, he said, marked by the demands of running a post 'under siege conditions' and the wider pressures of living in 'a demented environment, an Alice-in-Wonderland world, governed only by its own mad logic'. China then, he added was still in the grip of a nightmare, a regime under which the normal vices of a communist system had swollen to monstrous proportions. 'The standard lies and persecutions were now on an Orwellian scale; the tyranny both complete and capricious; the link with reality almost non-existent.'

Having read this revealing analysis of the background to my plight, almost as an afterthought, having caught up on the detail of Percy's narrative, I turned to the title page of *Experiences of China* to see if there was an indication as to the date when I originally obtained the book. There was: April 1994. What's more the date was written in Percy's own handwriting below a brief inscription that said:

To Tony: Who also experienced China. With warmest wishes, Percy Cradock.

The sight of this finally unblocked a memory obscured in the course of a busy life. I remembered I had indeed been invited by publishers John Murray to the launch party for the book in London. Another engagement that evening had allowed me to attend only fleetingly. During a few minutes at the party, I had managed to speak briefly to the book's distinguished author, who was surrounded by a deep throng of China Watchers pressing around his signing table.

Percy had signed the book for me with a warm smile, when I briefly got his attention and we exchanged just a few quick words before I departed. At the front of the book I notice today is a Latin tag from Virgil, befitting the publication of a former Cambridge don: *Forsan et haec olim meminisse iuvabit.* 'Perhaps even these things it will one day be a joy to recall.' Percy says he quoted it aloud wryly to fellow diplomats and other embassy staff as they crouched battered and apprehensive against a wall in sight of the burning British Mission on the tumultuous night of 22 August 1967.

My own love of writing was directly inspired during school-day translations of

Virgil and I feel perhaps, in our very brief exchange at that launch party, there was an instinctive shared appreciation of the sentiment of that quotation – both of us having been glad to have survived those surreal and dangerous late Sixties years in Peking with our lives, and well enough to continue our careers and tell our own respective tales. Yet also I am sure we were both consciously glad in retrospect to have been part of it. On reflection, my omission in not carefully reading the contents of *Experiences of China* before now is inexplicable.

However, no matter how late, the detailed understanding of the complexities of Sino–British hostilities in general and my personal part in them in particular, and how they were being handled in Peking and London during those strange years of 1967 and 1968, brings with it now a certain feeling of late closure. As the sparse entries in my shorthand diary for December 1968 which follow will show, in my own section of that 'demented environment, the Alice-in-Wonderland world governed by its own mad logic', I did not have any real understanding that anything had changed following that crucial second consular visit.

After anticipating with a growing sense of certainty that I would be released towards the end of l968, the severe and nearly unbearable disappointment that I was not to be freed had obviously left me drained of almost all feeling. In the days and weeks that followed, it will be seen that I did not communicate much with my diary, as I struggled to re-accustom myself to a new effort of endurance. But at Christmas itself, on Christmas Eve and Christmas Day small bizarre events in the form of what I will term a Christmas card 'bombshell' would carry a discernible underlying hint that a new and eventually climactic phase in my period as a hostage was beginning.

14
CHRISTMAS CARD BOMBSHELL

Sunday 1 December 1968
Plan - Remain calm to Christmas and beyond.

1   Keep busy!

2   On 2 December do accounts.

3   Write to Shirley.

4   Compile 31 small crosswords.

5   Study some Chinese each day.

6   Absolute self-control with no staring, etc.

7   Aim at 18 months.

Above all, keep busy and optimistic.

Saturday 7 December 1968, 9.15 pm

Yesterday three letters from Shirley, telling me how disappointed she was when she expected me to be released. I have been very touched by her buying a put-u-up. But it seems to me inviting disappointment to do things like that. It is now 11 days since I asked for a doctor. Perhaps my chest is slightly better. I have found the non-arrival of a doctor encouraging in a way. But I know in my heart of hearts I am only being messed around.

I have been reading a book called *Outline History of China* for the past ten days and have now finished it. I pray that something good at least will come in December. But I am prepared for a very miserable Christmas. I am trying to be patient to await some guidance from Shirley in her letters after the visit – if they arrive. It would not surprise me if they were stopped. I wonder what the cable that arrived on 3 December was for? It was not given to me.

I am living in a kind of vacuum in which I am inclined not to do very much and although worried about my health, the fact that a doctor won't come only makes me more unfeeling.

This really is a very strange period of a lack of feeling. I am no longer totally miserable, as I was after the visit of Percy Cradock. I harbour some hope, but my reason tells me there really can be none for some time. I suppose the nearness of Christmas and the fact that last year they seemed to recognise this helps me not to be too miserable. But I am really very lost.

Thursday 12 December 1968, 8.00 pm

Yesterday at lunchtime I pointed out that 15 days had passed since my request for a doctor and at about five o'clock a doctor came. He was older and gave me confidence. He gave me a good examination and diagnosed pharyngitis, and said that there was a possibility the pains in my chest were muscular pains. He said there were no symptoms of tuberculosis or even bronchitis (which the previous doctor diagnosed on 13 November). I was given pills to suck, cough mixture and an inhalant. Price: 12 yuan.

(As before) we would see how things went and if I didn't get better, we could have further examination, X-ray, etc., the interpreter told me when he came back with the medicine. I feel considerably relieved at this. I had begun to think that the doctor was being withheld because perhaps I was going to be released. So that at least was destroyed, but I feel little or no regret since I didn't really believe my 'theory'.

But I don't understand their wretched minds. Why keep me 15 days and then when I ask again, send a doctor almost immediately? My mood is still neutral. I am waiting for Shirley's letters to tell me of the reactions to the visit. I suppose I am hoping for something at Christmas – books or perhaps cables. I pray that December isn't just a blank. But I have no real hope of release.

My next point in time is 21 January, when it will be exactly 18 months. But I can't seriously hope for release until something further happens in Hong Kong or there are some negotiations on me. My prospects are still negligible. I suppose that is why I wait for Shirley's letters to guide my thinking. But I fear they will be tampered with. I began taking my various medicines today. Oh, what a wretched life it is. I have felt extremely frustrated physically recently, thinking of sexual activity and all it entails in a very intensive fashion.

Saturday 14 December 1968, 20.30 hours

(Mum's birthday)

There are several things to record. Yesterday morning I awoke to snow in the courtyard and on the tree. 'Oh just look at that!' came from me involuntarily, reminding me of my poem 'Snow in England', which I wrote some time back.

About ten days ago I saw that the latest addition to my dining room was a small white plaster bust of the Chairman on the table. Anyway, today's events: blackboards were changed; the old ones about 'Force at the core ...' and 'If we are attacked we will certainly counter-attack ...' were replaced by boards telling me how 'Imperialism is always doing evil things ...' and the old favourite, 'Lifting a rock only to drop it on your own foot ...'.

I was very kindly given a new portrait above my bed of Chairman Mao and Lin Piao. I also received two letters from Shirley, telling me the British Prime Minister spoke about me for several minutes on the night of 26 November. But the first letter of reaction to the visit was missing. The other letter said Don Ferguson, head of Visnews, visited her and he obviously scored a big hit.

Yesterday I had a big medical visit: two women doctors, an X-ray team, and a blood-test man. All crowded into this little room. During my talk with the doctors, I mentioned misery and lack of appetite and sleep. The examination was thorough. The X-ray equipment seemed Heath Robinson, supported on what looked like school high-jump stands and when they looked at my chest they used a kind of wooden box thing. The switch was done up with sticky tape.

I now await the results with hope. The reason for the visit baffles me. I can't be bothered to write a long diary about it. I hope something will happen before Christmas or during Christmas, but doubt if anything will.

Tuesday 17 December 1968, 9.30 pm

Today a cable was delivered while I was walking. Haven't been given it yet. I guess it is from Shirley on her birthday (yesterday, 16 December), but I don't anticipate it will say anything beyond, 'I love you.' What an angel she is! Of course, that is a mighty lot; I don't mean to cheapen it. Also today while I walked in the morning, a portrait of Mao that was put up over my bed a few days ago was moved over to the door. The one that has been by the table for a year was moved up over the bathroom door.

I have just completed the creation of my 279th crossword! My mind is fairly blank. I am hoping for something, however slight, for Christmas. But I am prepared for nothing. My mind still goes no further than 18 months at present. I am still really waiting for letters to show me something of the situation after Percy Craddock's visit. I suppose I think of next June as a release possibility now. But I am also hoping for something in-between and also ready for it to be almost any length of time.

Friday 20 December 1968, 20.00 hours

Yesterday the little translator came and told me the results of the medical. Nothing wrong, he said, with your lungs, liver or other organs. Diagnosis: pharyngitis. I asked for more medicine and it came later. I was charged 31 yuan 60 cents for the service.

Today I am hoping for mail tomorrow from Shirley. Yesterday I saw what appeared to be two big brown envelopes arrive with the papers and at first thought it was a wrapped magazine. I saw a coloured bordered envelope on the table a few days ago. I now live from weekend to weekend, hoping for mail. I still have no idea whether I have any reason to hope. I am vaguely hoping for something at Christmas; either a parcel, books, some cables or a visit – but I shall be not at all surprised if I get nothing.

I don't think beyond 21 January – the 18-months' mark. But in the back of my mind I am ready to go on until June or July now. On the fifteenth I asked for books and repeated the request yesterday. I was told I wouldn't be told that day. Fucking bastards!

There is very little to say. During the night I dreamed I was somewhere back home with my mother. I found the *Eastern Daily Press* file and looked at 27 November (the day after Percy Craddock's visit) only to find a column cut out. I asked Mother to look in the Evening News. She cut out something, but it wasn't it. I screamed at her that I had been in fucking solitary confinement for 16 months and wanted to know what people thought of it. It was a mad dream. I wonder whether I shout out in my dreams. I should think it's highly likely.

I have just looked through the photographs of Shirley and one of me. God, I am an empty vessel. I have finished *Death of a Hero*, which is really very good. Now I am reading about Chinese philosophy with the great emphasis on Taoism. I am so empty.

Monday 23 December 1968, 22.30 hours

This morning I asked if I could send Christmas cables. No reply has been given, so it is clear I shall not be allowed to. If any answer comes at all, it will be in about 12 days. I hereby write it off. Yesterday afternoon, with the paper, I was given a letter from my mum and the birthday cable of Shirley ('Love you on my birthday'). My mum's letter was dated 14 November and therefore had been held 36 days. It was the seventeenth letter and therefore two letters in between had been stopped. These people are really bastards. I now have little or no hope of having anything to mark Christmas this year. Perhaps I have a one per cent hope of a visit. But it would be quite out of character for the Chinese to allow it. My bitterness knows no bounds.

Mum told me of a visit to her by David (Chipp) on 14 December; he has been marvellously kind to her. There still seems no hope of anything useful happening to me in the foreseeable future.

Last night, a few minutes before I received the cable and letter, I called on God silently to let loose a thunderbolt at the guards! I cancelled the request almost immediately, but within minutes the letters came! This I found tremendously amusing. I shall clearly have to be careful about my use from now on of this secret weapon!

Saturday 28 December 1968

Now it can be told! The story of Christmas 1968! At lunchtime on Christmas Eve, to my surprise, Sao Kao said my request to send cables had been granted. This was little more than 24 hours after I had asked. I was surprised. I spent the afternoon between lunch and tea writing to Shirley, Mother and David Chipp. I checked the one to Chipp over and over again.

When Sao Kao brought tea, I handed them in. Immediately he came back again and started fumbling around trying to tell me something. Eventually I understood (he having stood up an old cable in the shape of a card) that the Foreign Ministry were offering me the chance to send Christmas cards! I didn't ask for this. It had not entered my head to ask for such a thing. I was amazed!

I said, 'Yes', and Sao Kao went off to buy some. I was walking outside when he returned. He showed me them and I was again amazed to see one with a vivid picture of mushroom cloud from an atomic or hydrogen bomb explosion on the front! (China's first successful test obviously!) I tried not to laugh as I walked afterwards, but then wondered whether the joke was not on me?

I thought of sending it to Harold Wilson, but decided against it and sent it to Gerald Long at Reuters. I wanted to write, 'Happy New Year – or else!' in it but decided not to because it might not get through.

I began writing the cards, in fact, before dinner, but didn't finish and continued during the evening. I sent one to Percy Craddock, apologising for my behaviour during his visit. The messages were brief and non-committal. On Christmas morning I handed them in when Sao Kao brought breakfast. He came back immediately with a cable and a letter from Shirley.

Late on Christmas Eve, about 10.00 pm, the bell rang and a cable was received by one of the guards; he went downstairs to get the date stamp to put on it as usual. Shirley's letter was written on the day of my visit and told of the very first reaction to Percy Cradock's report. Her cable, written in a slightly high mood, said she wanted me for Christmas as always. I ate practically no breakfast and also practically no lunch – which was fish and a piece of cauliflower – but I wasn't miserable.

I was very pleased to be able to send cards and this practically made my Christmas. Also the arrival in the morning of a letter and cable gave me something for Christmas. I solved the *Sunday Times'* crossword after lunch, which had come in Shirley's letter.

During lunch I saw two blue-coated cadres come in and that led me to believe that perhaps I was going to be visited; thus I was on edge with possible excitement and barely able to concentrate on my crossword. The cadres went upstairs and later downstairs too. The chief guard marched into my room to look at the temperature on the thermometer – I had switched on the electric fire.

I had risen a little earlier than usual (about 9.30 am) to have a bath. I tried to squeeze two of those things Shirley sent into the bath to make it scented, but they didn't really work. I dressed cleanly and put on my grey suit. When the guard marched in I was disappointed. But still I thought there would be something. But later the two cadres left and I thought I recognised one of them as the Foreign Ministry Service Bureau man who came with a man last May.

I wondered whether this meant something was being considered. But as before it may mean nothing. That is very likely. After bringing tea, Sao Kao returned once more with two cables – one from Gerald Long and one from head of the world desk, Ron Cooper. Long's was slightly more encouraging than last year's, but didn't really carry much intrinsic meaning, 'Fervent hope you will be reunited with your family before too long.'

I thought that was the end of Christmas Day's events. But there was a lot of telephoning between tea and dinner and after bringing in my dinner (meat balls and rice), Sao Kao came in again with the chief guard with my draft cables. I must change the date from Christmas Eve to Christmas Day, they said, and afterwards they could go!

They were back within 24 hours of sending them (to the Ministry)! I changed the dates and turned to set out my meal on the desk when Sao Kao came in yet again! This time he had the cards. They were all right too. They had come back in about eight hours – the same day! Incredible! I had given Sao Kao 190 yuan for the cables, watched by the guards; I gave him 10 more for the cards and he went off immediately to post them. I sat down to dinner and ate my meal hungrily, quite flabbergasted by the speed of events.

I was very hungry, not having eaten breakfast or lunch. I cursed myself for not sealing the cards and wished Sao Kao would come back for some reason. But I had forgotten about this by about eight o'clock. Then he suddenly came in and gave me back a little money. The cables had cost nearly 170 yuan. (Nearly £30!) But the place for the cards was shut and he had brought them back. I was very pleased and explained I wanted to seal them. (I really wanted to check they were in the right envelopes and that Gerald Long had got the atomic or hydrogen bomb explosion.)

I found this very amusing in my mind. After walking from 9 am until 10 am thinking only of cards and cables – thinking they would possibly reach my mother and David Chipp on Christmas Day – I sat down and began to read *Borderline* by Vercors. I had been saving this book to read on Christmas Day, but found I didn't want to start reading it until the normal time. I immediately thought it was very good and enjoyed reading it for an hour.

For the afternoon I had asked for some fresh tea and sugar and drank some in the afternoon, but I didn't eat any fruit. (I was disgusted to hear Sao Kao ask if it was all right before he brought them. It had been established long ago that I could have tea.)

I went to bed around 11.30 as usual, very pleased with the day really. It had been different to all others. I had been asking in my prayers that December should not pass without something to mark Christmas. I felt that my prayers had been answered.

Next morning, on Boxing Day, Sao Kao went off immediately he arrived to post the cards, after I had checked they were in the right envelopes and sealed them down. So everything turned out well. (Perhaps already the one sent to Percy Cradock has arrived; others will still be on the way, I expect.)

Boxing Day passed without incident except, as last year, dear Lao Chiao asked me quietly out of earshot of the guards, 'Christmas all right?'

I replied wryly, 'It could have been better,' but I am not sure he understood.

I tried to talk to him in the bathroom about his son and that Christmas was two days, but he was not particularly eager. Still afraid of his position, poor man.

For the past few weeks I have been managing to go on sleeping until after ten am, so I have re-arranged my morning somewhat. I now don't sit on the closed toilet for half-an-hour or more, writing or reading as in the summer, but wash and dress in the bathroom, and shave and 'open up' my door without doing exercises. I now do my exercises after the door has been shut for lunch.

This is much better and I have resumed doing the full course again. I enjoy this and usually get back in time to eat lunch in about 20 minutes before opening the door again. This way I have two closed doors between the guards and me for that period. I now eat breakfast in my dressing gown (over my clothes). On Christmas Day I did my exercises at lunchtime also. Boxing Day was without incident after the guards had paid a visit. Yesterday also was neither here nor there. I began to feel depressed in the morning, but threw it off as I did my yoga. There is no point. And I am trying to be optimistic about my chances.

I sang a few carols on Boxing Day afternoon as I walked, but not with much enthusiasm. Today I am hoping soon for some more letters from Shirley. Those that I saw being delivered last Thursday and Saturday haven't been given to me; it really seems that if I see letters, they are damned! I am really getting right behind with the news. It has been more than a month now. Dear God, let me have letters soon. And let me have some other improvements soon, like some books from Percy or something.

I half wonder whether something is not in store from the Christmas Day cadre visit. I am really on the verge of exhausting all my books now. For the two days before Christmas I read 'old stuff' at night for the first time. I began reading the short stories of Dennis Wheatley again. It looks like being appalling soon if nothing happens. I asked for books from upstairs again on 15 December, but I have heard absolutely nothing. I didn't really expect the Christmas cards to be anything but a very isolated incident.

I think that is all for Christmas 1968. I can't bear to think of spending Christmas 1969 here. I looked back to last year and found that it is exactly what I said then. I suppose if it is to be, it is to be! I can only accept what comes. But it seems much less likely that I will still be here next year.

REFLECTIONS - 14

Saturday 13 January 2007

To complete my account of that second strange and segregated festive season I spent in China, it seems appropriate perhaps to present here a surrealistic waking dream of Christmas presents dreamed by one who in reality could neither give nor receive them. It all started with him spying one of the many tiny gecko wall lizards that ran up and down the inside walls of the house at all seasons. The sight of one such little creature triggered something in his mind and his imagination was off on a wild Christmas shopping spree suddenly, no make believe expense was spared – and it took several days to complete the list. All he really had to give then were the creations of his mind – products of doubtful value. But to whom? Well perhaps to any of the bizarrre list of people who popped into in his fevered imagination – and then ultimately for the time being, to nobody but himself! Again the list was not written down, but carried home in his memory!

My Christmas List 1968

I'll get a gecko
For El Greco,
And a lasso
For Picasso,
Botticelli:
Colour telly
And this ash tray's
For Velasquez

While for two pins
For Rubens
I'd get loo bins

For Van Gogh
A Scottish loch
For Van Dyke
A Moulton bike
And for Dali,
P'raps a Raleigh
Plus for Goya
A destroyer

I won't be stingy
There'll be conjee
For da Vinci

For Cezanne
A Chinese fan
For Renoir
A Crunchie Bar
For Rembrandt
A potted plant
And for Gauguin
Whalebone probang

While to Constable
At luncheon
Give a truncheon

What for Gainsborough?
Give him Jane's bra!
To Raphael
La Tour Eiffel
To Matisse
A ten-year lease
With Monet
On Galway Bay

And to toothless
Canaletto
A false-setto!

Sample of early national and international news coverage.

*The eight-foot-square 'cell' (top)
photographed after slogans had been cleaned
off its walls ... and a view from the outside
(bottom) looking into that tiny space.*

*Inset: one window still partially blacked
out with Red Guard paint.*

My mother Agnes with Geoffrey Maw (on her left) on the steps of the Foreign Office in London where they delivered a petition with other members of my family ... and a sample page of my secret shorthand journal from November 1968.

'In that small cell I scraped my memory clean... tried to remember over several days the names of all the boys in all my classes at school. (Wensum View Junior football team, 1949, winner of league and knock-out cups... from left to right, back: R.Vincent, M. Franklin, A. Ewing, G.Wall, J. Howard, C. Hindle; (front) C. Buttifant, D. Bowgen, A. Knights, A. Grey (capt), B. Pinching, G.Smith.

A London stage designer mocked up an amazingly accurate life-size model of the eight foot square cell that shocked me with its authenticity when I stepped in and closed the door for a photograph.

最高指示

一切反动派都是纸老虎。看起来,反动派的样子是可怕的,但是实际上并没有什么了不起的力量。从长远的观点看问题,真正强大的力量不是属于反动派而是属于人民。

勒令

首都无产阶级革命派对英国帝国主义分子路透社反动记者格雷勒令如下:

一 格雷在我方警卫人员管制下必须老"实",不许乱说乱动

二 格雷必须在我革命群众贬定的范围内活动,不得超越

三 对我革命群众在格雷住所张贴的毛主席像,语录及标语等,不得涂抹撕毁

四 格雷必须严格遵守我国政府的一切贬定,不得有丝毫违犯,听候我国政府处理

以上所签格雷必须照办,如有违反一切后果由反动记者格雷本人员全个责住。

北京照相机厂红色造反委员签
北京中教育五七战线"红工兵"
北京小教联总部

一九六七年八月十六日

Above: The poster stuck all over me and the house by the invading Red Guards. Right: Its translation into English.

Highest Directive

All reactionaries are paper tigers. In appearance the reactionaries are terrifying, but in reality they are not so powerful. From a long-term point of view, it is not the reactionaries but the people who are really powerful.

Order

Proletarian revolutionaries of the capital, Peking, strictly order British Imperialist element Reuters reactionary correspondent Grey as follows:

1. Grey must always be 'reliable' under the control and supervision of our Public Security Bureau men and may not step out of line in word or deed.

2. Grey must live and remain within the limits defined by our revolutionary masses and must not go beyond them.
3. The portraits of Chairman Mao, the quotations and slogans, etc., stuck on Grey's house by the revolutionary masses must not be erased or torn down.
4. Grey must strictly observe all the decisions of our government and must not contravene them in the slightest degree; he must await further notice from our government.

Grey must act according to the above commands and should there be any contravention, reactionary correspondent Grey himself must bear the entire responsibility for all the consequences.

> Peking No. 1 Photo Machine Factory Red Revolutionary Rebels Council and all revolutionaries of the capital
>
> Peking Middle Schools Fighting Line 'Red Flag'
>
> Peking Primary Schools General Liaison Office.
>
> August 18th 1967.

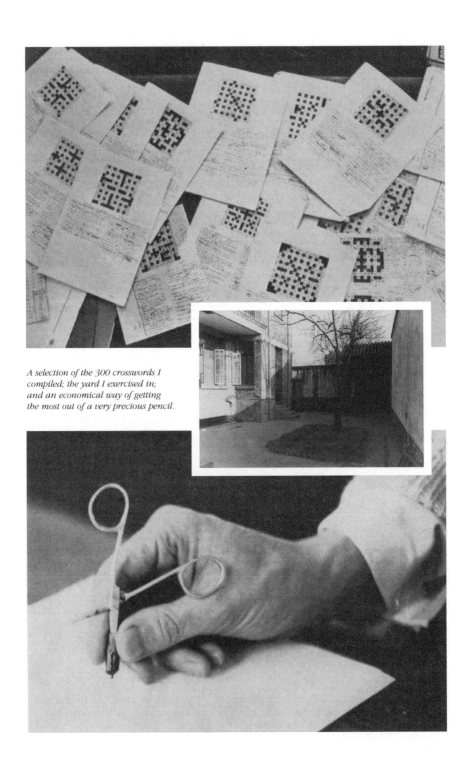

A selection of the 300 crosswords I compiled; the yard I exercised in; and an economical way of getting the most out of a very precious pencil.

250

PART THREE

1969

THE YEAR
OF
THE ROOSTER

15
CHINESE LESSONS

Wednesday 1 January 1969

Well, the bombshell fell on 28 December! Shortly after writing the last entry in this diary on that day, a new development occurred. The delivery of the newspaper to me brought with it the surprise of seeing my name splattered all over it. Sao Kao carried it in with the boiling water he now brings me regularly to inhale with to soothe my throat.

I didn't look at it immediately and remember thinking as usual, 'No bloody news in this newspaper.' Then I turned to the back page and caught sight of the Chinese character for 'correspondent'. There were two stories. I didn't see my name glaring out of one headline until later – but had only caught sight of it in the body of one article by the time Sao Kao brought my dinner. I was shaking slightly and he seemed to look at me expectantly.

I pointed to my name and said, 'Me?'

And he replied, 'Yes!'

He later said he 'couldn't understand', when I tried to question him further, but was not unpleasant. He said, 'Mr Wu!' and went out.

I went into the lavatory feeling this must mean something very bad. I ate almost no dinner. I kept looking at the two articles and could then see my name was plastered all over them. In one despatch from Hong Kong, I could see I was called 'an imperialist' and I think that a big headline on the other said I was 'a reactionary'. I looked at them over and over again in a kind of daze during the evening. I could also pick out a few recognisable dates in my chronology.

I prayed that nothing worse would happen to me. I also thought resignedly that if it made things clear, it might be a help. But largely my reaction was a fear of worse to come. After dinner the guards came to look in the room, which made me more uneasy. Next morning I was anxious to see if Lao Chiao behaved any differently towards me and rushed out of the bathroom quickly before he came with the breakfast.

To my delight there were six letters on my table with the breakfast and Lao Chiao seemed no different. I spent the day reading the letters over and over. I was very touched to hear that Barry had asked for photographs of me. Also that a French journalist, who often criticised China, had offered himself in exchange for me – to take my place. It was clear there was a big gap in the letters from 26 November to 30 November and another gap of a week in mid-December. So I have been denied a lot of information about the impact of my story.

The following day (Monday) I again returned to the task of trying to understand these two articles. I was able to find the meaning of a few of the characters and finally worked out that someone had said China had no legal basis for holding me. I carried on during the Tuesday (yesterday) and wrote out the characters I had found on a piece of paper. I discovered even more. I found that the headline did not refer to me as a 'reactionary' but referred to the British Government. I still can't understand it all. But it seems I am not slandered in the second article as I had thought. But it clearly is not good! Some references to my visit says something about my 'physical something being very good'; it seems that as nothing has happened since then – it means a confirmation of the *status quo*. I hope it makes things clearer to the British Government and I hope they will do something.

Most importantly the result has been to fire me with enthusiasm to learn Chinese. It has made me realise that the characters are not impossible to learn. The *Peking Review* has not been delivered this week and it looks as if it is being held from me, possibly because it contains translations of the articles. Last night at midnight I drank silent toasts in tea to my Mum, Shirley and myself. I realise that this year could be a long one but I do hope that my release will come this year.

Mr Wu was the name of the employed Reuters translator who had come to the office in the house every day during my first few months in China. When the political temperature around me began to rise, in the summer of 1967, and I became the personal target of demonstrations outside the house, he had suddenly stopped coming without warning and I had never seen him again. From that time I had to rely on getting detailed translations from fellow correspondents and diplomat friends. Sao Kao's mentioning his name after such a long time implied self-protectively that it was Mr Wu's job, not his, to translate things like this.

Barry is a nephew of mine, one of my sister June's three sons. The other two, one older one younger, are Mark and Robert. I had not seen much of them as they were still small boys and I had been abroad for most of the time when they were growing up. This request for a photograph of their distant 'long lost uncle' I found very touching at this moment.

Thursday 9 January 1969

There have been several 'events' since I last wrote. Today at breakfast Sao Kao gave me a cable sent in Peking – the first ever during my house arrest. It said, 'Thinking of you more than ever at this time, all our love', but wasn't signed. I asked Sao Kao to ring the post office and a little while ago he made three long telephone calls, and they said they would ring later. I imagined it might be from Annelise and Erna or the Swedes or perhaps even Mrs Craddock or even Mum. I wondered if 'more than ever at this time' (sent on 3 January) meant anything in particular.

After breakfast that delightful little lady doctor came again. It was 11 days ago that I asked for a doctor. She had another look at my throat and I asked what caused my pharyngitis. She said it was dryness. She almost smiled a few times. She stayed on as I walked (in the yard) and I heard the lavatory door open and she must have inspected. As I walked she left. And as she came down the steps our eyes met and I imagined I almost imperceptibly started a smile and I noticed an almost perceptible smile start on her face too. (I could be imagining it, of course.) But she was absolutely lovely. So tiny. As she examined my throat, I could breathe her smell, which was so fresh and fragrant, not the other awful one (not the familiar body smell of the guards). She must have bathed very well this morning. I breathed deeply to inhale the fragrance. I have hardly stopped thinking about her since.

Later Ma Tung-chih came with three little bottles of iodine and two lots of tablets for me to take. Before lunch Sao Kao came up to fix a pan of water on top of the radiator. I think the sweet angel really had wanted to help me! I had thanked her in Chinese ('*Hsieh-hsieh Ni!*') as she went out of the room and she had acknowledged it with a nod of the head. She had been much more friendly and self-controlled this time. Her age I can make no estimate of. Her hair was slightly more lovely this time, as if she had washed it today.

Going back a bit now, during 1 January to 5 January I have worked very hard at learning Chinese. Working every spare moment, I have made good progress. On the 6 January I wrote a ten-page letter to Mum and on the seventh in the morning Sao Kao gave me clean sheets, then lifted them suddenly as up he handed them to me to reveal a treasure of two cables, three cards and four letters! Cables from Shirley and (David) Chipp, cards from Shirley, Mum and June, and letters from Shirley.

I spent the whole day with them. I wrote the last two pages of my letter until dinner, then read them and the enclosures for the rest of the day. The enclosures included the cutting of a report of an incredible American Apollo moon shot at Christmas. It almost moved me to tears when I read that after these incredible orbits of the moon the US astronauts were on the way back and one said in a message, 'We feel like the crews of old-time sailing ships ... we shall be very glad to reach our home port.'

'We shall be glad to get you back,' was the reply. Tears welled up uncontrollably. How ridiculous! I almost cried, too, when I read the *Times* editorial on political prisoners, which said at one point, 'to give what every prisoner needs – hope'. I feel sure Shirley left it in purposely. She obviously reads everything carefully before sending it.

I was quite emotional as I read these things. In fact I was closer to tears than I had ever been before here. Yesterday I continued reading the enclosures (football pages, etc.) and spent several hours mending the big hole in the knee of my trousers. A real Heath Robinson effort! After my evening walk I did my accounts.

Thinking of the lovely little doctor and the cable has kept me from continuing my study, but I shall now resume it. All this unusual activity has given me a feeling that perhaps some change is coming. Sao Kao has been much friendlier recently. It began on the day my name appeared in the paper. He explained little things about the food for a few days. I showed him my cards from Mum etc. and yesterday he stopped to ask what I was doing in my sewing.

This of course may have no consequence at all. But it does help a little bit. I asked him if the doctor had looked in the bathroom and he said, 'Yes.' And he said she had said it was all right. So my mood is not miserable today. I hope for something really good, but of course, have no real basis for this.

Ma Tung-chih had become a regular visitor, when required for translating, and I had heard the other guards call him 'Comrade Ma'.

Saturday 11 January 1969

A short while after I finished writing the last entry on 9 January, Sao Kao brought in the *Peking Reviews* for 3 January. They contained translations of the two items about me in the *People's Daily* on 28 December. I read them once quickly before going out to walk, and during my walk, my reaction was very pleased.

The first read-through seemed to show firstly that there were no accusations against me, and secondly that the Chinese were embarrassed by the position and were lying with all their might and distorting things tremendously to make it look better for themselves.

Later I read them over again and continued to read them all day yesterday all the time. My interpretation of them finally is that they have given me hope. That China should pay some attention to public opinion is very encouraging and removes that fear I had of absolutely ruthless action. The suggestion is there that I will have to wait until the Hong Kong reporters are released, but it isn't absolutely stated. I feel perhaps there might be hope of the Hong Kong Emergency Regulations being lifted in the next few months. I don't think this will bring my release near, but I do hope for something perhaps in about three months' time or six months, say.

I was pleased that the Prime Minister and the Foreign Secretary had spoken out about me in London. At least the case is now in the open. I don't think there can be dramatic developments but I doubt if my conditions will get worse, as I thought before.

(Having said this, I now feel worried that something bad will happen because of my cockiness.) But anyway, I regard it as the hope which I prayed for at the beginning of the week. It gives me hope even if it is in the far future. I hope now that this year will see my release.

Friday 17 January 1969

This past week has contained two interesting things. On Tuesday 14 January I had a letter from Percy Cradock. This was the first letter from an 'outsider', beyond near ones and dear ones, since last April. He said he hoped to see me 'soon', which I feel was some kind of significant encouragement. On Wednesday I was allowed to go upstairs to get books and clothes.

This began in the morning with my request for shoes. I was not allowed to go upstairs myself. After Sao Kao had carried my shoes in to show the guards (how annoying – they needed mending), I closed the door for breakfast and at least four – possibly six – telephone calls followed, as my request was passed on to have the shoes mended!

Even after I was told I could have Amah bring down the shoes, I had to wait 'five minutes'. I got angry and told Sao Kao I also wanted clothes, showing him holes in my clothes and patches in my trousers. But eventually I told him not to ask for them.

I later saw the chief guard downstairs talking to Sao Kao at some lunch at the kitchen table. In the afternoon a long quiet conference took place in the dining room followed by the chief guard going downstairs to call Sao Kao, who was out.

When Sao Kao came in he told me, to my surprise, I could get clothes and books. (I hadn't asked for clothes.) Two guards watched me closely and I had to carry the books down myself, since they refused to let Sao Kao help. I forgot to get the *Playboy* magazines and cursed myself later. I feel that this was perhaps an answer to my second prayer for a 'supplementing of my hopes'. Together with Percy's letter, I believe it does show something.

I am hoping that perhaps there might be a visit in February or March or, if not, that the Hong Kong Emergency Regulations will be lifted in about March so that this can end. I am trying to be optimistic again. Meanwhile I have completed three lessons of Chinese from the *Teach Yourself* book and am into the fourth.

Tuesday 28 January 1969

Eleven days have passed since I wrote the last diary. Eleven empty days. Today is the fourteenth day without letters! It needs only tomorrow to make it the longest period ever without letters since I have been receiving them regularly. There is a little danger that they have been stopped now by the looks of things.

Today I expect to finish the tenth chapter of my *Teach Yourself Chinese* book. Last week from Sunday to Sunday I made a decision to show that I could work hard and for seven days got up at eight o'clock to work in the bathroom. Yesterday was the first time for seven days I didn't get up around eight o'clock. During that week I did four whole chapters, which was very good and it put me back to my target of ten this month. It gave me considerable satisfaction and it turned out to be a good thing to have done, in view of the lack of letters, which otherwise would have made me more depressed than it did. I am trying to let it not affect me, but it is difficult.

The night before last the 'smart' guard came in to look behind the door and try to tell me to open it further. I just stared at him and began to feel myself trembling. He eventually went out of the room. I expected a 'deputation' yesterday, but none came. I have opened the door slightly wider since to try to prevent this. I hate all contact with them.

Last week the guards spring-cleaned 'their' room. They washed the windows and I can now see a line strung across the room bearing several little flannels and towels! They also moved the radio and now use the cupboard where my liquor is, I think, for their water mugs. The constant banging of the door of the sideboard annoyed me at first. But I am now trying consciously not to let them affect me. The main reason for my early rising last week was the fact that the noise in the mornings made by the guards clumping up and down the stairs and arriving and singing and chanting their quotations made it impossible for me to sleep.

One morning I yelled out at the top of my voice because of a particularly loud editorial reading! In addition they now sing at all hours of the day, both together and singly, making a most ungodly racket. This I find very, very trying and have been on the point of asking them to stop the noise several times. These are indeed drab, dismal days.

There is some snow in the courtyard at present and the temperatures are around 23 and 24 degrees each day. There seems to be no hope. I keep asking for a real sign of hope. I felt my prayer had been answered with the *Peking Review* translation of 'The Grey Question' three weeks ago. I feel it was supplemented, as I asked the next week for permission to get books. Last week I asked for my hopes to be raised, but nothing happened. I am still asking for my hopes to be realised. I have heard nothing from Shirley this year. The gap is very big now. I have almost forgotten what it is like to read her letters.

Saturday 1 February 1969

Letters finally came at 6 o'clock on 29 January. There was a good one from Mum telling me of many friends' (including Mary and Emerita) writing to her and a dull one from Shirley, being silly about my not giving Vergil a message for her way back in early 1967 when he returned to London. It has been exactly 15 days in-between letters.

Yesterday I completed my revision of the first ten chapters of the Chinese characters I have learned so far. January was a big success from the study point of view. I wound up creating the old crosswords, which seems ages ago now. I added the last few to the file without checking the clues.

The main thing to report is that the noise made by the guards is now at an all-time high. They 'redecorated' their room, finishing a few days ago. It is now covered with different coloured papers with characters on them and with big green posters all down one side. Every day the louts sing time and time again, standing in front of one wall on which I suspect is written the national anthem. They all sing badly. It is deeply nerve-wracking.

Many times I have been on the point of asking them to keep the noise down, but I did not because I try to show myself completely unaffected by them. Also these days the 'Sniffing Bastard' stares at me all the time I am walking. This takes all the small pleasure out of the exercise periods.

The redecorations were also a big burden to bear. All day long there was an infuriating tap, tap, tap of nails and pins going into the wall as posters and slogans were put up. Their shrine is now a huge full-length picture of Mao in green, with red and yellow writing around the edge. Underneath is a big red poster. The great framed portrait was nailed over the door outside for a time, but has been replaced by a photograph with Lin Piao now. The doors of the sideboard are opening and closing all the time, as they put in and take out their cups. God knows what has happened to my liquor. I have a heavy cold. Yesterday I asked if I could get something for it from upstairs. No answer. Fuck them!

One day, one day! This is a terribly flat time that I am struggling against at present. I have planned to do another ten Chinese lessons this month. The redecoration of the room has been a depressing experience, since it indicates no sign of release or even a visit. This is a low point, I feel. There can hardly be any hope of release for at least six months. This is really wretched, and with my letters becoming much fewer, life has very little to offer. I enjoy reading *The Economist* and my Chinese learning. Life is otherwise empty. I have almost finished reading the book on the Chinese eighteenth-century poet, Yuan Mei.

'Sniffing Bastard' was a guard who sniffed perpetually.

I must have found old copies of the British news magazine, The Economist, *upstairs.*

Monday 10 February 1969

This entry today records two things. First, the winter is ended I think. The temperatures of the past two days have been 40 and 43 degrees. At present I have the window open during breakfast for the first time since last autumn. With this comes a new hardening of my outlook. It is now very clear to me that there is nothing to hope for in the next five months.

I looked up the old cuttings of the *Peking Review* two days ago and found that eight people in all were sentenced to three years, five of them on 13 September having been held for 45 days. This would date their release at the end of July this year, if they got the same remission as Hsueh Ping. Three others got three years in mid-August. So it seems until then there is no outlook.

Mother's letter told me of her trip to London, from which she got no satisfaction, which made it quite clear that the British Government, wretched swines that they are, intend to do nothing for me. They are heroically standing firm. So once again I must prepare to withstand the flat long months of the summer, without any hope, I think, of even a visit.

My letters are now cut to a minimum and my last three letters to home haven't been returned yet. The prospect is grim! This wretched 'no hope' outlook all the time and it is never-changing! How absolutely bloody flat it is! I am trying not to let myself fall into a depression now that I have reached this conclusion. I try to tell myself that perhaps there can be some explanation. I am not pleased the warmer weather is coming. I hate the prospect of another summer in these conditions.

My only consolation at present is that I am engaged in something – learning Chinese. The only plan I have for this terrible five-month period is, perhaps in April or so, to ask to be allowed to go upstairs. But I know it is quite hopeless. I look back to last year's diary to see if spring came at the same time. It did almost to the day. On 15 February I said that the last three days had been mild and I had taken off a sweater. So here we go again! If the others got four years, and if they get four months off a year, I might not be out of here in one year and two months' time. This is my summing up of the whole position. I expect little from the British Government now. The only thing I can hope for is that the Hong Kong Emergency Regulations will be removed and this will lead to early release. Otherwise I am still in for a hell of a time.

Damn and fuck the British Government! Please God deliver me to my loved ones soon, I keep thinking. I have had a rotten cold these past few days, but think it is slightly improved today. When I asked for permission to get some medicine from upstairs a week ago, there was nothing for two days and then a doctor came. Two days ago I asked for new medicine. Since then nothing has happened. Damn and fuck them, too!

Wednesday 12 February 1969

Yesterday, three days after I had asked for it, some medicine was delivered. I noticed a civilian man being led in during my breakfast time. As I was having breakfast, the door suddenly opened and the 'Basketball Player' came in to get the Mao sign-boards from my room.

After I had my walk, there were new boards written in good handwriting. During the walk the guy left. I didn't recognise him. It seemed he had been sent with the medicine, but at the same time he had been instructed to write new quotations.

They were, 'Riding roughshod everywhere, United States imperialism has made itself an enemy of the people of the whole world ...' and 'If the United States monopoly capitalist groups persist in pursuing their policies (the time will come when they will be hanged by the people of the world), the same fate awaits the accomplices of the United States.' I had thought there might be some reference to my letters, but no. Two letters from Shirley on Monday afternoon bore little of interest, except news of a thriller writer who had offered herself in exchange for me.

One guard wore a red undervest, with a large number on the back that was obviously a basketball-team shirt.

Friday 14 February 1969

Last night at dinner my February letter came back from the Ministry after only nine days! December and January letters both not returned. This seems to show some sensitivity, but not absolutely certain, I think. Also received a Valentine cable from Shirley.

Yesterday I had a haircut, and a new light was put up outside my room (this morning I asked for something to be done about it but they might be funny about it) and my toilet was mended. Shirley's cable tentatively shows that on 11 February there was nothing to hope for. So it goes on.

Thursday 20 February 1969

Since the last diary, the guards have refused point blank to do anything about the light outside my room. They claim to know better than I, how I sleep! Also on the night of the 17 February – the Chinese New Year – they sat up all night and played cards (with my cards from upstairs) and woke me every hour or so with their noise. I crashed loudly into the toilet once 'in protest'. The night before, they brought food in and had Sao Kao cook it and he ate with them at my table! I went to look when I heard the 'Basketball Player' go upstairs to get the cards.

Yesterday I shut the outside door after it had been left open for some time. I half-expected some reprimand for it, but I think they didn't see me (the outside door of the house is outside my room). Letters are long overdue again (11 days). I am past chapter 18 in my Chinese studies.

Still there is no hope or sign of anything. I am trying to reconcile myself to the prospect of nothing until July and August.

The decision of the guards, refusing to do anything about the light shining into my room from outside all night, has had me thinking of it almost constantly. It really got me into a vile mood. A few nights before, two of the swines sat outside my door talking loudly and I shouted at them. To my surprise nothing happened against me, but they gave it up almost immediately. I half-expected a general reprimand on all this. In the course of my reading and study I find myself increasingly wanting to check things over and over. This, I think, is a sign of nerves.

Today there is a light covering of snow.

Friday 21 February 1969

Today it is 19 months! Yesterday three letters from Shirley in which she tried to 'give me the facts'. Quite clearly I must look forward to another long, long haul. This threatened to depress me often last night and today, but I am fighting it. There is nothing in the immediate future to hope for. I am trying to carry on with the Chinese studies. Today and yesterday there is clumping up above as the guards wash their filthy sheets in the bathroom. This does annoy me!

Since the letters arrived yesterday, I have been 'writing' many interesting replies to Shirley in my head, but am trying to be reasonable before the real letter-writing time comes around. Most incredible thing was that my January letter reached home! It seems the Foreign Ministry men posted it, since it never came back here. I enjoyed very much reading an interview with actor Laurence Olivier from a cutting in the letters. Thank God for the letters anyway.

Wednesday 4 March 1969

(I am still as jumpy as ever about somebody coming in while writing this!)

Thirteen days have again passed without letters! It really is sickening. This morning I handed in a letter to Shirley, written yesterday. It will be interesting to see how long it takes to come back.

The snow is high in the courtyard, having fallen three days ago, and has thinned a little each day. But my walking at present is very restricted, because of the ice. Yesterday's letter to Shirley was a bit depressing, I suppose. This is a time of no hope in the foreseeable future. I have worked out that absolutely nothing can be expected before July or August and then perhaps only a visit. It may well be I shall be here this time next year with no other feeling except the present one.

I have reached Lesson 23 out of 40 in my Chinese studies. This is my only satisfaction. I have read a comprehensive survey of Japan in *The Economist*, but my reading is all at sea. I have asked for earplugs, because of the difficulty of sleeping in the mornings. There is nothing to say. I hope only for letters soon.

Friday 7 March 1969

I made today the beginning of spring. The temperature is above 40 degrees, the heavy snowfall is melting and today I got up early, bathed and put on my brown sports jacket and trousers and red sweater – it feels good. It was an effort to start a 'new era' and cast off the wretched feeling of wearing my worn old leather jacket and sewn-up trousers. But although it feels good, there is nothing to help me believe there will be any improvement. Quite the contrary.

Today it is now 15 days without letters – nearly the longest ever in normal times. And it clearly will go on for a few more days, possibly another week (if they haven't been stopped altogether). What a wretched time! What hopelessness with which to welcome spring. Please God bring me real hope of release. Please don't let me languish here another year without hope.

Monday 17 March 1969

A short note to record some satisfaction in progress with learning Chinese. I have today started on the Twenty-Eighth Lesson. But what is more satisfying is that I can now read all the characters daubed on the walls in the courtyard – and can also now read some of the poster about me in the lavatory. I am described as a 'reactionary' on it.

I have managed to read quite a few headlines in the paper recently. Progress is really very satisfying. Otherwise yesterday I received three letters from Shirley, very sweet but unremarkable. Her reply to my letter in February didn't arrive. On Saturday there was a visit from a man I thought to be from the Foreign Ministry. He seemed to be the one who came with the medicine and wrote the slogans in January.

Yesterday's letters were stamped with the date of 15 March. This seemed to me to indicate he had given instructions for me to get my letters earlier (in view of my complaint about this in the letter I wrote home, very specially expressed). I hope this was so. Otherwise the snow is melting fast now and I believe I won't be premature in thinking spring is soon to begin. But I have been surprised several times recently with new snowfalls. I am really ready for the spring now, and not annoyed at its going as I was a few weeks ago. My hopes see nothing except hauling through another summer, but I do hope for something in the autumn.

Tuesday 25 March 1969

My windows are wide open, birds are chirping in the tree, the temperature is well above 50 degrees and this is to record that spring has come. I sit with no jacket on, writing this. No letters have arrived for nine days. My hopes of fast mail haven't been justified, but I am still hoping.

The other fact is that yesterday I managed to understand every item on the foreign page of the newspaper and worked out a lot of details of names and countries, which help a lot. I have completed 30 chapters of my Chinese studies and am at present revising (today I am reading 1–30). I feel that even if I learn no more, already the learning has shown good results. I have been quite depressed recently, but have endeavoured not to let it get really bad. How I long for something to happen.

Wednesday 2 April 1969

I believe the Ninth Congress of China's Communist Party began last night. The radio was on again in the next room and soon lists of names were being read out. I thought I recognised Chu Teh and Chen Yi. Then the firecrackers and drums and gongs started in the distance. The guards excitedly shouted, '*Wan shou wu chiang!* (Life without end!) to Mao and later on jumped up and sang three revolutionary songs – including 'The Helmsman' and two others extolling Mao.

Drums and gongs quickly became louder, the police came and went and there was an air of excitement. I was reading the thriller novel *Midnight Plus One* by Gavin Lyall and enjoying it greatly, so was little affected this time by the noise. I slept quite well and was only once woken, about 2 am I suppose, by drums and gongs. The wireless went on well after midnight. This morning it began again after I got up.

While I was walking, I saw the tall flags going by in the street above the wall. I saw through the opened gate that some of the marchers – it opened when the guards came and went – were carrying what appeared to be flowers. The flags said, 'Long live our great leader!' It is much earlier than I expected.

On my personal front, it is a record 17 days since I received mail. Things are very bleak. There seems little likelihood of mail either. I have reached Lesson 33 in the Chinese studies and have got quite a lot out of this, although I find it a drag to have to drive myself on to study it every day.

I have just, this lunch time, had a bath, leaving myself ten minutes or so to eat a fairly wretched meal of bad eggs, cabbage and tough meat before opening the door. The very first beginnings of leaves are visible on the trees. There is no possible beginning of my release, or of the slightest change in my circumstances. Well over 20 months now.

The Ninth Party Congress, taking place much earlier than outside political observers including myself would have expected, were a clear and hopeful sign that the worst excesses of the Cultural Revolution were being tidied up and that some semblance of order was at last being restored nationwide - although officially the Chinese hierarchy insisted that the mass movement known as the Cultural Revolution endured in the broadest sense for all of ten years from 1966 to the time of Mao's death in 1976. Primarily the Congress, by referring to him constantly as his 'closest-comrade-in-arms', officially confirmed Defence Minister Lin Piao as Mao's successor.

Chu Teh, a venerable Marshall of the People's Liberation Army, had been a member of the elite five-man Standing Committee of the Party Politburo and this early radio announcement probably announced his relinquishing that powerful post. Chen Yi, another Long March general, had been Foreign Minister at the time I arrived in China and therefore was the man ultimately responsible for my situation. He was attacked and struggled by Red Guards, suffered ill health and never resumed his full role at the Foreign Ministry, so Chen too was probably among those announced as 'standing down' from his party posts in the lists where I fancied I heard their names mentioned.

Saturday 12 April 1969

Yesterday two letters from Shirley and one from Mum came after 26 blank days. They gave me more letters together than usual, seemingly because both Shirley's letters were practically meaningless. All but two of her numbered letters in March (about 12) had been stopped. Mum's numbering showed that two had been stopped, one including a letter from June. How wretched these swines have become! I promise to relate it if I ever get the chance. I shall in particular write about the guards.

I was able to read the Chinese in the newspaper when it was announced the next day – the Party Congress – and the arrival of the *Peking Review* confirmed that I had understood all the important parts. I am at present on the Chinese proverbs lesson, number 38. So I am near the end of the task I set myself at the New Year.

The tree in the yard is covered with small bright green leaves. Yesterday it was 70 degrees for the first time since last October. I looked back to last year's diary and find that at this time last year the tree was in blossom and it is exactly a year since I had that 'mystical experience'.

My ideas have hardened in the last few days to thinking that perhaps in five months there will be a possibility of something happening. Of course I still continue to pray for a miracle. From Mum's letter it seemed she was quite depressed. It is almost 21 months now. How wretched for her too!

I have a very strange intuition of antipathy from the Information Department over my letters and everything else. I realise I am writing far less diaries than before. The last few days I have been quite depressed, but am trying to keep it from assuming bad proportions. Recently I have read *Tortilla Flat* (John Steinbeck) and *Midnight Plus One* (Gavin Lyall) again. Both were enjoyable. I hope to God my letters will come more regularly. A letter containing eight crosswords to solve was a big spirit-raiser.

Friday 18 April 1969

Two days ago I had three very cheering letters from Shirley. Cheering first because they arrived only five days after the last ones – one was posted on 9 April which meant it reached me in 7 days – and secondly because they contained interesting news. This was that the Chinese Foreign Ministry had said I was being granted the 'concession' of having books when they met the new British Chargé d'Affaires, who has arrived here. Also I was told that there was a piece in the papers about my asking for information about what goes on.

One of the replies was Shirley's reply to my March letter, so this was nice too. She also said she loved me very 'beautifully' and also she had strong hopes for September. All these things cheered me up immensely after these terrible 26 days without letters. Also I am trying to think of time now as only three or four months before I can start hoping again.

This year some months don't seem to have lingered so much. I think it seems now a month goes much quicker than before. Yesterday I finished

Chapter 40 of my Chinese book, thereby completing my task! This has pleased me a lot. So I am feeling much better at the moment, although of course there is a lot of difficult time to go.

John Denson took over as Chargé d'Affaires in Peking on the departure in early 1969 of Percy Cradock.

Saturday 19 April 1969

Yesterday a single letter from Shirley! Only two days after the last delivery and it was only posted on the 12 April! So it was a six-days' door-to-door delivery. This is the answer to my prayer for some kind of 'new occurrence in my life this week'.

On Wednesday, the same day as the three letters came, two little cadres visited before and during breakfast to chat with the guards. Could this mean a consular visit before the month is out? Cadre visits before have always been succeeded by consular visits.

Yesterday I had my hair cut short. The guards, for about a month now, have been saying little 'prayers' before the big green portrait of Mao. It seems to be a pledge to study harder tomorrow, more like 'prayer' than ever before. Also the 'Basketball Player' now sports a Mao badge the size of a small saucer on his chest and my prediction about 'cartwheels' is slowly coming true. (I had jokingly predicted to myself much earlier that all Chinese would gradually disappear behind cartwheeled-sized Mao badges!) Please let this improvement continue to progress.

Sunday 27 April 1969

In the past week I have finished the 40-lesson course of Chinese, read it through in one day, polished off another little Chinese language book I found here in one day, learned the songs 'The East is Red' and 'The Helmsman', of which I had the words and music from old copies of the *Peking Review*, and gone over the communiqué of the Ninth Party Congress.

All these things have made my knowledge of Chinese considerable. Yesterday I read the third and final communiqué of the Congress in Chinese. But it doesn't say anything really interesting.

Yesterday I got two letters from Shirley and one from Mum, all three containing almost nothing. They show no hope of an early release and only confirm my feelings about things. It was during last week that two cadres visited and it is this, with the early arrival of letters – yesterday's reached me in ten days from end to end – that makes me believe there might be a visit in May. But of course there might not.

At the moment there is an infuriating brushing sound going on just outside the door as one of the guards is washing his coat on a chair. They have been hammering on their bicycles in the yard since early (about 8 am) this morning. The coat-cleaner is 'Pervert Jaw'.

It was on Thursday night that the end of the Congress was announced. There was an excited running about by the guards – they went upstairs to try to get my radio working – then later the drums and firecrackers started. Finally they locked the outside door and sat down to listen to the radio blasting out over the rooftops around midnight.

They again couldn't resist shouting '*Wan shou wu chiang!* in unison. The celebrations went on all night, but quite incredibly after going to bed around 1.15 am, I slept through. I was woken once or twice, but soon went to sleep again. It was only around 10 am that they woke me properly.

The guards brought in a portable radio to plague me with. Yesterday's communiqué really gave little away. Now we must wait for the publication of the reports about the meeting, which I expect around May Day. This week I have read for the third time the *Moscow and Peking* book about the basis of the Sino–Soviet dispute and am about to begin reading the crucial letters of conflict exchanged between them. I am more or less decided to ask for more books soon. The sun is shining; summer will soon be here.

REFLECTIONS - 15
Sunday 14 January 2007

The sun was shining; summer would soon be here, I wrote as April 1969 ended. An upbeat summation of another four hard winter months during which, in modern sporting parlance perhaps 'I ground out a result.' In one-on-one combat, I fought the Chinese language to a draw, it could be said.

It was not a beautiful game; my memory of it is crouching huddled in a padded 'blue-ant' Chinese jacket in the penumbra of the scullery, early morning after early morning on a rickety wooden chair by the loo, copying out repeated versions of each Chinese character around the white margins of the *People's Daily*, because I had no other available paper to use at that time. Some panes of the scullery windows were still painted black and the early morning winter light was almost always dull and sometimes yellowed by the sand storms from the Gobi Desert or the Shansi loess hills.

Looking back now I seem to myself a bit like some kind of latter-day troglodyte in those gloomy conditions, working flat out, after delaying it for so long, to arm myself with some rudimentary knowledge of the language of my captors. I was spurred on initially by the fright of having seen my name splashed all over their main newspaper and this again triggered the long-term paranoia that never really left me, of being put on a contrived trial and transferred to an even worse prison somewhere in China's great hinterland. Well, I am glad now at least something inspired me to get over my lethargy.

I am surprised to find from the diary entries that I rose only at 8 am. In my memory it had become much earlier and I thought I had possibly forced myself to rise at perhaps 5 am or 6 am to scurry through into the loo, so as to put two closed doors between me and the guards when they were at their most distracted, roaring out their early day propaganda songs and quotation-chants in my dining room.

In any event, secretly mastering 1200 Chinese characters unaided from a standing start, without my own personal instructor, became an achievement that in retrospect gives me more satisfaction than almost anything else I achieved under those strange circumstances of imprisonment. That it allowed me from then on to read first-hand each day the officially sanctioned domestic and international news in the chief party newspaper gave me a very satisfying feeling of being less at sea as far as the political environment around me was concerned.

Although the official full English translations of the news stories about me and Britain arrived in the *Peking Review* quite soon after I started this Herculean solo task, calming that fear of a trumped-up trial on spying charges, the desire to fully understand and know the contents of the pink poster slapped on me and the walls of the house on the night of the Red Guard invasion became my burning ambition. That I was able eventually to read and translate exactly what my 'crimes', if any, were said to have been, before the posters were scraped off the walls, provided me with a great personal satisfaction.

In the normal course of events, new Reuters correspondents in China had taken daily lessons in the Chinese language from a teacher visiting the house. (Now I am sure the dozen or more Reuters staff in China are invariably selected from among qualified Chinese speakers, but such animals were much rarer in those days.) This practice of taking daily lessons on the spot had ceased before my arrival, like so many things during the chaos of the Cultural Revolution, so I missed even an initial grounding in Chinese during my first four months of reporting from Peking.

Looking back at all the 23-day and 31-day plans of that long spell of solitary, it can be seen how many times I formulated the wish to make amends for this and learn the language – then immediately shirked it, through laziness or the lowness of mind I experienced. That I managed to achieve some small mastery of the convoluted Chinese characters before it all ended, salved my conscience on that score.

Overall, it helped me feel I was conducting myself with the maximum discipline and effort too, an important morale-booster in itself. Even the very nature of the diary entries during those first four months of 1969 reflects that a fundamental change in attitude and focus had taken place. Creating crossword puzzles and writing short story fiction had both been immensely important previously in fighting the emptiness. Yet suddenly the 31-day plans, which had ritually been inscribed at the start of each month, no matter how threadbare in intent, disappeared completely, never to return. There was only one plan for those four months – to learn Chinese.

And the regularly inscribed time of day disappeared from each diary entry too. It seemed everything was being pared down in the learning effort and eventually I also wrote that 'each day does not seem to linger as long as before' – so time was passing more swiftly, it seemed, due to my absorption in the intense task of memorising the complex pictograms.

A lot of these ancient and fascinating symbols had been modified and simplified under the Communist regime in the Peoples Republic of China, although they still remained unsimplified in Taiwan. So in addition to learning the original unsimplified version in my *Teach Yourself Chinese* book, I then had to work out which ones had been changed and to what, and then learn the new simpler versions in order to read the newspapers.

At the beginning of April, unexpectedly an historic Ninth Congress of the Communist Party of China was suddenly announced and held – and this too added a feeling that order and sanity were to some extent returning to a China that had become severely deranged during the previous two years or so. The Eighth Congress had taken place 15 years before in 1954 and there had been times when Mao seemed intent on smashing the Party itself nationwide as part of his wild campaign.

This development added for me an extra dimension of reassurance that a return to normal life for China and me was more likely than something worse. I could see, however, as April drew to a close, that my imprisonment was not likely to be all over in the next five minutes. Nevertheless those gruelling months of application to the secret learning of Chinese in the depths of that winter of 1969 helped move me towards feeling that perhaps at last I genuinely deserved something better. As May Day dawned again, there was a significant feeling of momentum towards the light.

16
GETTING BACK FROM THE MOON

Thursday 1 May 1969, May Day

The sun is blazing outside, a fresh breeze is blowing, and there is the sound of marching as crowds converge on the Square yet gain for May Day celebrations. Yesterday the temperature was 74 degrees and today it is about the same. I have discarded my pullover; the summer has begun. Yesterday the new Politburo list was published in the papers. Lots of new names.

The speech of Lin Piao was published two days before and a new Constitution was also published. There were the usual celebrations with drums and banging through the night. So the Congress is over, all bar the publication of any of Mao's speeches. But I don't see what they can add.

So far the whole thing is rather damp squibbish, although I haven't been through Lin Piao's report. (Great shouting of 'Mao Tse-tung' at present, as more marchers go by in the street outside. Also a gang of boys from the nearby moat around the Forbidden City – where they swim – just climbed up into my view to steal fruit from the trees over the wall.)

I made my own lunch in the room here today with stuff left for me, since Sao Kao went home at 12 noon to avoid the crowds.

I look back on my four months' of effort to learn Chinese with some pride. It has made a great deal of difference to my life – and I have again done it all in secret. I have been busy almost every day for four months. I have resolved to go on and study all the writings of the Congress word by word. I can now read the papers quite well. I have completed the first two communiqués and have today begun the third. Yesterday I asked for more books from upstairs. I was told to 'wait a minute'. I look on the four months of summer as I did last year, to be endured, to bring me near to the time of hope. I half expect a consular visit in May. I do so want to be free!

Sunday 11 May 1969

It is about 3 o'clock on Sunday afternoon and I am fuming with anger as a high-pitched voice in the next room reads aloud an editorial, frequently mentioning the name of president Liu Shao-chih and reactionaries. It penetrates very acutely and I have just flung the book I was reading into the air in extreme anger. Sometimes self-control is on the verge of slipping. These past ten days there has been a change, not for the better. Three new guards, all young and stupid, have taken the place of 'Barry' and 'Basketball Player'. The arrival of these new brats has lead to new annoyance. First of all their voices – two of them high-pitched and one just breaking – sound extremely 'puberty-stricken'. This last one particularly spits a lot and very loudly, probably to express his incipient 'manliness.'

There has been an increase in study lessons and also a new outbreak of singing lessons among the guards. They sometimes take place at 7.30 in the morning! At lunch and dinner they ride their bicycles round the yard. They are extremely childish. Also bikes have been mended constantly in the yard in the past two weeks with much banging and hammering.

The weather has been very wet these last two days; today the temperature is 41 degrees. I looked back to last year and found it was 84 degrees on these days. Two days ago I had letters from Mum and Shirley, but no news. My request for books on 30 April is still unanswered. How pathetic! I'm not so sure I shall get my visit now in view of all this delay.

Again, as last year, I think only of enduring the four months – May, June, July and August – before I can hope for release. The awful thought of not being released this time but having to go on another terrible year is in the back of my mind. It's too horrible to contemplate.

I am just finishing reading the polemics between Peking and Moscow, in pamphlet form, and relevant newspaper editorials and it has been very interesting. This week I have worked out what the poster in the bathroom says, with less than ten characters remaining unrecognisable. I have already worked out what characters signify various countries and their capitals in the *Peoples Daily*. I read of de Gaulle's resignation in Paris in the Chinese press and was very pleased at my ability.

The past two or three days I have begun slightly to lose my appetite, I don't know why.

Sunday 18 May 1969

Another Sunday – another week and still absolutely nothing! No letters for nine days, although I had a cable on the 12 May from Shirley saying her letters were 'boomeranging' and being returned to her. Yesterday I had a big stare-out with the particularly obnoxious little new guard, the one that spits all over the place. He thought he would be very clever and stare at me from the gate end. I stared back constantly and even walked up to look at the thermometer right at his side.

Afterwards I decided there would be no more of this ridiculous nonsense, although I was pleased that I found I could still do it without getting nervous. I was delayed so long before being allowed out that Sao Kao put my dinner in the room and went home while I was still walking! How very smart they are!

It is now 19 days since I asked for books. The seeming promise of April that letters would arrive earlier has not been fulfilled. During the week I finished working on the new Constitution in Chinese and have also now almost learned the poster in the next room. Today I successfully made up a bed in the lavatory – with blankets on the floor – with a view to trying it out to escape the tremendous noise made by the guards in the dining room in the mornings. There really is otherwise nothing to say. The temperatures have been in the 70s this week, but not high because of the winds. Time must just pass.

Wednesday 21 May 1969

Today it is my 'anniversary' again – 22 months – and today for the first time it has become bloody hot. Temperature leapt into the 80s and to 85 degrees for the first time. Got hair cut short and washed it immediately. Yesterday I had four letters from Shirley. Nothing actually interesting, except that two were posted on 10 March, so were over two months' late! More interesting was the return from the Foreign Ministry of my letter to Mum after only 15 days, which pleased me a little.

The other thing I want to record is the increasing encroachment of the guards. Yesterday they took bikes into the dining room to repair. They now constantly mend and fool around in the yard as I walk back and forth. Every day they bang and make noise. At this very moment there is banging in the next room as they fix up summer blinds, which I saw one bring up from the kitchen in a great bundle a while ago. Two went upstairs for a while this afternoon.

A couple of days ago I had shock and tingling feelings in back and shoulders and was quite worried for a bit. I have also had pains in my kidney region, which have worried me a bit. Otherwise nothing interesting to report. I still wonder whether I might get a visit, perhaps next week. Still no books.

The summer began today as far as heat is concerned. (Strawberries for meals for past three days, pineapple last week.)

Wednesday 28 May 1969

There has been some development and I have a bloody headache! Today the slogans were removed by a great gang of workmen, but my rising expectations were not allowed to go too far because soon the sound of hammering came from above, indicating the windows were being nailed up, which shows I am not to be released.

Today's activities were a climax to a little 'period' of unusual activity that began on Monday afternoon with Sao Kao handing me letters from Mum and Shirley. Mum's mentioned that Gerald Long had written to her saying he had 'a little bit of encouraging news'. This started me wondering, because of the exact nature of the words she had used without being specific.

For several illogical reasons I had expected a visit on Tuesday 27 May. Mum's letter made me think this was so. Then on Tuesday morning, as I got up, the gate bell rang and I had recognised the words '*Tien Pao*' (telegram) shouted out by one of the guards as he called Lao Chiao up to take it.

It was the Wednesday cable from Shirley, which I was given at breakfast. During breakfast two cadres left after a quiet talk with the guards. I thought this meant a consular visit, for sure. At dinner time the real surprise was when Lao Chiao handed me a card from Shirley in which she said, 'Most hopeful speedy reunion since Hong Kong concessions'.

This really set me off and I couldn't eat half my dinner. I was ready for something today, but didn't know what. The attitude of the guards on Monday and Tuesday indicated something was up. Then, as I opened the door today, the bell rang again and the two cadres arrived. I later saw them looking round the house and concluded that it was about repairs.

Then after lunch another bell rang and a gang of workmen suddenly arrived. At once they started cleaning the walls in the courtyard with brushes and my hopes rose. Later they came inside and went upstairs and were everywhere. Then I heard the nails going in. My door was shut all the afternoon and I just sat feeling rather fed up at the sound of the nails. I expected some announcement. But nothing came.

I was told to go outside very late and saw that all the slogans in the passage and on the walls up the stairs had been removed. The only ones left are in my room. I think I heard the man saying they would come back tomorrow. In the courtyard were some old flags from the demonstration I watched long ago outside the British Office. (The staff probably had kept them downstairs.) And lots of new emulsion paint for the walls.

Even the outside walls facing the street and the gate outside were cleaned. My guess is that I will be moved into nailed-up quarters upstairs tomorrow, when they come to clean my room. I am not able to see what it means. I am trying to look at it roughly this way: last week there was nothing, this week something has happened. It may not be release but at least something has happened. I am trying not to be too disappointed.

Friday 30 May 1969

Well, today something happened! I rose early and had a bath, since I was expecting something. After opening the door of the room, I went into the bathroom and checked over the poster I wrote out last night against the original on the wall. Then I had a peep through the keyhole and saw the 'Old Guy' coming in with Ma Tung-chih (Comrade Ma, the translator).

I hid this copy of the poster and came out. They came in again and the 'Old Guy' read from a paper and Ma translated. It said, 'We have several things to tell you this morning. Each day, between 10.30 am and 12.00 noon and between 4 pm and 5.30 pm, you will be allowed to go either to the courtyard or to the three rooms upstairs, but you must first tell the guards. You must not open or close the doors or windows yourself. You must not go onto the balconies. You may take your radio and your books with you. You may close the door of your bedroom.'

Shortly after this I went upstairs, after indicating my wish to do so to the guards, and found it still in a bit of a mess, with Amah cleaning. I came down, had breakfast and afterwards went outside and walked for about 15 minutes, then went upstairs again. The first thrill was to find my radio working. I didn't expect it to work after so long and half-expected that was why they said I could have it.

During my first trip up alone I had noticed a view of the golden roofs and the nearest gate of the Forbidden City and with something of a thrill I saw on the walls of the Forbidden City characters that I could read for the first time 'in the flesh' as it were after my studying! I could only get Chinese on the radio and didn't have much time left except to find the radio's leaflets and bring them down with a copy of *Encounter* magazine. I had forgotten how to work the radio and had to re-familiarise myself with it.

At lunch a letter from Shirley came, but although written on 22 May, it contained no news and I threw it down in an illogical temper. I regretted this later and read it carefully. At around three I heard my first voice speaking English on the radio, an American report on the 'Brooklyn Dodgers ball game' (baseball). Soon I got the American Forces Network news about the Paris Peace Talks, the Vietnam truce, Prince Charles's Investiture in Wales, etc. It was truly great! But could I get the BBC World Service?

At 4.15 pm I went outside to walk by choice, then upstairs again. My first act then was to seek out the old *Playboy* magazines. Yes, still there!

But I didn't bring them down immediately in case I was inspected. I put them in the lounge. I checked and found no more useful books remained up there. I had read all the good ones. I checked quickly through my desk and found old letters there, but didn't really have enough time to do much.

When at last I got the BBC World Service news, I heard that there had been big tidal waves in Shantung province. It was so great to hear the news! I also heard a review of the British newspapers. I came down with an old copy of *Nova Magazine* and two copies of *The Economist*. The pictures in *Nova* were very sexy after my long monkish existence.

I tuned in to listen to the news on the hour in my downstairs room and also heard some music – declined to listen to the Mozart Players, but got in on the Dave Cash music programme because a cricket commentary was ruled out by rain. I heard the Beatles' latest single, called 'Get Back'. ('Get Back to where you once belonged!') It was so splendid to hear this and to hear news and radio newsreel programmes again! Robert Elphick from Vienna on the Czech crisis was very interesting. This has been a very good day for me! I only hope and pray that it will soon lead to bigger and better improvements.

Thursday 12 June 1969

Just two weeks of 'upstairs freedom' and I have today finished clearing up. I have thrown away letters and burned them and Reuters stationery and thrown away old papers. I have cleared up and fiddled around for nearly two weeks, doing nothing else. I have heard my name twice on the radio – once in connection with the Gerald Brooke case and again last night in connection with the British Foreign Office 'taking no new action' about me.

These are small signs, but I must still clearly think of being here several months more. It is marvellous being able to listen to the radio. I have brought up all my books from downstairs and taken down old news cuttings and every readable page of old newspapers. All these things have added a new dimension to my life.

On 4 June there was an incident of staring with the young guard. Next day the interpreter came to tell me I had been arrogant and impolite. I should confess if I was guilty. I said I didn't intend any impoliteness and was told to pay attention to it. Today Lao Chiao was allowed to open windows for me at my request. Now I think I am settling in to this new state of affairs. Letter yesterday from Shirley said she was annoyed at my writing twice to Mum. How ridiculous! My time is more occupied but I am more lazy.

Gerald Brooke was a Briton arrested and put on trial in Moscow in the early 1960s for smuggling banned political pamphlets into the Soviet Union. He became a bargaining counter for Soviet spies and, while in East Berlin, I wrote a world exclusive report about Brooke, which I obtained from an East German lawyer who led such secret negotiations for Moscow. The report revealed that Moscow was trying to swap Gerald Brooke for Peter and Helen Kroger, two top Soviet Cold War spies held in Britain - but the British Foreign Office had 'rebuffed' his initial approach. The story won exclusive Reuters front-page headlines in all British newspapers, so hearing of new moves in this story I had originated a few years later was of particular interest to me. The latest news said that the Soviets were still trying to swap Brooke. Also the similarity between my situation and his - we were both by then prisoners in the two leading communist countries of the world - added a further dimension of identity.

Monday 23 June 1969

Last night I heard my name for the fourth time on the BBC in 'From Our Own Correspondent' in a piece about tourists abroad. I have become obsessed with the plant in the garden during my walks in the past two weeks. I have long ago finished 'clearing out', but on about the 19 June the little guard ordered me to stop my record player while it was playing and I was mad for two days. Twelve days have passed and I haven't heard about my improvements on the radio. Shirley's letter was very upset. This diary is very difficult to write, so I will keep it brief. (It is now being written upstairs, where I am still very concerned about guards coming in to look.)

The plant was a climbing vine and stood at one corner of the flowerbed and was quickly, at this season, growing up a rough wooden frame. I found myself very drawn to helping its tiny outstretching tendrils find new and helpful holds on the frame each day and I always paused a lot and inspected it intently during my walks. As it flowered and flourished and grew all the way up the frame in quite a short time, I developed a very strong affection for it and a feeling of closeness with it.

Monday 30 June 1969

Big change in spirits! On 25 June my news was on the radio. My new conditions are known. Later Mum broadcast a message and I think I was a bit surprised and embarrassed by her saying, 'I love you very much.' But it was very, very wonderful to hear her. My name was also mentioned on 'Outlook'. Next day (Dennis) Healey in Hong Kong said he believed I would be released in October and it was announced that other Chinese were to be released.

This seems to be it! I was quite calm because it is still three months and that is quite a long time. I don't know whether I can expect a consular visit or not, or anything else. At present I think I must just be patient. Diaries are short because I still fear 'intervention'. God, please let it be soon!

'Outlook' was a popular daily BBC World Service magazine programme fronted on different days by three different presenters, including veteran

broadcaster, John Tidmarsh, who later became a good friend. The programme more or less 'adopted' me from this point onward and I often heard personal messages and references to me on it over the succeeding weeks.

Sunday 13 July 1969

On 4 July I received a cable from Gerald Long and Mum, and two days later others from Shirley and June. On 11 July the guards' room was redecorated. Two days before, they began taking down the Mao pictures and on the eleventh they also took down the one on the door. The room is now clear except for one picture, a Mao portrait on the wall. It looks very much like a consular visit is coming, I think. During the past two weeks I have listened to the Wimbledon tennis men's final and cricket Test matches and yesterday I got new batteries for my radio with great relief. Reception had become poor. I am still going on doggedly as there is lots of time to go yet.

Thursday 17 July 1969

Since my last diary, written in this new book upstairs on about 12 or 13 July, things have happened as I expected, but much quicker. At lunchtime on 14 July I first noticed Lao Chiao going in and out of the courtyard gate a couple of times and I guessed it was curtains and chair covers he was fetching from the cleaners.

Then the furniture started coming down from upstairs and the side-door was unlocked. I then knew it was 'consular visit' day. I immediately changed into my white trousers and a clean shirt, having already had a bath at lunchtime by coincidence. Then there were several rings of the bell and three civilians came in and later the two familiar interpreters.

The interpreter was much milder in his tone this time. Instead of reading stiffly from his paper as before about things like, 'We have been informed ...', he rather shyly and quietly said, 'Well, the British Chargé d'Affaires is to visit you at three o'clock. I have some points.' I nearly laughed at the change in tone.

Then the usual ones about using clear English, no cameras or tape recorders and no documents or food.

'You must obey the directions of the Public Security Bureau,' he added gently.

There was no mention this time of reserving the right to terminate the interview at any time. He ended by saying, 'You can go through five minutes before three o'clock.'

The guard came in and out of my room to look at me, but didn't stop as before and I was motioned through to the dining room at five to three.

Wires (to the assumed recording equipment) snaked away down the stairs to the basement, and in the room I noticed wires going into the waste-paper basket and out of the window. I stood up to get a glimpse of John Denson and Roger Garside as they arrived in the courtyard and saw the new Chargé d'Affaires was white-haired.

The most interesting thing to come out of the interview was the date of 3 October this year and the fact that the Chinese had indicated in London – via their Chargé d'Affaires to a Foreign Office man on 19 May – that I would have my freedom of movement restored when the last Chinese 'news worker' in Hong Kong was released. Their prison terms had been commuted 'in a review of the sentences', I was told.

Overall the interview didn't have such impact as the previous two. All I really wanted to know was the date. The meeting was allowed to run on almost 45 minutes and there was a distinct impression that my visitors didn't know what to talk about. It was interesting that they had asked for the visit only on 10 July and it had been granted without an equivalent visit to Chinese prisoners in Hong Kong.

We talked about who was still living in Peking, about the British Office here and the fire's after-effects and about the visit of a Pakistani delegation here and about the planned Apollo moon shot and my radio and several subjects of general interest. I said there was some trouble from noise, but really John Denson didn't seem much interested in conditions and I said there seemed to be no point in making a song and dance about them now anyway.

It was very pleasant to see them, but it had almost no emotional impact this time. I simply wanted information from them. The visit was the lead item on the BBC World Service news at seven and nine and 12 o'clock this evening, based around the fact that I was expected to be released in early October and looked fitter and more relaxed.

Next day on the programme 'Outlook', I again heard Mum talking on the telephone and couldn't hear all of it but heard her mentioning my treatment for 'a nervous throat' and about how I could walk without surveillance now. I think she said I was thrilled about that. John Tidmarsh said he hoped I could hear it – how very nice of him! Sam Pollock, who reviews the newspapers on the programme each day, said after reading out the *Daily Telegraph* headline, 'That is too good a news item to dismiss in a headline.'

Tidmarsh said, 'Yes, it is good that his ordeal is coming to an end.'

The outcome of all this is that I am trying to settle down to the two and a half months' heat without being too impatient and making it go too slowly. God, please let it come quickly. Yesterday and today I have thought of little but the Apollo mission, which is now on the way to the moon. God protect them and return them safely!

Sunday 20 July 1969

This day is one of the most exciting of my life in a sense – the American astronauts are just on the brink of stepping onto the moon. May God please keep them safe and protect them. Grant them success and safe return.

Meanwhile 'back on earth'; yesterday I got lots of letters from my Angel and Mum. There was a nice 'fisherman' card from Shirley and in her letters she finally became herself again, back telling me how despondent she was about the long delay in receiving my letters. My July letter to her has now been at the Foreign Ministry two weeks.

On 18 July something quite extraordinary happened. There was an earthquake while I was in the bath! Gave me a big fright and I jumped out of the bath without either washing or waiting to see if I was imagining things. My toothbrush was swinging steadily on its hook. This assured me I didn't imagine it.

As I write I am listening to the radio, which is all commentary about the astronauts etc. from America. My mood is completely taken up with the moon trip at present and will be until they return safely. Otherwise it is an important matter of getting to the end of July; then there will be just two months to wait.

I had suspended my toothbrush by a piece of cotton through its end on a metal support for a glass shelf that had long since disappeared from above the sink.

After jumping from the bath in alarm, I really thought I might have mistaken movement of the water I was lying in for an earth tremor. But the toothbrush went on swinging gently back and forth with an eerie steadiness for at least two or three minutes – a sight I will never forget. Much later whenever I tried to make the toothbrush swing like that by pushing it sideways, it always stopped moving quite quickly. Seven years later a massive earthquake shook Peking and north-east China just before Mao died, killing hundreds of thousands of people.

Monday 21 July 1969

What an incredible, wonderful, unique day! My excitement in following the moon landing and walk was intense; and interest almost never flagged during the day. I left my dinner uneaten for almost 90 minutes and walked only a few minutes in the morning. I heard all the main things as they happened here in my downstairs room, including Neil Armstrong's 'one small step for man' as he climbed down from the spacecraft. I feel I am following every step and stage of their return.

It was also a two-year anniversary for me. On 21 July 1967 I was put under house arrest here! On this day I have received a letter from an unknown friend or sympathiser, and also my letter to Shirley was at last returned to me from the Foreign Ministry for despatch.

Friday 25 July 1969

Today is the most 'unwholesome' of the summer so far. It is 83 degrees inside and 81 outside and has been heavy, dark and cloudy all day. Water spills everywhere in the bathroom, from the pipes. My prayers were both answered yesterday, when the three astronauts were safely returned to earth and Gerald Brooke was also released! I had prayed for both these things for a long time – very hard, too. The sweat runs down my neck and chest as I write – this is truly wretched. Please roll on a break in this weather.

On the radio, both at eight o'clock and five o'clock on the BBC World Service news, I heard it said obscurely that the Chinese Foreign Ministry said that some time ago they had issued some proposal about me – but the upshot of it all was still that I was expected to be released in October. So time seems to drag. The noise from the next room is a great torment. The last few days they have had lecturers of a senior rank from headquarters.

Thursday 31 July 1969

I feel some satisfaction on reaching the end of July. After the consular visit of John Denson and Roger Garside, I had noted that it was two-and-a-half months to go and now the odd half-month is past. Now I think of it as two solid months to endure. And I have planned to be more active in the next month.

In the past two or three days I have read harder in order to concentrate more. Strangely I find it difficult to concentrate and work for more than a few minutes. On the 26 July I had a nice letter from Shirley in which she sort of said she had been ridiculous in some past letters and she also told how she had heard of the Denson visit. I do love her and look forward to seeing her.

May God grant me patience and speed the time of my release. Last week the guards had lots of big sessions with lecturers from headquarters. This week they have been reduced since Sunday, with only three men on duty all the time and I have been wondering if this is the start of something new. It is now raining outside and the humidity has lifted for the first time in about ten days and this is a great relief.

REFLECTIONS · 16
Monday 15 January 2007

Of the three momentous changes for me that occurred during the months of May, June and July in 1969, the most important by far was regaining access to the outside world via my short wave radio. It opened up my terribly closed-in perspective for the first time since 18 August 1967, and to hear that the world was still functioning roughly as before in all its flawed beauty and wonder – and I was again a part of it, no matter how remotely – was an uplifting change of massive proportions.

It was of course on, a smaller scale, wonderful to be told on 31 May that I could henceforth chose between certain times to go outside and walk in the courtyard or go to the three rooms in the upper part of the house without being ordered to do so, or being escorted. All that close and supervised restriction had been a living nightmare. A tiny morsel of freedom of movement was being restored to me – and although it may have been comparative and small, it was like getting at least one of my arms out of the terrible straitjacket for the first time.

I hadn't got the jacket off completely by any means, yet it was noticeably more comfortable than before. It was also extremely good to receive another consular visit from John Denson and Roger Garside on 14 July – and to be told confidently that the date of my release would almost certainly be early October. And to chat fairly relaxedly with them for three-quarters of an hour was also a small but significant privilege.

And that my new limited freedoms allowed me to become aware, as it happened, of the historic first-ever moon landing by the Americans – on the precise second anniversary of my imprisonment – was quite breathtakingly extraordinary. None of these three events could I ever have anticipated. I never formed any idea of how precisely my imprisonment in that house would be wound up – yet all these developments were totally unexpected. They perhaps allowed me eventually to emerge into the full light of day without undue bewilderment.

Later, when hostage-taking became more widespread and the British hostages in Lebanon for example, including John McCarthy and Terry Waite, were flown home, I believe they were taken to RAF Lyneham in Wiltshire and protected from the outside world for some time while they regained their equilibrium and talked things through with sympathetic counsellors and doctors. Their ordeals of course were much longer, harsher and more severe than mine and they were constantly in the hands of individual guerrilla groups. Perhaps because I was arguably the first western hostage of the modern political era and all this was unfamiliar territory, no such 'quarantine' arrangements were suggested in my case, although I was asked at some point early on back home if I wished for psychiatric help – and promptly refused. I remember that I had a very stubborn feeling – rightly or wrongly – that I did not wish to allow anybody else to get inside my mind while I was still sorting things out for myself. I believe I read that Brian Keenan had taken the same line, despite being offered the opportunity to undergo a period of counselling and seclusion.

Being allowed access to a short wave radio and being permitted to move more freely in the house, did begin to provide me with a kind of controlled recovery period. Although it was not the conscious purpose of the Chinese, in doing this they certainly allowed me the time and space to begin gathering my wits and absorbing, before I emerged into it, something of what was going on in the rest of the world in general and what was being said about and done about me in particular.

At first I was fascinated to see in this diary, as I 'processed' the previous three months, that when I left that downstairs room where I had been held for so long, I found I could not concentrate on anything at all for more than a few minutes at a time. I became strangely nervy in a larger space. This would happen on a larger scale after I got home but perhaps in Peking, during that first tiny step out of the void, it was partly because the guards tended to come to look at me more in that unfamiliar upstairs area and this made me feel even less secure because I had things to hide. I wrote very little in the final stages of this diary, as a result of a heightened fear of its late discovery. Perhaps it was also my nervous system going into a kind of spasm on its way to returning to normal.

Reading again today in mid-January 2007 how I identified with the American astronauts as they prepared to return home after having travelled further into space than anybody before them, I am surprised how close that identification came. I clearly felt a great affinity that I too was preparing in a strange way to return from my own personal visit to an 'alien' world, as far from my familiar haunts in some ways as the moon was for the US spacemen. But perhaps we have also forgotten just how emotional those days and nights were when we were able to follow 'live' how that extraordinary first adventure into space was successfully completed.

In any event, those final months of comparative new freedoms, it is clear to me now, served as a kind of rudimentary 'heat shield' for my own personal 'lunar module', which helped me not to burn to an instant crisp as I began re-entering the dense earth atmosphere of normality after so long out in rarefied mental and physical 'space'. Before reading the entries for those past three summer months of 1969, I had no recollection in which order or on which dates those three major events I have cited had occurred. Unravelling the sequence and rediscovering my reactions once again has been fascinating.

Equally, even now, I have no detailed recollection of what the last two months or so hold in store. As I head into re-reading them again, I have a sense of moving towards the moment of release with almost as much anticipation as when it was physically happening.

17
THE ENDGAME

Sunday 10 August 1969

Tonight has become very humid again after an interval of better weather. The cicadas are buzzing outside and the temperature in here is 81 degrees (almost 12 o'clock midnight). Yesterday I received a really nice big bundle of letters from Shirley telling how she thought things would be when I got home. There is otherwise little to say. I am daily trying to read old copies of *The Economist* and learn the poster that I forgot before.

As I write, the sweat is forming on my forehead for no reason except the humidity. I feel that I have now got a sizeable piece of August under my belt. I look forward to it becoming cooler.

Monday 25 August 1969

I have just looked back and found it is 15 days since I last wrote a diary. In that time I have finished reading all *The Economist* magazines and read two books, *Stories of the Long March* and *Reporter in Red China* by a predecessor of David Oancia, representing the *Toronto Globe* and *Mail*. I am at present reading *A History of Classical Chinese Literature*.

I am becoming more aware of the growing closeness of the time now and for the past week or so I have been counting the days and weeks. Today it is five weeks and one day to the end of September. I expect this consciousness of time will become greater as it gets shorter. Apart from the slight discomfort in my throat, I am all right. Last night the bulb of my lamp broke and the guard I call the 'Young Swine' again had a game putting on and off both the corridor light and the outside light. I punched my hand several times in simulation of what I would love to do – and it reminded me again how much I am still a prisoner.

The fifth Test match is on in England, but rain is spoiling my listening.

Reception on the radio is mixed, but generally not too bad. Shirley's letter of yesterday had something very interesting in it. She said that if I wanted five thousand women in the first week, she would try not to have a nervous breakdown: very out of character but this made me love her more if anything!

I had letters almost every day last week – quite incredible. Apart from wishing the time away furiously, there is little to say. How I long to be home in England. It seems to be becoming possible now.

Thursday 28 August 1969

Two days ago on the 26 August on 'Outlook' on the BBC World Service, I heard my dear mother! I had been alerted the night before by John Tidmarsh's fellow presenter Robert Reid saying the interview would be broadcast then and in it she spoke about knowing that I had heard her last message and about John Denson's letter to her in which he had spoken about my 'fortitude' etc.

Robert Reid sent very best wishes from all in the 'Outlook' studio, which was very nice, and said he hoped I had heard it all loud and clear. Dear Mum was really very good in her interview and sounded very confident and sensible. They began by repeating the message they had originally sent for my birthday and said it was a birthday message with a difference. Mother said how I had been allowed to get new batteries for my radio, and how I had heard Test matches and the Wimbledon tennis. She also said something about getting new reading materials, but it wasn't clear.

She said she pinned her hopes on early October, because the last Chinese prisoner was getting two years' remission. I remember thinking very fondly how she passed quickly over the strange words 'Chargé d'Affaires' and she was really very good. I love my dear dear mother! It was such a splendid thing to hear and I must thank all the 'Outlook' team personally when I get home.

Friday 5 September 1969

Two days ago on the BBC World Service news it was announced that the first of the remaining 11 Chinese 'news workers' had been released in Hong Kong – earlier than I had expected such a development. The man in question was an editor and publisher. It was very low key in the news, but correspondents said it could 'open the way for the release of Grey.'

This morning three cadres visited and looked around upstairs, which seemed to indicate some movement again. I don't expect anything really before exactly one month today. I pray nothing intervenes to prevent it turning out all right.

Last Friday there was a heavy, heavy storm, which broke 13 windows in the house and put the lights out for over an hour. My mood is very calm, but I now count the days off almost before they arrive. I have been reading, in the past week, the back numbers of the *Far Eastern Economic Review* and now have three to go.

Sunday 7 September 1969

On the afternoon BBC news today it was announced that another four Chinese had been released in Hong Kong and that the other six would be released within the next three weeks. Yesterday I was mentioned in a *Daily Telegraph* editorial about an American Ambassador being kidnapped in South America. I feel things are coming within reach now. I give thanks for all the good things granted to me.

Monday 15 September 1969

Since my last note, eight days ago, two things have happened. On 12 September I spent a whole day upstairs, as my two rooms downstairs were redecorated. I returned about nine in the evening while they were still wet. I hadn't walked at all that day. On the same day, on the news I heard that another five Chinese news people had been released in Hong Kong. So there is now only one man left, and the news said he was due for release in 'less than a month'.

How I am waiting very impatiently for the time to go by. Today I finished re-reading through the news cables I had sent from here and the various newspaper cuttings from around the world sent back to me. Before that I had read through the Reuters Editor's Review and before that I finished reading all the *Far Eastern Economic Reviews*, having earlier read through all the copies of *The Economist*. So now I feel right to start on some relaxing reading – *Playboy* and some re-reading of my other books, perhaps.

Wednesday 24 September 1969

For the past two days I have had a severe cold, blowing my nose all the time. For the past two or three days, I have been reading again *Charterhouse of Parma* by Stendhal and enjoying it very much although I am reading it slowly. Before that I read the two *Playboy* magazines and enjoyed them too. Two days ago I received the sad news of Alfred's death. Poor dear Alfred, I had thought to visit him in Berlin. Bless him! I hope to see Gaby in London soon.

I have been trying to make out how things will work out when the time comes to go. It is nine days today and things seem to be getting near. Shirley's letters two days ago said there were indications that I should not return by my 'out-route' – meaning, I think, that I came in via Hong Kong – which strengthened my suspicion that it will be expulsion without seeing anyone in Peking.

Before this, I had been thinking of the other possibility of some freedom here, but now it seems less likely. The question now seems to be – if I am released next week – what difficulties there will be about leaving. I am not particularly impatient now and time seems to be going quite well.

Alfred Kluebs was the German-born, English-educated Reuters resident correspondent in West Berlin during my time in East Berlin and his wife Gaby worked as a doctor then. Alfred was a very good correspondent, well versed in Berlin's history, had a lovely sense of humour and had been a very kind mentor and guide while I lived in East Berlin. Gaby had looked after any minor ailments while I was there and both became very dear friends.

Saturday 27 September 1969

Today there are six days to go. Last week I started feeling as though it will really happen at last when on 'Outlook' Sam Pollock read out a headline from the *Daily Mail* saying, 'Grey free next week!' It was a story by their diplomatic correspondent, John Dickie, quoting the Chinese 'Legation' in London.

Being in the hoped-for last week seemed to mark a new stage. (It is now almost ten o'clock on Saturday night and the bloody fucking bastards in the next room are playing their fucking radio with the clashing cymbals and stupid bloody screeching of a woman. It does infuriate me, although it isn't very loud.) Outside in the street there is singing of 'Down with the Soviets and the Americans', as the crowds go by for another practice period for National Day. I am getting on well with the *Charterhouse of Parma*, but feel a little impatient.

Wednesday 1 October 1969

Yesterday afternoon, just after lunch, a ring of the bell and two cadres, one in army coat and hat and one in fur collar overcoat – came and stayed for a short time. Later another blue-clad cadre arrived and stayed nearly two hours, and left holding a package in front of him. I hope this was the beginning of the long-hoped for end. Yesterday I received letters from Mum and Shirley. Mum's told me of a meeting she had had with Doon Campbell. Today I have been alone feeding myself (in the National-Day absence of cook Sao Kao) and now perhaps only a short time remains. I am somewhat apprehensive of the possible method of release and of course, until the moment comes, still doubtful about it happening.

Doon Campbell was news manager at Reuters when he interviewed me for a post with Reuters in 1963 and later became editor. He hired me and later became an assistant general manager to Gerald Long. He was an heroic correspondent, who was the youngest and first British journalist to wade ashore on the Normandy Beaches on D-Day, despite having been born with only one arm. He later covered the assassination of Gandhi in India, exclusively interviewed Mao in Chungking before he led the Communists to victory over Chiang Kai-shek and, last but not least, he flew out to Asia to meet me and escort me home after my release. Doon was a very dear friend who died recently and is much missed by all ex-Reuters correspondents of his era.

Friday 3 October 1969, 11.15 pm

A day of some tension. The first mention on the radio was on 'Radio Newsreel' last night at eight o'clock with Hong Kong's Anthony Lawrence saying 'Anthony Grey may be free soon.' It was not put in the news and was dropped from the next 'Newsreel' and I was annoyed and wondered whether it was a mistake.

I was up for eight o'clock this morning to hear the news (awoke at 7.30 am), but nothing on that bulletin or 'Radio Newsreel'. Did exercises early and had a bath and wondered whether I would be interrupted. While I was walking in the yard, there was a buzz at the bell and guards came out looking excited and buttoning their jackets. I got a slight headache with the tension.

I managed to get the three o'clock news and heard, halfway through, that the man in Hong Kong had been released. Then in the four o'clock 'Radio Newsreel' there was more detail, but I lost most of it with bad reception. The five o'clock news revealed that diplomats had been turned away from my house here in Peking 'three times during the day'. (That was a French News Agency report.)

There was a mention on 'Press Review', because of a *Daily Telegraph* article talking of personal freedom. I was on 'Voice of America' at six, and by seven o'clock I was still first in the news on BBC and this time they said that my 'phone was still cut'.

In the eight o'clock 'Newsreel' they had managed to add that China's Foreign Ministry was closed today. Nine o'clock and I was still on top of the bulletin. Then in 'Outlook' the first item was an interview with John Osman, who said attempts had been made to help me through Tanzania and Pakistan, but some diplomats had said possibly it didn't help. Osman also said he thought no journalists expected help from the Government.

Then Sam Pollock mentioned the *Telegraph* freedom editorial again, saying, 'All papers headline the story.'

At 11 o'clock I was still the first item in 'Radio Newsreel', with the announcer saying, 'Still no news of Anthony Grey's release.'

Then, in the middle of the programme, he came in with a news flash – in a very excited voice, saying Reuters correspondent in Moscow had come in to say that the Chinese would speak to British diplomats tomorrow. (This riveted me because the announcer said it so dramatically.)

I am waiting now for the midnight news to hear it again. (Anthony Lawrence, for the BBC in Hong Kong, said it was not known whether Grey would leave immediately or what route he would take.)

Saturday 4 October 1969

Today after lunch I was driven to the Foreign Ministry where the following conversation took place. A cadre, unknown to me, read a statement, which was translated by the familiar Mr Chi.

'We have called you here today to make an announcement. On 21 July 1967 your freedom of movement was restricted because of the illegal and unjustifiable detention of correspondents in Hong Kong. On many occasions the British authorities were told that if they were all released, your freedom of movement would be restored. And we must make it clear that what we say counts. All the correspondents have now been released. Your freedom of movement is therefore now restored.'

What did this mean exactly? I asked.

Mr Chi replied it meant all conditions for me were as before July 1967.

AKG: 'But my accreditation expired in September 1967.'

Chi: 'That is your affair.'

AKG: 'Could I have my accreditation renewed?'

Chi: 'You may apply.'

AKG: 'Will it be granted?'

Chi: 'You may apply.'

AKG: 'What is the position of Reuters?'

Chi: 'All is as before.'

AKG: 'The lease on the house expired two years ago, what about that?'

Chi: 'Take it up with the department concerned.'

AKG: 'Visas?'

Chi: 'Use the normal channels. If you have any queries you can make enquiries of the Information Department.'

AKG: 'Could I make some notes of our conversation?'

Chi: 'Certainly.'

I jotted some quick notes on the above exchanges then looked up again at the officials.

AKG: 'Am I free to walk out of the door?'

Chi: 'We suggest you go in the car that brought you here.'

AKG: 'Am I not allowed to walk?'

Chi: 'The car will take you to the door of your house.'

AKG: 'Then I am not free to walk?'

Chi: 'We suggest you take the car.'

I was driven back to the house in the Public Security Bureau car and deposited on the pavement outside, free at last to move as I wished. Roger Garside from the British Office, who had visited me with both Percy Cradock and John Denson, was waiting to shake my hand outside the house. I went inside and straight upstairs to my old office and wrote a few more notes of the conversation at the Ministry before I did anything else. Then I asked Roger Garside if he would drive me to the Central Telegraph Office so that I could cable Reuters in London saying I was free.

I eventually left Peking by air five days later, on Thursday 9 October, flying first to Shanghai and then onward by Pakistan Airlines out of China to Dacca. I arrived in London on the morning of Sunday 12 October, after a two-night stopover in Karachi.

REFLECTIONS · 17
Thursday 18 January 2007

Being free again in those early days of October 1969 in Peking, after more than two years as a hostage, resides in my memory even now as a strange, very intense and dreamlike period. It was elating, bewildering and overwhelming all at the same time. Yet I found myself compelled to do everything possible not to show those feelings to others, since above all else I wished to be seen as 'normal', as having survived with my sanity and good sense intact. So I still find all these years later, there are no words to describe adequately what I felt at first.

I believe Winston Churchill – who was taken prisoner briefly during the Boer War in South Africa in 1899, whilst working as a foreign correspondent – once said that until we lose our freedom it is impossible to appreciate fully what freedom really is. That I can certainly confirm from my experience in China, is very true.

My first overwhelming feeling as I was deposited on the pavement outside my house from the Public Security Bureau car on that afternoon of 4 October 1969 was one of immense relief. I was vastly relieved that the need to endure the sanity-threatening isolation unaided was over at long last.

For quite a long time after my release, I can remember wincing inwardly every time I heard in a news bulletin that anybody had been sentenced to any term of imprisonment for any crime at all, so appalling had I found my own innocent loss of liberty. No matter how deserved the punishment, no matter how severe the crime, the thought of any human being having to face a sentence of years locked away from the world in a prison cell made me recoil with a deep frisson of horror. Imprisonment for whatever reason seemed, during those early days of release, to be the worst form of human torture imaginable. In a strange way, for quite a long time, regaining my freedom made me feel even more acutely how awful it had been to lose it.

In addition to re-familiarising myself with freedom, I found there were so many other unexpected factors with which I had to come to terms. So much had changed so quickly during my time shut away from the world. In that relatively short historical period a real 'cultural revolution' had begun in fashion, music, the arts and socially in Britain and some other Western countries.

Shoulder length hair on young males, a burgeoning new drug culture, inspired and encouraged to some extent by the wild popularity of the ground-breaking Beatles, full frontal mobile stage nudity in extraordinary new landmark productions like *Hair* and *Oh Calcutta!* and all the extraordinary new ramifications of the bourgeoning 'Permissive Society' made me feel as out of touch with everyday life as the fairy-tale character Rip Van Winkle waking out of his famous dreamless sleep of 100 years.

The first stimulating shock on this front in Peking was the advent of the mini-skirt and the replacement of stockings by sheer, all-in-one tights. Nubile female diplomatic secretaries in the office and social milieu of Peking were casually and routinely revealing unprecedented swathes of their lovely lower limbs and I genuinely did not know where to rest my gaze, standing or seated. Whether it was the sensory deprivation of two very drab years alone, or that sense of heightened perception that had caused me to find the suits and coloured neckties of my first two diplomatic visitors at 15 Nan Chihtze so stunning, I am not sure. But at first it sometimes felt as though I was moving through a vivid, colour-enhanced dream world, where the tints and shapes sometimes needed toning down.

I lodged during those first few nights of freedom at the apartment of second secretary George Walden, who later became an education minister in Mrs Thatcher's government – and later still today a leading London newspaper columnist. When two English secretaries casually dropped by George's apartment for a drink with us on the second evening of my freedom I could not help but exclaim at one point that they looked to me, 'Just like angels!' And I really meant it. They did, appearing ethereally beautiful and surrounded by a tangible aura of pure female energy.

After that, as already indicated, I became a bit more guarded. Desperately wishing to be found 'normal' by those around me was an enormous struggle because everything was at that time seemingly so wonderfully 'abnormal' and intense to me. Walking idly in the streets of London later, I found myself staring up at the giant advertising hoardings, the big red double-decker buses and in fact people, buildings and everything in a totally new way. I struggled to explain it to myself and could only say inwardly, 'I feel I am seeing everything differently as if with the eyes of an artist that I was not before.' Such feelings persisted for a long time and have recurred intermittently over the years; sometimes even today I will occasionally feel some echo of that intensity when my attention is drawn to some striking or arresting sight.

My status too had changed fundamentally, I quickly realised during those first free days in Peking, and this added a totally unexpected new area of challenge and tension. The foreign correspondent who had taken up his post in China as a relatively anonymous individual had been transformed, through no merit or fault of his own, into the subject of a worldwide news story. The former newshound, accustomed to hunting safely in numbers with the press corps pack, had been separated out – had become the fox, the hunted one, unconsciously hiding out in a diplomat's apartment most of the time, getting used gradually to being out of a figurative strait jacket. Journalists from all over the world, meanwhile, were inundating the switchboard of the British Office around the clock with questions about me, in those first days following my release.

All wished to know what I'd had for breakfast, what I was doing, saying and other tiny details of my daily existence. That was the main reason why I stayed on for five days in Peking before leaving to head home to Britain. 'Grey chats on and on and on,' said one memorable British tabloid headline about my first meeting on the afternoon of my release with Chargé d'Affaires, John Denson, and a group of other British diplomats. It was not long before I became hoarse and started to lose my voice, although I have no recollection now of anything that I said.

I know I absently drained several cups of black coffee that were served to me while I was talking and these strong, unfamiliar potions sang through my relatively pure bloodstream with a great disruptive effect on my metabolism. So much so that I had to quickly revert for several days to the pure unadulterated hot water I had been accustomed to drink daily from the giant Chinese vacuum flasks of my captivity.

George took the photographs of the inside of the house that appear in this book. I think he went back on his own to do this. I remember going back only once with him to say farewell to the cook, Sao Kao, the 'boy', Lao Chiao and Amah, Mrs Hou. George said he saw tears in the eyes of the amah as I shook their hands and this information moved me deeply. I too experienced a fierce illogical rush of nostalgia as I prepared to walk away from the house for the last time.

Part of it may have been that I felt a deep compassion for those three decent, ordinary Chinese, who had to work closely around me, mostly in unnatural silence for two years and show, at least under the gaze of the guards, a consistent, silent hostility. Also I had spent such a long and extraordinary time in that strange house that perhaps some sense of its deeper long term importance for me was mixed into my curious rush of sentimentality as I finally left it.

International coverage of release news.

The long-awaited 'happier climes' ... pausing (top) before a giant portrait of a young Mao Tse-tung during a first tentative walk in a Peking just after my release ... and a more relaxed sunny autumn moment two weeks later in Ruskin Park, Camberwell, London, with Shirley.

297

More happier climes: A thirty year gap separates these pictures of myself, my mother Agnes and my sister June: the first (top left) taken in Norwich in 1939 or 1940, the second in a London hotel, the day after my arrival home, 13 October 1969. Top right: my father Alfred, who was divorced from my mother in the early 1940s, remained discreetly silent throughout my captivity. I later met up with him for the first time in several decades.

With Shirley at St Ouen on our 'secret' wedding day 4 April 1970 in Jersey, Channel Islands.

Shirley again, autumn 1973, Hyde Park, London with Doxa, the Alsation dog we adopted in Jersey ... and snapped in joyous mood in November 1974 on the day we learned she was expecting our first daughter Clarissa.

My mother Agnes (top) smiling in her Norwich garden in 1975 and Clarissa and Lucy aged nine and six, pictured at Kensington Preparatory School, in 1984.

Even more happier climes ... author waves (top right) from Gate of Heavenly Peace during first return visit to China, January 1988 ... completes London marathon (top left) in the year 2,000! Time: just over six hours!! And as it now looks today in the fast-changing China of 2009, my modernised former prison house at 15 Nan Chihtze. Inset: 1967 façade.

Postlude

Looking back now over the past forty years I find a heavy antique chest of drawers remains vividly in my memory as an emblem of that first day and night of comparative freedom. I was free, but nevertheless still had to make my way of out Beijing and China's clutches. So on my first night sleeping at George Walden's flat, I could not resist dragging a heavy chest of drawers across my bedroom door. I knew I was acting strangely as I did it, and tried to do it quietly without George hearing, but I was still not convinced I was entirely safe from re-arrest or invasion by Red Guards or the Public Security Bureau. Even back in London, at a Reuters 'safe house' in Camberwell, the first time I was left alone there, I found myself uneasily watching the garden wall and wondering whether I might see Chinese swarming over it to take some kind of vengeance on me for what I had already been saying in print and on radio and television about the experience. It takes a long time for the conditioning of the hostage state to exit fully from the system.

A big corps of British and international pressmen had gathered in Hong Kong, I was told on my first night of freedom in Peking. They were waiting for me to me emerge from China at whichever exit I chose and I struggled more than a little to come to terms with these heady new circumstances. I heard that these fellow journalists all rushed to Phnom Penh at one point to wait there when it was rumoured I would depart in that direction on Cambodian Airlines. Freedom itself, even doing very little, was intoxicating enough and I found I was more than a little apprehensive about plunging into this unfamiliar maelstrom of potential interrogation and photo-opportunities with erstwhile colleagues.

In those first days of liberty, in fact I listened intermittently during the day to George's classical music collection. After a largely music-less two years, I found myself wonderfully soothed by the 'Concerti Grossi' of Handel and light pieces by Telemann which I had never listened to before

– and I was greatly amused by tracks from my own LPs of Peter Cook and Dudley Moore, rescued from the house in Nan Chihtze, their covers still splashed with congealed Red Guard glue.

One memorable evening I attended a special showing of a film of the US moon landings put on especially for me at the British Office, located then in the neighbouring former Residence that had not been burned down. These pictures of men on the surface of the moon greatly augmented the dream-like quality of the time. I also walked one morning through the eerie, still-charred ruins of the burned out British Office next door and sometimes strolled in a nearby Peking park with George. All this was of course conditional freedom, since I still had to get safely out of China.

George Walden eventually flew with me, as a kind of chaperone, as far as Pakistan when I left via Shanghai on a plane of Pakistan Airlines. He ordered some champagne and I managed a single sip of celebration as we crossed out of China into I think Burma's air space.

The waiting international press corps at last tracked me down at Dacca and flooded on board my plane for the first time at the airport. There was some initial tension and raised voices for a while as Reuters assistant general manager, Doon Campbell, who had come out to escort me home, came on first and tried to keep them at bay. On landing he had sent a dramatic and terse message to me on the plane saying, 'Stay on board! Terminal full of pressmen.'

Doon, a popular and gregarious Scot who had been the first and youngest British war correspondent ashore on the Normandy beaches on D-Day and had later reported the assassination of Gandhi from India, was famed during his reporting career for always wishing to be first with the news. Now he found himself in the strange and unfamiliar position of doing his best to keep the press at bay from their story, and stifle and delay reporting.

Reuters wanted to get me home safely and put out a good exclusive blast about my experience on its own wires – but it could not ignore those pressing for immediate news who were also all Reuters clients anyway. Eventually the newshounds on the plane, with Doon's agreement, appointed a 'pool' man to come and squat beside my seat and do a short solo interview about how I was feeling. He then passed details to all the others on board so they could file stories to their newspapers and broadcasting outlets.

On disembarking, after a further leg of the flight, at Karachi airport, I found another seemingly massive crowd of local and international photographers and journalists waiting. The London *Times* correspondent later endeared himself to me by observing in his report that I descended the plane's rear steps there wearing an expression that was 'a mixture of amusement and bewilderment'. I remember thinking fleetingly as I was caught up in the crowd that in a curious way, being mobbed by a sea of yelling photographers and journalists with bright lights flashing in your face was not unlike the night when the Red Guards broke into my house – different intentions yet similar effects!

Doon had personally hired me after an initial interview at 85 Fleet Street in 1963, and he was accompanied by another Scottish friend, Reuters Beirut correspondent, Ian MacDowall. Nicholas Moore, the resident correspondent in Pakistan, was also on hand and they had tried to protect me from the crowd of journalists by hurrying me unobtrusively down the rear steps of the plane into a waiting car. This plan misfired and the wild scrum ensued when the journalists, who were grouped around the plane's front steps, spotted me and rushed towards us, cutting us off from the car. This led to a headline in one of Pakistan's leading newspapers saying, 'Reuters and UK Mission Weave Hollywood Drama Round Freed Reporter'. The story added that I had landed 'in an aura of excitement associated with Hollywood's sex symbols'.

I was whisked away from the airport eventually to the palatial surroundings of the British Deputy High Commission, where I stayed for two nights as the guest of Tony Stout and his wife. The plan was for me to rest and try to recover my appetite and ability to sleep, both of which had deserted me. I have recollections of burly, turbaned, white-uniformed house servants waiting deferentially on me and my hosts – and sometimes me alone at late breakfast in splendid isolation at a massive dining table – in the manner befitting the British Raj in its heyday.

When I at last boarded a BOAC Boeing for London 48 hours later, in addition to 'the aura of a Hollywood sex symbol' which was perhaps now fading fast, I took away with me from Karachi two further unexpected benefits – one of London's leading literary agents and the offer of an OBE. Tony Stout had come to my room while I was again resting one afternoon to inform me that Her Majesty wished to make me 'an Officer of the Order of the British Empire'.

During the darkest moments in Peking I had speculated about whether some kind of award might be offered me if I survived and in my embittered frame of mind I had then told myself in no uncertain terms that if this turned out to be the case after nothing was done to bring about my release for so long, I would scornfully and publicly decline it.

In the event however, I found my frame of mind had changed completely. My profound feelings of relief at having at last been freed, apparently sound in mind and body, were so great that all illogical past feelings of bitterness and resentment had completely evaporated, to be replaced by something approaching a serene equanimity on such matters. Later many press colleagues expressed surprise that I was not angrier about the British Government having done nothing for so long to help me.

I suppose if anything, my anger whether logical or justified or not, was expressed in that tiny memorised cameo piece that appears earlier in the Reflections section of this book, following Chapter 12, entitled 'The Play'. Perhaps writing that got any such feelings out of my system. So I did not refuse Tony Stout's conveyed offer in Karachi and in the event a visit to Buckingham Palace with my mother and Shirley, to be invested with the O.B.E. only four weeks or so after arriving home, was to bring a memorable conclusion to the first phase of my homecoming for us all.

I would not see until much later a short report by a lobby correspondent that appeared in one of the leading British quality dailies shortly after my arrival home, summing up the whole situation very succinctly in terms reminiscent of 'My Play.' Under the heading 'Battle Honours' the journalist quoted 'the Westminster and Whitehall grapevine', which almost certainly meant a Foreign Office spin doctor of the day who, under the now defunct 'lobby system' was then able to insist on anonymity. The 'grapevine' warned that because the Reuters man in Peking had been awarded the O.B.E., it was not to be assumed that any other of the ten or so Britons still detained in China at that period in late 1969 would be offered anything similar. They were described as 'involuntary prisoners' whereas I, according to the grapevine, had been 'a hostage in a game of diplomatic blackmail'. In this so-called game, the Chinese had attempted to make the British administration in Hong Kong come to heel just as they had successfully forced the Portuguese colonial government to do in Macao, the only other remaining foreign colony on Chinese soil. Similar riots in the two colonies had both been stage-managed from Peking, said the lobby correspondent, reminding readers that it was the 1967 riots in Hong Kong which had led to the imprisonment there of the dozen or so pro-Communist 'newsworkers' – and that after the release of the last one, Wong Chak, my release had followed forthwith. 'What it amounts to,' added the correspondent shortly, 'is that Anthony Grey, by slogging it out, doing his yoga exercises all those weary months was enabling the British Government to stand up to Chinese blackmail. There was no surrender to Peking pressure as there was in Macao – but it all depended on the endurance of one man – who now gets the O.B.E.' Simple as that.

It was in those same palatial surroundings in Karachi where I first heard of the O.B.E. offer, that I also met for the first time Michael Sissons, deputy head of the then small, august London literary agency A.D. Peters & Co., which represented household names like J.B. Priestley, Arthur Koestler and Margaret Drabble. Michael had been selected by Reuters from a number of agents who had applied to represent their correspondent-turned-hostage in negotiations for book, television, radio and newspaper rights that were likely to arise connected with the story. He had flown out to Hong Kong to await my exit from China amongst the press corps and, although I was greatly bemused by all this when he arrived at the Deputy High Commissioner's residence in Karachi to suggest A.D. Peters & Co represent me, I gladly accepted this second unexpected offer. Michael Sissons later became head of a greatly expanded agency, now known as The Peters, Fraser & Dunlop Group, which represents stage and film actors, directors and producers and sports stars well as writers, and he became my agent for the next 30 years or so.

On the flight home the air of unreality grew again when fellow passengers and the pilot plied me with requests for my autograph! Because I had done absolutely nothing for two years this came as a particular surprise. That a pilot who could reliably fly and land a massively complex Boeing jetliner heavily laden with hundreds of human souls should want my signature frankly astounded me. It seemed more appropriate for me to ask for his signature.

Because I was so unfamiliar with any kind of movement, I kept my window blinds drawn during the whole flight. Consequently, when invited to the flight deck by the pilot as we passed over Mont Blanc and Switzerland, I found the sight of the snow-covered Alps far below so dizzying I had to return quickly to my seat and settle back sheepishly beside the drawn blinds. Until we touched down at Heathrow and the brakes slowed the aircraft to a survivable speed, I was not absolutely certain the ordeal was successfully ended.

Gerald Long, came aboard with other Reuters executives to greet me, Foreign Office representatives waited at the bottom of the plane's steps on the tarmac to welcome me home, they said, on behalf of Foreign Secretary Michael Stewart. Among them I was very touched to find Percy Cradock, the man who had opened the publicity floodgates for me at a stroke.

A press conference had been arranged in the airport terminal and because of the jet lag and everything else, I moved through the crowded room and among the cameras and bright lights feeling a little like a sleepwalker. A Sunday newspaper had offered to serialise my story and a deal had already been agreed, and because Reuters understandably wished to put out some kind of major story of my return home in the next day or two, there were conflicts and I believe I was briefed to say as little as possible to the flurry of journalists' questions at the airport.

Then I was out into the fresh air of an overcast English October Sunday morning with a large, strangely silent crowd of people watching me intently as I walked slowly towards a waiting car. I think there was some scattered applause and a friendly shout or two. 'Have a good rest now!'

and, 'Get some colour back in those cheeks!' Being suddenly in the limelight after a long spell in outer darkness was both very touching and not a little unnerving.

A convoy of press vehicles closely pursued our car into central London, where rooms had been booked at the Charing Cross Hotel at the end of The Strand. There I was privately reunited with my mother, my sister June and Shirley, and I met Geoffrey, my mother's new partner for the first time and immediately liked him. Journalists and photographers again 'door-stepped' the front entrance to the hotel and Reuters posted a man at a desk in the corridor outside our rooms to ensure privacy.

Shirley's first words to me, I think, were slightly Pinteresque. 'You've still got nice teeth, haven't you' she said and perhaps could have been forgiven for thinking that they might have all fallen out by that time!

In due course in our room we all watched the Heathrow airport scenes of my arrival on the evening television news. It was the second item following on after disturbing, unfamiliar images of fully armed British troops in battledress being deployed, I think for the first time, in single file in the streets of Belfast.

Later the hotel manager showed us a 'secret' basement exit that opened directly into the mainline Charing Cross railway station, near the platforms, and my sister June, Shirley and myself gave the press at the front door the slip, and walked anonymously and happily arm in arm along the Embankment beside the Thames in the evening darkness.

That was my first real taste of unobserved freedom on English soil. Much later in the evening, using the same 'escape route', Shirley and I slipped out of the hotel again and took a cab to her flat just off Baker Street. Crossing that familiar threshold in York Street W1, I felt then for the first time I was really 'home'.

I'd kept no base of my own in London after taking up my first Reuters post in East Berlin, but most of the fictional short stories I had written in captivity were set deliberately in London because the capital was where I wished most intensely to be. During all that time alone in Peking, London was, I felt, my natural place of domicile. Before I went to Berlin, Shirley and I had shared our time out between my flat in Battersea and her York Street home. So in the words of the popular new Beatles song of the moment 'Get Back', I had come at last, like Jo-Jo, 'back to where I once belonged'.

Or to put it another way, in the vernacular of those silent mantras, which I had memorised and repeated to myself every single day throughout my long incarceration, 'Something good' had truly come at last – and I knew I had finally arrived back in those poetic, long-promised 'happier climes'.

CONCLUSION

'Man's inhumanity to man makes countless thousands mourn,' was the headline placed above the first newspaper serialisation of the story of my enforced two year stay in China. In the years since that first bout of modern hostage-taking involving myself and ten or more other Britons in China, the inhumanity displayed in the field of international hostage-taking and terrorism has escalated almost beyond belief. From this distance in the autumn of 2009, the late 1960s now seems in some ways like a comparatively innocent age.

The coastal waters off the coast of Somalia are the latest setting for new forms of hostage taking. As I write, a British couple who were holidaying on their yacht off the African coast are being held in captivity after being taken at sea a week ago by a group of Somali 'pirates'. A ransom demand of approximately £4 million was brazenly demanded via a phone call from their captors to the BBC Somali Service. Similar pirate groups have been capturing and ransoming container ships and their crews in that area and beyond over many months. On land in the Middle East, a period of time similar to my own spell of captivity has passed since five Britons were taken hostage in Baghdad by a large gang of local terrorists dressed in police uniforms. Sadly, at least three and possibly four of the men who were bodyguards to the fifth man, Peter Moore, a computer specialist, have already lost their lives in captivity and some of their bodies have already been given up in Baghdad by the terrorists. As in my case, the British Foreign and Commonwealth Office have from the start issued advice to families and the media that the best way of helping these men was not to publcise their plight unduly. The public has not even known the full names of the men for most of the two and a half years they have been held. The fact that it is believed that only one of them remains alive is an indication of how unsuccessful such a ploy has been.

That above quote about 'man's inhumanity to man' comes from a

Robert Burns poem *Man Was Made to Mourn* and it remains as apposite now as it was forty years ago. It is perhaps also appropriate to emphasise here that such inhumanity also inevitably has a deeply traumatic direct effect on women with close ties to those directly targeted. Each time a hostage is taken, it also becomes a case of 'man's inhumanity to women' too, because the women suffer greatly – in some ways more acutely than the hostages, due to the fact that they remain free and yet helpless to secure the freedom of their loved ones. Their caring back-up, as my diary illustrates over and over again, is likely to be a crucial part of any hostage's successful survival. Consequently my gratitude to both my mother Agnes and Shirley for their close love and support during and after Peking remains, and will always remain, boundless.

That is why it is vital for me to celebrate their memory here before ending this story because both these major players sadly died within a few months of each other in 1995–1996. Shirley died in November 1995 from cancer, during a brilliant sunlit autumn at a peaceful hospice on Clapham Common. We had wed on 4 April 1970 exactly six months after my release and our marriage lasted 22 years. After a divorce in 1992, I moved to a house of my own a mile or two away from the family home in Kensington and we remained close friends and a close family.

Our two daughters, Clarissa and Lucy, with their boyfriends and myself were all together with Shirley at the end and a few months later in March 1996 we held a Service of Thanksgiving for her at St Brides' Church in Fleet Street which was full for the ceremony. Two lifelong friends who also hailed from her native Yorkshire, Jean Merritt and Paddy Hands, spoke movingly of Shirley's sterling qualities as a friend, a lecturer and a mother and many letters of tribute were read out from absent friends in Germany and other foreign parts.

Jean, who had taught with Shirley in Yorkshire after university and later became head of Heathfield School in London, recalled that Shirley had been, along with my mother, the very first of what by 1996 had become a long line of those who suffered and strove to release their loved ones held hostage. 'Shirley provided unfailing support and the bridgehead for Tony to see beyond his current fate,' said Jean. 'She was always certain about what was right for him in his predicament and what she should do to assist the Foreign Office in securing his release. I always admired her self-sufficiency, her independence and her self-reliance – all qualities which were to be of such tremendous importance during the difficult times she had to face in her life.'

I thanked Shirley in my eulogy, not only for her marvellous help and fortitude under duress during my time of captivity, but also for her extraordinary love and support in the days, months and years following my release. Shirley also played a vital role in my writing for well over two decades, always being the first to read the manuscripts of my books and novels, and invariably providing wise counsel and constructive criticism. Her unexpectedly early death left a big void in the lives of Clarissa, Lucy and myself, as well in the lives of her family and many friends at home and in Germany.

Only a month after the service for Shirley, in early April 1996 my dear mother, Agnes, died in Norwich at the age of eighty-six. Agnes had contracted cancer within a very short time of my return home. The stress she suffered during my period of captivity had obviously affected her health adversely but she fought the illness and held it at bay with enormous courage for 20 more years, supported always with the greatest loyalty and patient loving kindness by Geoffrey Maw, whom she had met in Scotland whilst I was in China. I have said before that she deserved an honour of some kind more than I did, deserved at least to be Agnes Grey OBE for all her courage and persistence and determination. Geoffrey was equally staunch in his loyal support of her and he survived her for more than twelve years and died in 2008 on the afternoon of Saturday 4 October, the thirty-ninth anniversary of my release.

I paid a heartfelt tribute at her funeral to the heroism Agnes had displayed in campaigning constantly for my freedom in a situation in which she could scarcely have imagined becoming involved. 'Door-stepped' by national and local media representatives many times at home and at her place of work, Agnes also took family petitions for my freedom to Whitehall, supported by my sister June and some of my nine uncles and aunts; she gave television and radio interviews to foreign and national broadcasting networks and newspapers in London, and managed as best she could to handle a long drawn-out and traumatic period of anxiety. It seems highly likely that the undermining of her previously good health was connected directly to the stress of those two difficult years. Yet even after that, she would remind us from time to time that her philosophy could be summed up in the single phrase, 'I see every day as a gift' – and that statement of optimism is perhaps her best and most inspiring epitaph.

*   *   *   *   *   *

'Looking at life from where you are now, how much do you think your experience in China cost you?' a friend asked me as I was finalising my reflections for this book.

I realised on hearing the question that I had never truly taken overall stock of my hostage experience looking at it in terms of 'costs'. On reflection, my mother's resultant poor health was the most obvious hidden cost and a high one at that. The ordeal, I suppose, also cost me just over two years of normal free life between the ages of twenty-nine and thirty-one, which in some ways is the prime of a man's life – yet I have always thought that cost could so easily have been much, much higher. It could have been 100 per cent, because I could so easily have been killed at that time in China when we now know something like three million Chinese lost their lives in the massive turmoil of the Cultural Revolution. I had always thought it was a bonus to have survived. Life does not come with any printed warranty or guarantee and sadly international journalists have since then much more frequently been targeted and lost their lives as front-line victims in the world's open and terrorist conflicts.

I often reminded myself during that time, cut off from the world, that nobody had forced me to go to that danger zone. I was not a conscripted soldier being sent anywhere against my will. I had jumped at the chance with a great passion when offered the post in Peking, as it was a dream assignment for a young ambitious foreign correspondent near the beginning of his career. So I could not and never did blame anybody else for what had happened to me. Neither was I ever under any illusion that British government policies were going to be easily and quickly altered simply to bring about the freedom of a single hostage.

The experience obviously wrought some big philosophical changes in me and it also perhaps additionally unbalanced and over-sensitised me emotionally and socially for some time after my release. Yet, in a close loving relationship once free, I was able gradually to overcome the worst of these excesses. Perhaps we all edge our way forward through life, shoring up and doing makeover jobs whenever necessary on any personal emotional insecurities and shortcomings in our own process of continuing personal growth and refinement. I did not after a few years of recupertion feel at any great disadvantage on that score.

The personal health difficulties I mentioned briefly in the Introduction to this book took me by surprise with their severity in the early part of 2007. Perhaps I should not have been surprised, given that I had fought a number of battles over the years with attacks of depression of varying lengths of time and intensity. Perhaps I should have been more wary in view of the the nature of the work I was doing in reviewing the diaries dealing with those past challenges in China. Until then, as I wrote earlier, I had never sought any medical assistance and as I struggled in 2007 at first on my own, to deal with those depressive feelings that were more intense than ever before, a strange phrase appeared in my thoughts. I felt a wish, I told myself 'to be consoled by the community' and even now I am not sure of the real meaning of this expression or why it sprang so insistently into being in my mind.

By taking my problems for the first time to members of the medical profession and consultant psychiatrists, and accepting treatment, which in my case took the form of National Health Service 'Rehab', I suppose that, in effect is what happened. My original decision on my release that I did not need any psychiatric assistance now seems palpably unwise. Possibly by wishing not to appear 'weak' in seeking assistance and therefore always somehow eschewing it, something beyond my own recognition had built up over the years that needed to be dealt with.

My GP memorably said to me at the outset that the longer you leave a hungry dog locked in a cellar unfed, the more dangerous it is going to be when you do eventually let it out. So perhaps digging into the past in these diaries was effectively opening that cellar door at long last and dealing with the ravening 'unfed dog' that had somehow been neglected for too long. Perhaps that deed box at my bank was the 'cellar' and my diaries were indeed the 'hungry dog'. I knew 'it' and 'they' were there, and I occasionally did think about taking them out and doing something with them, effectively nourishing them in some way. But I didn't unlock them until the autumn of 2006 and then in a manner of speaking, they metaphorically sprang at me in one bound, and bit me quite hard!

The toxic wound, treated once, but perhaps not throughly enough, made itself felt again earlier this year in the spring of 2009, causing me suddenly to seek some more urgent first aid. This time, for some reason a deeper conviction remained afterwards that the wounds had been fully dealt with, and my thoughts returned slowly and naturally it seemed, to this book. Suddenly it appeared right then as the fortieth anniversary of my being freed approached, to go ahead with its publication. Rather than returning the 'dog' again to its lonely cellar unfed, I was now figuratively feeding it and taking it openly for a walk in the full light of day, letting it cautiously off the lead to run free even, when appropriate, to wag its tail and make friends with strangers. Greatly glad to be alive and well, a quiet feeling of gratitude has grown in me for the fact that I am living in a country where such treatments are freely available as a right -- and that there are many things about life in Britain today, despite our manifold problems and anxieties, that make it a place of very special value to live.

So overall, my 'excavation' of these diary entries – my own personal and very modest Terra Cotta Army if you like – now leaves me above all else with a sense of simple gratefulness, a renewed sense that what I experienced in China has in effect proved itself in the end to be a kind of delayed action privilege. The diaries have reminded me that we almost certainly reach a more desirable level of being when we succeed intermittently in practising our own particular form of 'momentism' to use my invented brand name from the days in the eight-foot square cell. Setting aside our normal hurried and sometimes scrambled thinking processes, we can possibly become more intensely aware of the purity and wonder of the present moment, and in the resulting stillness, in the freedom from the distracted rush and tumble of our days, we can sense more clearly the constant background presence in and around us of that which is indefinable and infinitely good -- and far greater than our individual selves.

Whether we become aware of it or not, or allow it or not, this life essence, I have come to believe, has the power to imbue our whole being with its inherent goodness, beauty, joy and compassion – and in short it enables us to access what has been called in a time honoured phrase, 'the peace which passes all understanding.' That was, I am sure, at the heart of that unforgettable 'magic moment' in mid-April 1968.

Each new moment – or perhaps it is really the same one and only moment – is always springing into existence in its own unique way to be relished, savoured, enjoyed. It becomes the metaphorical gateway to our inner selves, the gate through which we can pass into awareness of the infinitie serenity that underlies all nature and our daily reality. This is perhaps the true 'Gate of Heavenly Peace' which I first dimly discerned withiout realising it in so many words in that prison-house close to the golden-roofed landmark of that name in the heart of China's capital. Perhaps indeed the original name of the Gate and its adjoining Square of Heavenly Peace springs from a similar emotional awareness of these profound and ultimately indescribable truths among China's ancient Taoist sages and emperors who were responsible for their naming.

I can't help wondering if, by using as often as possible this personal gateway into the inner realms of a purer consciousness, might not each one of us begin at last to transcend our destructive egotistical selves? The more we succeed in that, surely the more our everyday thoughts will be led in more peaceful and harmonious directions whenever they reactivate. Possibly our own lives, our society our world, our understanding of its many dimensions and our true awareness of them, might also become clearer. If this is possible, is there not still hope that life on our planet might at long last be transformed dramatically and lastingly for the better?

On another front, the deep appreciation of freedom itself that I felt on my release, has remained in me ever since, varying only in degrees of intensity. I felt a great gratitude for life's simple beauty from that moment of 'rebirth' at the age of thirty-one. I could never for long see any point in being embittered or resentful. Discovering the old Chinese proverb, 'To regret the past is to forfeit the future', fairly early on in my homecoming, hit the mark to great advantage and I have never forgotten that. Increasingly as time has gone by and certainly now at this concluding moment of intensive review, I feel that, in the long term, the advantages, the experiential 'profits' of being cut off from the world as a hostage, have eventually far outweighed the costs.

Norwich, England
3 November 2009

Acknowledgements

While preparing this book for publication I have received truly invaluable help, much sound advice and always generous and kind support from my family and a group of very special close friends and colleagues, for all of which I am deeply grateful. They include primarily my two daughters Clarissa and Lucy, Angela Hind, John Clements, Hilda Beaumont, Paul Dickson and Illuminée Nganemariya, Les Collings, Maura McCarthy, Jamie Wardley, Michael Webster and Nawal and Treeva Fenwick. Indeed all those mentioned above and below helped enormously in their own unique ways. My love and very warmest thanks go to them all.

Mavis Giles heroically did the basic spadework of bringing the whole diary into publishable form by retyping it word for word from its original 1971 transcript. Bridget Lely edited the manuscript with the meticulous care which is her well known hallmark and John Weston generously helped with some basic Chinese language queries.

Others to whom I'm also very grateful in different ways include: Janet and Jon Stewart, Sasha and Ruby Norris, Kim Davenport, Ed and Sally Middleton, Colin and Susan Chapman, Stephen Cross, Matt Rushmere, Steve Wyatt, Dr Richard Pannett, Dr Shelagh Axford, Dr Tina Laczko-Schroeder, Dr R. Wesby, Brian Higham, Angie Barnes, Annette Willett, Jim Banting, Rachel Davenport, Tony Ellis and Lizzie, John Entwisle, Robert Fisk, Isabel Ingram, Gloria Siegert, Neil and Jean Merritt, Jenny Smith, John and Jan Peart, Nina Judson, Robert Kendall, Robert Carter, Mark and Sue Carter, Barry Carter, Michael Bland, Walter and Peggy Mussett, Neils Eiffers, Paul Thomas, Graham Barber, Lloyd and Rosemary Fraser, Rosemary Peach, Raymond and Gillian Brown and Paul, Sonja Haggett, Terry and Maureen Beaumont, Wang Difei, Paul Ward, Marcus Wenner, Daphne Wise, David Alexander, Michael Nelson, Vivien Carver, Barry May, John Tidmarsh and Chris West.

By chance and unknown to me at the time, my elder daughter Clarissa, at the age of thirteen or fourteen, inadvertently became the first person to read the full diary outside of myself and Shirley, who had helped me with its transcription. It was the late 1980s and off school for the day with a passing illness, Clarissa came across a backup copy of the original loose-leaf transcript that had somehow been deposited for safekeeping in a bedroom drawer. She idly began reading the start of it – and in the absence of anyone to consult, took the initiative and went on to read every word of it through much of the day.

She had never read anything before about my time in China and on finishing the transcript declared herself 'intrigued and fascinated'. I was at first more than a little perturbed by the fact that the diary included unseemly cuss words and other stark, unedited, private reflections and what on earth must she have thought of all that? Clarissa however re-assured me with aplomb that it was all 'cool' and okay. 'Raw' was one word she used approvingly several times in talking about it – and 'very readable'. That first unscheduled appraisal became something of a family 'event' that we have all often smiled about since. So thank you particularly, Clarissa, for that early vote of confidence! It perhaps was a more important step than we realised at the time towards this eventual publication of the diary.

Finally the Tagman Press and I wish to thank all copyright holders for permission to reproduce their work. Every effort has been made to trace all known copyright holders. In particular we gratefully acknowledge and thank the following publishers for permission to quote excerpts and references from their publications: *The New Diary – How to use a journal for self guidance and expanded creativity*, by Tristine Rainer, published 1978 by Jeremy P. Tarcher/Putnam, a member of Penguin Putnam Inc, New York; *Mao – The Unknown Story* by Jung Chang and Jon Halliday, published 2005 by Jonathan Cape, London; *Experiences of China* by Sir Percy Cradock published 1994 by John Murray (Publishers) Ltd, London.

Reviews of *Hostage in Peking* by Anthony Grey

'How a man can survive in a state of stunning emptiness and isolation, and stay alive in spirit as well as physically, is the essence of this exceptionally fine and memorable book ... What Grey had to face was psychological pressure of a most insidious kind. It is a book, in short, about a singular triumph of mind, one not to be missed.'

The Observer

'It is important that his book should be read in full to understand the nature of the regime in power in China ... One leaves his book remembering the sublime courage of a man and the shame of a nation.'

Daily Telegraph

'A detailed, pungent and never wearisome description of his captivity in Peking ... In many ways it is a vignette of a very remarkable and turbulent passage of Chinese history repeated in a thousand ways albeit with different facts ... It is likely to be a popular volume in the libraries of Western countries for a very long time to come.'

South China Morning Post, Hong Kong

'His book has turned out to be remarkable and readable. It is the story of the absolute isolation of one human being. This in itself makes it important – but it also pleads the cause of liberty and human dignity.'

Frankfurter Literatur Rundschau

'Our unwilling representative in their midst met undeserved disaster with such dignity, such courage.'

The Times, London

'It is a magnificent story, magnificently told – a book that is gloriously easy to review because all one basically needs to say is just: Read it! His integrity is demonstrated by his resolute recording of all those inevitable moments of weakness and despair which he eventually so triumphantly overcame.'

The Church Times

'It is a graphic and moving tribute to the survival of the human spirit under the most inhumane conditions.'

Belfast Telegraph

**Acclaim for the short stories of *A Man Alone*
now republished as *What is the Universe In?***

'The subjects are imaginative...graphic...and a sharp vein of humour runs
through the book'
The Times

'His stories are macabre fantasies, nightmares of reality, that are both
extremely funny – and extremely frightening.'
The Birmingham Post

'Without exception polished pieces of writing which make
excellent reading.'
Christchurch Press, New Zealand

'As the expression of a man in solitary confinement under the pressure of
uncertainty and fear, these compositions possess a remarkable buoyancy'
The Scotsman

'Thoroughly readable, sometimes moving, sometimes amusing and
usually concerned with elemental themes: the brevity of human life or
the strange tricks played by destiny... Powerfully conceived'
British Book News

'The book reveals a man, who incredibly retains his sense of humour and
remembers his home city with sensitivity and longing...It gives a startling
insight into his character and personality.'
Sunday Times, Wellington New Zealand.

'Since there is an obvious basic talent the stories have a good deal of
technical as well as personal interest.'
The Guardian

Acclaim for Anthony Grey's international best-selling novels

Saigon

'This superb novel could well be the *War and Peace* of our age. By using a technique of historic progression Anthony Grey does for the Vietnam wars what Leo Tolstoy did for the Napoleonic wars ... Brings readers closer to the social and political upheaval that overturned Vietnam than perhaps any novelist has done before.'

San Francisco Chronicle

An epic novel of terrible importance ... Like James Michener and James Clavell, Mr Grey is a master storyteller. Unlike them, however, he has something pertinent to say and does so in distinguished fashion.'

Kansas City Star

'Long overdue epic masterpiece of twentieth-century Vietnam. The author balances political intrigues and wartime horrors with a story of human sensitivity and love.'

Advance Library Journal, New York

Peking

'A magnificent epic novel of modern China ... worth reading solely as a factual reminder of the chaos and calamity of China as a quarter of the world's people struggled and suffered towards modernity in the stormy and cruel decades between 1920 and 1980.'

Toronto Star

'Grey, a superbly accomplished writer, weaves a masterly tale of triumph and tragedy ... marvellous detail, erudite, imaginative and instructive sequel to his previous best-selling novel *Saigon*.

Western Australian

'A moving, authentic, tautly written saga of forty years of blood, sweat and tears ... conveys brilliantly the workings of the Chinese Communist system in its dealings with foreigners and dissidents.'

Los Angeles Times

Other books by Anthony Grey published by The Tagman Press

Autobiography
Hostage in Peking Plus

Short Stories
What is the Universe In?

Novels
The Jersey Stratagem
The Bulgarian Exclusive
The Chinese Assassin
Saigon
Peking
The Bangkok Secret
The Naked Angels
Tokyo Bay

The Tagman Press

The Tagman Press was founded in 1998 initially to publish books that
challenge convention – *Books to Inspire and Transform*. The Tagman
logo, a red heart superimposed on a white triangle, is a modification of
an early symbol of infinity.

In August 2006 Tagman merged with CLE Print Ltd and moved its
headquarters to St Ives, Cambridgeshire. Its list has now been expanded
to publish a wider range of general fiction and non-fiction titles.

For a comprehensive description of new and backlist book titles and
audio-visual products, please visit our website at www.tagmanpress.co.uk
To contact Dr John Clements directly email: john@lifewisecoaching.org

Further copies of this book and all other books published by
Tagman may be ordered direct by mail from:

The Tagman Press
Media House, Burrel Road,
St Ives, Huntingdon, Cambridgeshire PE27 3LE

You may also call our credit card hotline on 0845 644 4186
or fax us on 0845 644 4187

or email us on sales@tagmanpress.co.uk

or you can buy directly online from www.tagmanpress.co.uk